EXAMPLES & EXPLANATIONS

Legal Writing

Legal Writing

Terrill Pollman

Ralph Denton Professor of Law
Director of the Lawyering Process Program
William S. Boyd School of Law
University of Nevada, Las Vegas

Judith M. Stinson

Clinical Professor of Law
Sandra Day O'Connor College of Law
Arizona State University

Richard K. Neumann, Jr.

Professor of Law
Hofstra University

Elizabeth Pollman

Teaching Fellow
Stanford Law School

Wolters Kluwer
Law & Business

Copyright © 2011 CCH Incorporated.

Published by Wolters Kluwer Law & Business in New York.

Wolters Kluwer Law & Business serves customers worldwide with CCH, Aspen Publishers, and Kluwer Law International products. (www.wolterskluwerlb.com)

To contact Customer Service, e-mail customer.service@wolterskluwer.com, call 1-800-234-1660, fax 1-800-901-9075, or mail correspondence to:

    Wolters Kluwer Law & Business
    Attn: Order Department
    PO Box 990
    Frederick, MD 21705

Printed in the United States of America.

1 2 3 4 5 6 7 8 9 0

ISBN 978-0-7355-9730-3

Library of Congress Cataloging-in-Publication Data

Legal writing : examples & explanations / Terrill Pollman . . . [et al.].
    p. cm.
    Includes index.
    ISBN 978-0-7355-9730-3
1.   Legal composition. 2.   Law—United States—Language. I.   Pollman, Terrill, 1948–

    KF250.L398 2011
    808'.06634—dc22

                                             2011014576

About Wolters Kluwer Law & Business

Wolters Kluwer Law & Business is a leading global provider of intelligent information and digital solutions for legal and business professionals in key specialty areas, and respected educational resources for professors and law students. Wolters Kluwer Law & Business connects legal and business professionals as well as those in the education market with timely, specialized authoritative content and information-enabled solutions to support success through productivity, accuracy and mobility.

Serving customers worldwide, Wolters Kluwer Law & Business products include those under the Aspen Publishers, CCH, Kluwer Law International, Loislaw, Best Case, ftwilliam.com and MediRegs family of products.

CCH products have been a trusted resource since 1913, and are highly regarded resources for legal, securities, antitrust and trade regulation, government contracting, banking, pension, payroll, employment and labor, and healthcare reimbursement and compliance professionals.

Aspen Publishers products provide essential information to attorneys, business professionals and law students. Written by preeminent authorities, the product line offers analytical and practical information in a range of specialty practice areas from securities law and intellectual property to mergers and acquisitions and pension/benefits. Aspen's trusted legal education resources provide professors and students with high-quality, up-to-date and effective resources for successful instruction and study in all areas of the law.

Kluwer Law International products provide the global business community with reliable international legal information in English. Legal practitioners, corporate counsel and business executives around the world rely on Kluwer Law journals, looseleafs, books, and electronic products for comprehensive information in many areas of international legal practice.

Loislaw is a comprehensive online legal research product providing legal content to law firm practitioners of various specializations. Loislaw provides attorneys with the ability to quickly and efficiently find the necessary legal information they need, when and where they need it, by facilitating access to primary law as well as state-specific law, records, forms and treatises.

Best Case Solutions is the leading bankruptcy software product to the bankruptcy industry. It provides software and workflow tools to flawlessly streamline petition preparation and the electronic filing process, while timely incorporating ever-changing court requirements.

ftwilliam.com offers employee benefits professionals the highest quality plan documents (retirement, welfare and non-qualified) and government forms (5500/PBGC, 1099 and IRS) software at highly competitive prices.

MediRegs products provide integrated health care compliance content and software solutions for professionals in healthcare, higher education and life sciences, including professionals in accounting, law and consulting.

Wolters Kluwer Law & Business, a division of Wolters Kluwer, is headquartered in New York. Wolters Kluwer is a market-leading global information services company focused on professionals.

To Ben and Elizabeth and JP
—TP

To my beloved and the three finest sons a mother could ever have
—JMS

For Lill and Alex as well as my coauthors and
our colleagues in the legal writing field
—RKN Jr.

For Pollman, supra.
—EP

Contents

Acknowledgments

Terry Pollman thanks Linda Edwards and her Advanced Writing Group of 2010 for helpful comments on the first chapters she wrote. Thanks also to her legal writing colleagues through the years at the William S. Boyd School of Law and to the law school for research support. Jordyn Raimondo, Jason Bacigalupi, and Charles Gianelloni have her gratitude for research assistance. Finally, she will always be grateful to her coauthors who made it fun to work together.

Judy Stinson thanks Laura Curry, Tamara Herrera, Carissa Hessick, Zig Popko, Doug Sylvester, and the Sandra Day O'Connor College of Law at Arizona State University.

Richard Neumann thanks Matthew Allen, Courtney De Witt, Rachael Ringer, and Kristin Stranc for their research assistance.

Elizabeth Pollman thanks Jeanne Merino, Norman Spaulding, and Stanford Law School for support and guidance. In addition, many thanks to past and present fellows involved in the Stanford Law School legal writing program for inspiration.

We all thank Linda Berger for allowing us to use the copyright and fair use problem she created. We know we are fortunate to be a part of the legal writing community, where so many great teaching ideas are so often and so generously shared. We hope that if we have forgotten to acknowledge an individual, you will understand that after years of teaching in such a generous community we are sometimes no longer sure where each idea originated or how many wonderful colleagues have added to it. Thanks to Kelli Bonds for excellent secretarial assistance. We also thank Wolters Kluwer Law & Business, especially: Carol McGeehan, Peter Skagestad, and Sarah Hains, as well as Jay Harward from Newgen and Michele DeAngelis. In addition, we are grateful to the anonymous reviewers who read drafts of the manuscript for Wolters Kluwer and made many valuable suggestions. (It really is anonymous; you know who you are, but we don't.)

Finally, the authors acknowledge the following for permission to use material reprinted in this book:

"Rockin' In The Free World"
Words and Music by Neil Young
Copyright © 1990 by Silver Fiddle Music
All Rights Reserved. Used by Permission.
Reprinted by permission of Hal Leonard Corporation

Legal Writing

Introduction

CHAPTER 1

How to Use This Book

Focus on the user and all else will follow.

—*Google slogan*

Google built a thriving business by making its products *useful* and *pleasingly easy to use*. We've tried to do something like that in writing this book.

Your memos and briefs will be more effective if you write them with the same goals in mind. Think about the reader's needs, just as Google has thought about yours. How can you make your memos and briefs *useful* to the reader? And how can you make them *pleasingly easy to use*?

This is the mantra for all writers: focus on the reader and create a document that's most usable for that reader. Your reader is your audience. In this book, for example, we've written in a more conversational tone than in a formal legal writing document because we think this will make it easier for you to read and use. When you can identify a specific reader—like your own legal writing professor—you'll need to pay attention, above all else, to that individual reader's priorities. This book explains what many professors typically consider to be effective writing, but you'll need to pay attention in class and ask questions in teacher-student conferences to tailor your document to the expectations of your audience—the reader who is also your professor. As with other books in the Examples & Explanations series, if we seem to be saying something different from what your professor says, your professor is right.

HOW THE BOOK IS ORGANIZED

The organization of this book generally follows the organization of typical first-year legal writing courses. Most courses first cover objective writing (which some call predictive writing) with students writing office memos, and then persuasive writing, with students writing motions and briefs. We've also included a section on revising and rewriting, because those skills are necessary to all good writing.

Most of this book's chapters are divided into four sections:

A typical chapter's first section — "What You Need to Know" — explains, as simply as possible, the essentials about a part of the writing process. Writing is a complex art. Sometimes in our attempt to give you what you need quickly, we necessarily simplify some of the finer points. For the most part, we cover, at a basic level, the essentials — the things everyone in a legal writing course must master. We've tried to keep things as straightforward as possible, to make the material accessible and quick to digest. Later, as you mature as a lawyer and writer, you'll pick up more subtle nuances. Learning to write is a lifelong project.

The next section — "How to Do It" — provides a step-by-step procedure for accomplishing the writing task that is the subject of the chapter. Not everyone follows the same steps to accomplish a purpose, but *we illustrate at least one way to think through* the particular parts of your writing project.

A typical chapter includes Examples that ask you to evaluate the effectiveness of a sample piece of writing.

Examples are followed by Explanations for you to check your work. How you use these examples and explanations will determine how much value the book will hold for you.

Throughout the book, most of our examples come from two hypothetical problems. One involves a vehicular manslaughter prosecution in which the defendant used a cell phone while driving (Appendix A has the details). In the other hypothetical problem, a popular singer alleges a copyright violation by another singer, who might in turn raise an argument based on what copyright law calls the fair use defense (Appendix B has the details). In many instances, you'll be able to follow the examples just by reading through the chapter in which they occur. But wherever you need more information or want to understand the example more fully, the facts and the relevant law are in the Appendices. In addition, some examples use fictional cases for illustrative purposes.

HOW TO USE EXAMPLES

Social scientists have learned much about how using examples helps you learn. Here are some of their findings.

Learning through examples can help you become a better writer. In law school, when you face a new writing assignment, you actually face two tasks. The first is to write a successful document for the assignment in your course. The second is to examine what you learn from the experience of producing that one particular assignment and then to use what you learn as you create new documents. Researchers have identified a problem with this process: the task of writing a new document takes up so much "cognitive load," or mental energy, that students have little left to spend on learning from the assignment. This research suggests there is great value in observing and thinking about writing when not simultaneously tasked with creating.

Passive observation helps little. Students learn best from examples when they "self-explain" as they observe. While the research makes clear that students can learn from examples, it also shows that those who *actively engage* with the example learn much more than those who observe passively. As you work through the book, talk with yourself silently about what you see and the choices you make.

The best strategies for "self-explanation" include observation, evaluation, and reflection. We've designed the examples in this book to provide all three ways to improve learning from examples. The step-by-step model in the "How to Do It" sections invite you to actively explain to yourself what you're *observing* as you work through the process. Check your work against our explanations of the steps. And it's especially important for you to *evaluate*—and to *reflect* on your evaluations—as you complete the questions in the "Examples and Explanations" portions of each chapter. As you compare your "self-explanation" to the explanations offered at the end of each chapter, reflect on the general rules you should learn from the chapter. This reflection will help when you next face the task of writing.

HOW TO USE THIS BOOK

Legal writing professors sometimes hesitate to give students examples because occasionally students use them poorly. We stress two things:

- Please do *not* imitate one of our examples without thinking about whether it's appropriate to your assignment. It might work for your assignment . . . or it might not. Decide.

- And please do not imitate an example just because it's in the book. Some of the examples illustrate ineffective writing and ask you to identify the mistakes in the example. Know what you're doing and why you're doing it.

By using the "self-explanation" technique as you work through the examples, you'll develop the ability to view your own work critically. You'll learn to articulate reasons for the choices you make in your writing, which will help you work while writing as part of a team. Be as specific as you can during this self-explanation. For instance, "This way of structuring the Question Presented helps me present the crucial facts in a convincing way." Learning to examine your own writing critically and to reflect on your choices is essential to becoming an effective legal writer.

Although this book necessarily oversimplifies some of the finer points about legal writing, we hope that it helps you improve in the areas where you struggle. Remember that writing is an art. Formulas will help get you started and can definitely improve your final work product, but writing involves a lifelong learning process. Your dedication to the craft and willingness to continue observing, evaluating, and reflecting is what will make you a truly gifted legal writer.

CHAPTER 2

Transitioning to Legal Writing

The transition from college to law school can be significant. The skills you've developed will be helpful in law school, but a few things will be different. For instance, you'll very likely need to study more. And the writing you'll do in law school (and law practice) differs in some respects from what you did in college. You have probably always been a good writer. The good news is that you can be a good legal writer, too. This chapter highlights a few of the differences between writing for undergrad and writing for law school and provides some tips to succeed.

WHAT YOU NEED TO KNOW ABOUT TRANSITIONING TO LEGAL WRITING

Writing in law school takes a lot longer than writing in undergraduate school. It isn't just the actual act of writing that's slower; the entire thought process is, for most students, far more challenging and time-consuming than they are accustomed to. Legal writing requires more than describing, summarizing, or categorizing. You'll get faster over time, but at first, this process will be surprisingly slow. In law school, writing will take longer than you expect.

Therefore, don't wait until the weekend before a memo or brief is due to start writing. Start early—much earlier than you're used to—so you'll have time to work through the analysis and refine your predictions or arguments. The process of writing helps us think, and therefore you need to start writing early enough to help you think through the problem. Then, you still need enough time to communicate that analysis to the reader—the part you're probably used to thinking about as the "writing."

Good legal writing is concise. Have you ever switched fonts to make your paper longer? Or added a word or two to key paragraphs to make them drop to the next line? Writing assignments in college often include page minimums. Writing assignments in law school and law practice, on the other hand, generally impose page *maximums*. And you should never vary from the specified formatting to make your text fit within the limit. Your goal is to make the paper as concise as you can and still say everything that needs to be said. This will take practice, but you'll get better at it just by recognizing that your goal isn't to make the document as long as possible. Chapter 28 explains how to write more concisely.

Legal readers expect your writing to be formal. In college, writers often have some flexibility with their tone. In law school and law practice, though, you'll almost always write in a formal tone. Avoid contractions, for example. (This book uses them a lot—but we aren't submitting this material to a judge or senior law partner.) In addition, avoid the first person (no "I" or "we"), even though the reader knows it's your prediction or argument. Use last names, don't omit articles (the, a, an), and otherwise think about making your writing more formal than your usual spoken tone.

Minimize the use of quotations, but quote key statutory language. Most of what you discuss in memos and briefs will be cases. Even though a court has some inherent credibility, don't quote its every word. Instead, determine what a particular case holds and express that holding in your own words. Of course, sometimes a court uses wonderfully helpful language. When that happens, quote it. But make that the exception when discussing cases.

When discussing statutes, quoting the relevant language is required. Statutory language is significant because the words the legislature chose affect the meaning of the law. But quote only the words that must be interpreted, not vast blocks of statutory language.

So remember: quote key statutory language, but generally paraphrase cases.

Avoid "elegant variation," unnecessary legalese, and other distracting stylistic choices. In college, students sometimes want their writing to sound "flowery" and interesting. They vary their use of terms to make it less monotonous or to sound smart. With legal writing, the subject matter is often complex and it's important to express your ideas as clearly and simply as possible.

Use terms of art—the key terms that the statute or cases use repeatedly—and use them consistently. Don't vary them just for the sake of breaking up the monotony. Similarly, avoid legalese *unless* it's one of those "terms of art." The movement to "Plain English" has caught on with force in legal writing, and most legal readers expect your writing to omit unnecessary legalese. It's also a good idea to avoid any writing style that might draw the reader's attention, like split infinitives. If the reader has to stop and wonder why you've written your document the way you have, chances are the reader isn't able to fully focus on your substance. And that means your writing isn't fully effective.

Use past tense to discuss the client's facts as well as the facts and holdings of other cases. But legal writers generally use present tense when stating a rule of law. For instance, "The court found the defendant had acted in self-defense when he punched the victim and held that he was therefore not guilty of assault. A defendant who uses force against another because he reasonably believes that the other person will imminently injure him acts in self-defense and does not commit assault." The first sentence talks about the case's facts and holding, and is therefore in past tense. The second sentence states the general rule of law, so present tense is used there.

Courts don't "feel," "think," or "believe." They "hold," "state," "find," "reason," "conclude," etc. Courts are institutions, not people. Even though judges are people, we presume they act objectively. Talk about what they reasoned rather than thought, what they held rather than believed, and what they found rather than felt.

HOW TO MAKE THE TRANSITION FROM GOOD WRITER TO GOOD LEGAL WRITER

Using the cell phone manslaughter problem in Appendix A, we'll walk you through the process of using the tips from this chapter.

Problem

> *Here is a quick overview of the cell phone manslaughter problem (for details, see Appendix A).* Allison King used her wireless phone, without a hands-free device, while driving in dense fog on a winding road on the edge of an ocean cliff. King placed the call to warn her friends about the dangerous conditions, as they would be meeting later. While she was making the call, she hit and killed a bicyclist. The prosecution will attempt to convict King of vehicular manslaughter by showing that she drove while committing an illegal act (driving while using a wireless phone without a hands-free device) and with gross negligence. King will argue that her actions fit within the emergency exception to the wireless phone prohibition; she will also argue that she did not act with gross negligence.

Step 1: Start working on your assignment immediately after you receive it, not days or weeks later. Because it will take longer to analyze, much less actually write, memos and briefs in law school, start early. Read the materials, think about them, and consider outlining your analysis. Chapter 6 explains how to organize that analysis.

Step 2: While writing, think about quoting key statutory language, being concise, and using a formal tone. Legal documents—even intra-office memos—are formal documents. It may sound stuffy at first, but you'll get used to the expected tone. Review good samples in your textbook or those provided by your professor to help get a feeling for what good legal writing "sounds" like.

Following these guidelines, you might transform this problematic statement of the rule:

> People are found guilty (convicted) of vehicular manslaughter when they kill another person unlawfully, and when they don't have malice when they commit the killing. Furthermore, this killing has to happen while the defendant is driving in the commission of an unlawful act, and that act can't be a felony, and the defendant has to have gross negligence. Cal. Penal Code § 192 (West 2008).

into this statement of the rule:

> Vehicular manslaughter is manslaughter—"the unlawful killing of a human being without malice"—that occurs when "driving a vehicle in the commission of an unlawful act, not amounting to felony, and with gross negligence." Cal. Penal Code § 192 (West 2008).

Note how much shorter the second rule statement is, and how it quotes the key phrases in the statute. The first rule statement includes some of that key language, but it doesn't use quotation marks—and that is problematic. Quote, use quotation marks, and keep the rest of your writing formal and concise.

Step 3: Rewrite—again and again and again. In college, it might have been enough to write a paper in a single draft, proofread it, and turn it in. In law, you can't be an effective writer unless you go back to your draft many times, each time seeing it with a fresh eye and reorganizing it and rewriting paragraphs and sentences. It might take four or five drafts to write an effective memo or brief and several more drafts after that to write an excellent one. This will continue for the rest of your career.

Step 4: Review your writing to ensure you've used the appropriate writing style, tense, and word choice. Avoid distracting stylistic choices, like varying terms. Remember to use past tense for everything that already happened, but present tense for rules. Finally, keep in mind the role that judges play, and think about how you describe what it is they do.

Consider the problems in this paragraph:

> Allison King uses her cell phone for "emergency purposes" within the meaning of the statute when she calls her friends to warn them that the fog and low visibility make it dangerous for them to drive on Highway 1, the road she is driving on. Like the defendant in *Newton*, who calls his wife's obstetrician while driving to the hospital because his wife is in labor, King calls her friends to help protect them and others by trying to keep them off the aforementioned road. The *Newton* court felt that this reason was serious enough to be excusable. The same thing should happen in King's case.

With some rewriting, you might improve it like this:

> Here, King used her cell phone for "emergency purposes" when she called her friends to warn them of the dangerous driving conditions. Similar to the defendant in *Newton*, who called his wife's obstetrician while driving his wife to the hospital because she was in labor, King called her friends to protect them and others by keeping them off the road. The *Newton* court's holding that the call was made for emergency purposes suggests King's call was likely also made for emergency purposes.

The second paragraph is not only shorter, but it's also easier to understand.

EXAMPLES

Review the following examples. Choose the best answer and explain to yourself why you've chosen that answer. Then read the explanations in the last section of this chapter to check your work.

Example 2-1

Copyright protection includes an exception herewith for "fair use." The third factor of said exception concerns "the amount and substantiality of the portion used in relation to the copyrighted work as a whole." 17 U.S.C. § 107(3) (2006). In *Fisher v. Dees*, the court believed that "many parodies distributed commercially may be 'more in the nature of an editorial or social commentary than . . . an attempt to capitalize financially on the plaintiff's original work.' In such cases, of which this is one, the initial presumption need not be fatal to the defendant's cause. The defendant can rebut the presumption by convincing the court that the parody does not unfairly diminish the economic value of the original." 794 F.2d 432, 437

(9th Cir. 1986) (internal citations omitted). Similarly, in *Mattel, Inc. v. Walking Mountain Productions*, the court felt that we "assess the 'persuasiveness of a parodist's justification for the particular copying done,' recognizing that the 'extent of permissible copying varies with the purpose and character of the use.'" 353 F.3d 792, 803 (9th Cir. 2003) (citations omitted).

This is an . . .

A. effective paragraph because it sounds like it was written by a lawyer.
B. effective paragraph because it quotes the cases extensively.
C. ineffective paragraph.

Example 2-2

Mark didn't commit assault, much less one that was "aggravated." True, he hits George with a pole, but George swings at him first. Plus, Mark thinks (and this seems reasonable) that George has a knife. Therefore, Mark's actions are in self defense, and he isn't guilty.

This is an . . .

A. effective paragraph because it avoids legalese by being easy to read and not too stuffy.
B. effective paragraph because it keeps the story active by using the present tense.
C. ineffective paragraph.

Example 2-3

King is not likely to be found guilty of vehicular manslaughter in California. "Manslaughter is the unlawful killing of a human being without malice." Cal. Penal Code § 192 (West 2008). Vehicular manslaughter is manslaughter that occurs when "driving a vehicle in the commission of an unlawful act, not amounting to felony, and with gross negligence." Cal. Penal Code § 192(c)(1) (West 2008). There is no question that King's driving killed the bicyclist and that she acted without malice. She probably did not, however, commit an "unlawful act" or act with "gross negligence."

This is an . . .

> **A.** effective paragraph because it quotes only the necessary statutory language and uses proper tone and style.
> **B.** ineffective paragraph because the sentences are too short and choppy.
> **C.** ineffective paragraph because there are too many quotations.

EXPLANATIONS

Explanation 2-1

A is wrong. The characteristics that make it "sound like it was written by a lawyer"—the legalese—actually make the paragraph ineffective. For instance, "herewith" is legalese and adds nothing to the substance of the sentence. Use plain English unless you're writing about a particular term of art. **B** is also wrong. Quote relevant statutory language, but quote sparingly from cases. The reader expects you to synthesize and summarize the material. These topics are covered in more detail in Chapters 7 and 8. *C* is correct. This paragraph is ineffective for the reasons A and B are wrong. In addition, this paragraph refers to what a court "believed" and "felt," and those terms aren't used when describing a court's actions.

Explanation 2-2

A is wrong. Although avoiding legalese is good, legal writing uses a more formal, professional tone. For instance, use last names and avoid contractions. In addition, use terms of art—like "aggravated assault." **B** is also wrong. Using the active voice and following the traditional subject-verb-object sentence structure is generally easier for readers to follow. But that doesn't mean you shouldn't use present tense. Past tense (writing about things that happened in the past as if they already occurred) is different from passive voice, which often omits the subject or places the subject near the end of the sentence rather than at the beginning. The incident with the pole already happened, so describe it using the past tense. *C* is correct. For the reasons stated in A and B, this paragraph could be more effective.

Explanation 2-3

A is correct. This paragraph quotes the key statutory provisions. It also uses terms of art, like "unlawful act" and "gross negligence," consistently. The style is crisp and not distracting. **B** is wrong. Short sentences in the active voice often work best in legal writing. **C** is also wrong. Although you should rarely quote from cases, quoting key statutory language, as noted in A, is necessary.

Objective Writing

CHAPTER 3

Overview: Office Memos

Your first major writing assignment might be an office memo or part of one. This chapter provides some tips, some common pitfalls to avoid, and an overview of the audience, purpose, and format of an office memo.

SOME TIPS FOR PLANNING YOUR TIME

Writing legal memos takes a lot more time than you might think. One of the most important things that you can do to ensure that your writing process goes smoothly and that your finished work product is good is to start on your assignment early.

You'll seldom write a memo from front to back. Although office memos typically follow a certain format (Heading, Question Presented, Brief Answer, Facts, Discussion, and Conclusion), there's no prescribed order for the actual writing of an office memo. Once you've researched the issue and read the sources, it's up to you whether to start by drafting the Heading and proceeding in order, or whether to start by drafting sections that are located further back in the memo.

Once you've got a working draft, make sure that the sections of the memo work together. For instance, you might write the Facts before the Discussion, but you'll need to edit the Facts afterward to ensure that all of the facts that you use in the Discussion are also included in the Facts. Writing is an iterative process.

Even if the assignment calls for a "first draft," don't hand in your actual first draft. Many professors will ask you to write the same memo or brief twice—once as a "first draft" and again as a "final draft." Between the two, the professor might give you feedback on the first draft to show you ways to improve your work in the final draft. Plan to revise your memo many times before handing it in, even as a first draft. And after your professor provides feedback, revise several more times to produce the final draft. (Note that not all professors will ask you to turn in both a first draft and a final draft.)

Proofreading isn't the same thing as revising. Your revising process should be rigorous—read your document and ask yourself, for instance, whether it has all the required components in the proper order, whether each component accomplishes its purpose, whether you've included extraneous information that doesn't help answer the question presented, whether your organization is clear and logical, whether your analysis is thorough, etc. After thoroughly revising the memo, proofread for more detailed, stylistic points such as grammatical errors, typos, punctuation, proper citation, etc. It will likely take several rounds to polish your document to meet the profession's high standards.

SOME COMMON PITFALLS

Pitfall: Misinterpreting or misstating the applicable legal rules. You might be able to avoid this problem by reading the authorities carefully enough. Make sure to budget enough time to read them multiple times. If you're struggling with constructing a rule or explaining a rule, see Chapters 7 and 8. Sometimes, students misinterpret the applicable legal rules because they don't yet understand weight of authority. To get additional practice with weight of authority concepts, see Chapter 4.

Pitfall: Organizing by authorities rather than substantive points. Keep in mind that you need to synthesize the authorities rather than catalog them like a book report. For help with constructing a synthesized rule, see Chapter 7, and for help with organization, refer to Chapter 6. Once you have a good structure for organizing your analysis, remember to use strong "roadmap" paragraphs and topic/thesis sentences to communicate that organization clearly to the reader. For more on these topics, see Chapters 12 and 27.

Pitfall: Using a persuasive, argumentative tone rather than an objective one. To avoid this, imagine how you'd feel if you make a recommendation and your employer relies on it to spend time and money on a case that turns out to be weaker than your memo said it was. You're not doing the requesting attorney or your client any favors by burying or ignoring a weakness in your client's case.

Pitfall: Using a lot of waffling language. Edit out unnecessary waffling from your predictive analysis. For instance, words like "seems," "appears," "suggests," and "may" suggest the writer is hedging and lacks confidence in her analysis. Although no prediction is certain, aim to minimize the amount of waffling in your memo to the extent you can do so and maintain accuracy. It's generally okay to use words like "probably" and "likely" to express that you're making a prediction. Those usually aren't viewed as waffling.

Pitfall: Not thoroughly explaining all steps of the analytical process about how the law will likely apply to the facts. You probably need to be more explicit in explaining your analysis than you initially think. Some professors, much like your former math teachers, will tell you to "show your work." If you think your case is similar to a precedent, explain the similarities in detail. If you think the other party has a strong argument that the precedent is distinguishable, then you should likewise explain that in detail. Even if something seems clear to you, it might not be obvious to the reader, who may not have read or be as familiar with the legal authorities as you. Imagine yourself in the reader's shoes when deciding what to include and not include. It's important that your analysis doesn't jump to conclusions because the reader can't follow your thought process and, consequently, won't know whether she agrees with it. For practice with legal analysis, see Chapters 9, 10, and 11.

More generally, it's also helpful to keep in mind why lawyers write memos, who is the typical audience for a memo, and how a memo's format makes it most usable for the reader. The rest of this chapter briefly addresses those topics.

AUDIENCE AND PURPOSE OF AN OFFICE MEMO

An office memo communicates legal analysis about a specific legal problem or question. Typically, an office memo is predictive—it answers a question about how the law would likely apply to a particular set of facts and predicts the outcome. For instance, a memo might address the question of whether under federal copyright law a court would likely conclude that a certain song that parodies another song falls within the fair use exception to copyright infringement.

The information communicated in the office memo usually serves as a basis for making a decision about how to proceed in a case or situation—either to help make a client's planning decision (for instance, how to organize a business for certain tax consequences) or to help a lawyer make a strategic decision (for instance, whether filing a certain motion would likely be worthwhile). Typically, junior attorneys or summer clerks write office memos for more senior lawyers at a law firm or office, although sometimes clients or others also receive a copy.

A good memo fully and objectively evaluates each question presented without arguing for or against a certain outcome. The tone is neutral. Your role as the writer is not to persuade the reader of any particular argument or result, only that your analysis is objective, thorough, and accurate. The reader wants to get as accurate a sense as possible of the facts, the law, and the likely outcome in order to make an informed decision about how to proceed. Assume that the reader hasn't read any of the legal authorities you discuss and doesn't know the relevant facts.

OFFICE MEMO FORMAT

Legal memos vary in their format. Some law firms or attorneys have a preferred format with specific section titles, ordering of sections, and the like. Sometimes preferences vary given the circumstances. For instance, if the requesting attorney wants to minimize the time spent on the memo and doesn't need a formal document for the client or file, she might ask for just an email with the key points of analysis and legal authorities. Sometimes attorneys prefer a more conventional, formal memo, such as when a copy of the memo is going to the client or when the memo addresses a question that arises frequently in similar cases.

Most legal writing courses require students to write a formal memo with the following components: Heading, Question Presented, Brief Answer, Facts, Discussion, and Conclusion. The Heading is simply the top part of the memo with the "To," "From," "Date," and "Re" lines. Chapters 4 through 15 discuss the other memo components in more detail—and the skills you need to write them—and provide examples and explanations.

Once you learn how to write a good memo in the conventional, formal format, you can adjust the format as circumstances require in practice. If you're assigned to write a legal memo in your summer job, it's often wise to ask the requesting attorney if she wants a full formal memo or something more abbreviated and if a sample memo in the preferred format is available to use as a reference. Remember, regardless of the format you use in practice, do thorough and accurate legal research and analysis.

CHAPTER 4

Choosing Authority

It's the first day of class and it feels just like your fifth-grade civics lesson. "What are the three branches of government and how does each of them make law?" And you thought law school would be more sophisticated than this! But—regardless of whether beginning law students think this is just "background" material—understanding where law comes from and how much weight you give it is the key to legal analysis and organizing the documents you write.

In fact, social scientists have studied the differences in how practicing attorneys and new law students read cases. One of the key differences between the two is that practicing attorneys pay much more attention to where the law is from—the jurisdiction, the branch of government, and the level of the court within the jurisdiction.[1] This is different from the way students typically read cases in the casebooks used in many of your other classes. In those law school classes, jurisdiction and court level matter little because casebook professors focus on broad legal principles or doctrines in

---

1. Several authors have explored reading strategies for law students. *See, e.g.,* Dorothy H. Deegan, *Exploring Individual Differences Among Novices Reading in a Specific Domain: The Case of Law*, 30 Reading Res. Q. 154, 161-62 (1995); Laurel Currie Oates, *Beating the Odds: Strategies of Law Students Admitted Through Alternative Admissions Programs*, 83 Iowa L. Rev. 139 (1997); Ruth Ann McKinney, *Reading Like a Lawyer: Time-Saving Strategies for Reading Law Like an Expert* (2005); Leah M. Christensen, *Legal Reading and Success in Law School: An Empirical Study*, 30 Seattle L. Rev. 605 (2007).

the abstract. In your legal writing class, because you're working on a specific problem and using sources for a specific reason, you'll read cases the way you will read in practice.

Terminology Notes: "Mandatory authority" is also known as "binding authority." "Persuasive authority" is sometimes called "nonbinding authority."

WHAT YOU NEED TO KNOW ABOUT CHOOSING AUTHORITY

"Primary sources" are more important and useful than "secondary sources" when writing practice documents. Primary sources are the texts produced by the three branches of government: statutes, treaties, case law, administrative regulations, and executive orders. The Constitution itself is also a primary source. Your professor might ask you to exclusively cite primary sources. Secondary sources, on the other hand, are texts about the law written by scholars or commercial companies, and may differ in how much weight they carry. Because they merely comment on the law, secondary sources are rarely important enough to cite in practice documents like memos and briefs.

Two hierarchies govern your decision about which sources carry the most weight and which you'll cite first. You'll need to take both into account as you decide which sources to use and how to prioritize sources in your writing.

The branch of government hierarchy: This prioritizes the importance of various primary sources—which branch's law governs or trumps others. The Constitution's text trumps everything else. But after that, it's complicated because "judicial review" confers on courts the enormous power to decide whether statutes and regulations are constitutional. That's part of the "checks and balances" that make it impossible to say that the primary sources from one branch are always more important than another. But if the constitutionality of a statute or regulation is not at issue, then the following list shows the priority that governs which sources to use and which to put first in your document:

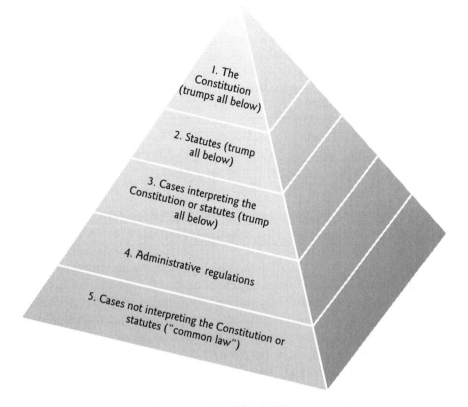

This means that if a statute is constitutional, it carries more weight than any of the cases interpreting the statute. Courts interpreting the statutes are "bound by" or must follow the statute's text. And if the statute is constitutional, set it out first in your writing, even before cases from the Supreme Court that interpret it.

The case law hierarchy: This prioritizes cases within one jurisdiction or from different jurisdictions. A decision from a court within the jurisdiction where your assignment takes place is usually more important than any decision from a different jurisdiction. The United States contains at least 52 jurisdictions: the federal government plus each state and the District of Columbia.[2] Here is the common pattern for weight of authority of the courts within one jurisdiction:

---

2. There are still more court systems if one includes the tribal court systems on Native American reservations across the country.

1. The court of last resort (*usually the "Supreme Court" of that jurisdiction*)[3]
2. An intermediate appellate court (*in most but not all states*)
3. Trial courts (*whose decisions are published in the federal system, but usually not in the state systems*)

Type of Court	Federal	State
court of last resort	U.S. Supreme Court	most states call it the (State Name) Supreme Court
intermediate appellate court	the Court of Appeals	most states call it the Court of Appeals or something similar
trial court	U.S. District Courts	states have a variety of names for trial courts

Some states and the federal system segment the intermediate appellate court into geographic divisions. Remember that the decisions of an appellate court in the state whose law governs is mandatory authority, while decisions of other states' courts are persuasive only.[4] That's true regardless of the courts' ranks within their respective states. Thus, if you're writing a memo set in California, a decision from the California Court of Appeals (an intermediate appellate court) is "more important" and should usually appear in your analysis *before* a case from the Michigan Supreme Court.

Mandatory authority includes decisions from any court that might decide an appeal from the court where your case is being or would be litigated. Work from the top down on these lists while addressing authority in writing. Usually you will address or summarize all "mandatory authority." You'll put it first. Ignoring mandatory authority is a bad idea because courts must follow it. Further, no matter how similar the facts may be to a case from outside your jurisdiction, use cases within your jurisdiction before citing cases from outside your jurisdiction. One caveat: Under "stare decisis" lower courts are bound only by the precedent case's holding and not by anything unnecessary to the decision. Statements a court makes that are unnecessary to the decision are called "dicta."

---

3. If you've watched *Law and Order*, you know that the New York Supreme Court is not the court of last resort, but instead a trial court. In New York the highest state court is the Court of Appeals.

4. Note that each state's rules about weight of authority are themselves a matter of law and they can vary by state.

The relationship between the federal system and the states' systems is a complex one, but except for constitutional issues or "diversity jurisdiction,"[5] usually the two systems operate separately. These questions are more complicated than we can easily summarize here, but generally, if you're in federal court with a federal issue, you'll rarely cite to state law. If you're in state court on a state law question, you'll rarely cite to federal law. In state court, sometimes you'll get questions that implicate constitutional rights or federal statutes. For example, state law usually governs the crime of burglary, but a burglary trial in state court may need to address whether the defendant's federal constitutional rights regarding search and seizure were respected when the police gathered burglary evidence. In cases such as those, you'll cite federal law in state court.

The date of a source of law can also affect the weight of the authority. If two sources are of equal weight using the previous lists, the more recent source is usually more important. A more recent source may change the law and make an older source of questionable value. For example, the legislature may amend a statute and make earlier cases interpreting the statute irrelevant. Or a higher court may overturn or reverse earlier decisions, making them questionable sources.

HOW TO CHOOSE AUTHORITY

Using the copyright and fair use problem in Appendix B, we'll walk you through the process of choosing authority.

Problem

> Here is a quick overview of the copyright and fair use problem (for details, see Appendix B). Young is suing Olds for violating the Copyright Act when Olds wrote a song based on Young's original, "Rockin' in the Free World." Olds' song uses the structure and many lyrics of the original but changes the original song's political message. The music of the two songs is not at issue, only the lyrics. Young expects that Olds will argue that his song is a parody that falls under the fair use exception to the Copyright Act. The court will consider the relevant factors set out in the fair use statute, 17 U.S.C. § 107 (2006): whether the copy was transformative and targeted the original; whether it took more than necessary of the original; and whether it will interfere with the original's market.

---

5. Diversity jurisdiction allows parties from different states to litigate a state law issue in federal court in a case when a substantial sum is at issue. It involves special circumstances that you'll learn about in Civil Procedure.

Step 1: Make a list of all the available sources of law. For cases, note the court that decided the case and when it was decided. For statutes, you'll need to know the dates when the statute or amendments to the statute took effect, because cases interpreting the statute may be irrelevant if the cases interpreted a different version of the relevant part of the statute.

In the copyright and fair use problem, copyright is mentioned in the Constitution. But unless the Constitution's wording is at issue, do not write about the relevant constitutional provision. Appendix B includes several sources of law. Remember that Young, the plaintiff in our problem, is considering filing suit in a federal court in California, which is geographically part of the Ninth Circuit. For purposes of illustration, we'll add several sources to the list. Following are the available sources of law, in no particular order:

- *Fisher v. Dees*, 794 F.2d 432 (9th Cir. 1986).
- *Campbell v. Acuff-Rose Music, Inc.*, 510 U.S. 569 (1994).
- Barton Beebe, *An Empirical Study of U.S. Copyright Fair Use Opinions 1978-2005*, 156 U. Pa. L. Rev. 549 (2008).
- *Dr. Seuss Enters., L.P. v. Penguin Books USA, Inc.*, 109 F.3d 1394 (9th Cir. 1997).
- *Leibovitz v. Paramount Pictures Corp.*, 137 F.3d 109 (2d Cir. 1998).
- *Mattel, Inc. v. Walking Mountain Prods.*, 353 F.3d 792 (9th Cir. 2003).
- 17 U.S.C. § 106 (2006).
- 17 U.S.C. § 107 (2006).
- *Abilene Music, Inc. v. Sony Music Entm't, Inc.*, 320 F. Supp. 2d 84 (S.D.N.Y. 2003).

Step 2: Start with primary authority and apply the list of hierarchy of authority between primary authorities from different branches of the government. The list includes a federal statute, and its constitutionality is not at issue. That tells you where to start. The first source of law you'll mention in your memo will be the two provisions of the federal copyright statute, 17 U.S.C. §§ 106 and 107, which trump the case law that interprets these provisions. You'll start by setting out the parts of the statute that apply.

Step 3: Next look at the list of cases and apply the list of hierarchy of authority to those. Remember that cases from your own jurisdiction and any courts that are mandatory authority for it will be most important to the analysis. Your list has many federal cases and no state cases. If there were a state case on the list, you would probably put it last on your list of cases to use, or not use it at all, because it would not be mandatory authority on a federal issue like copyright. In the federal courts, the U.S. Supreme Court trumps all courts below. So use *Campbell* before the other cases. (But remember that before citing *Campbell*, you'll state and cite the relevant portion of the statute.)

Next, after choosing any Supreme Court cases that apply, consider the fact that the plaintiff is considering bringing suit in a federal court in California, which is geographically in the Ninth Circuit. Cases from that circuit will be more important to us than other federal cases. The Ninth Circuit cases are:

- *Fisher v. Dees*, 794 F.2d 432 (9th Cir. 1986).
- *Dr. Seuss Enters., L.P. v. Penguin Books USA, Inc.*, 109 F.3d 1394 (9th Cir. 1997).
- *Mattel, Inc. v. Walking Mountain Prods.*, 353 F.3d 792 (9th Cir. 2003).

Discuss these cases only after discussing the more highly ranked authority represented by the statute and *Campbell*. Deciding how to prioritize these cases can be complicated and there may be no clear answer. Here, the U.S. Supreme Court addressed fair use in detail in *Campbell*, and that case will trump or may have changed earlier law. *Campbell* was decided in 1994, so the *Seuss* case and the *Mattel* case are probably more important than the other Ninth Circuit case on the list because *Seuss* and *Mattel* were decided after *Campbell* and will take the Supreme Court's *Campbell* decision into account. Therefore, plan on using *Seuss* and *Mattel* instead of earlier cases in ordinary circumstances.

Cases from the federal intermediate appellate courts will be more important than cases from the federal trial courts. If you have enough cases from your own jurisdiction to present a good picture of the law and address most of the issues in your analysis, you might decide to ignore other circuits. In contrast, if you have scant authority from the higher courts in your jurisdiction, you'll likely want to use out-of-jurisdiction cases to fill out your analysis. But either way, you'll usually address those cases *after* you've addressed mandatory authority.

Finally, consider whether the cases from the trial level federal courts will help you. Often the lower courts will be the place to look for fact-based reasoning that will fill in the gaps left by higher courts. Sometimes that's very useful. But usually you'll discuss such decisions *after* you've addressed mandatory authority.

Step 4: After planning your analysis using mandatory primary authority, consider whether persuasive primary authority or secondary authority adds something important that is currently missing. Remember that primary authority—authority written by a governmental agency and regarded as "the law"—is usually more important than secondary authority—commentary written by a scholar or commercial company to explain the law. But primary authority, when it's not mandatory, is only persuasive. When you haven't found adequate mandatory authority to support your arguments, you may decide to use persuasive primary authority, usually cases from lower courts in your jurisdiction or cases and statutes from other jurisdictions. When you use persuasive primary authority, use it after you've addressed the mandatory authority from your jurisdiction.

Although secondary authority can help you find mandatory primary authority and understand an issue, it rarely adds something important that you can't find in your primary sources, which have precedential value. In fact, some legal writing professors discourage citing secondary authority in memos and briefs for this reason. Here, the law review article is helpful as background reading for the writer, but it's not worth citing in your writing because it likely would not carry weight with a court. Occasionally, a secondary authority is such a well-known, respected text that jurists consider it influential, such as the Restatements of the Law.

Step 5: Using the priority of authority you've established for the section, you can start writing. Most sections of your memo on the copyright and fair use problem will start by quoting the relevant part of the copyright statute. Then you'll need to formulate a rule that explains how the cases have interpreted the statute on the particular issue this section addresses. (For help with that see Chapter 7 on Constructing a Rule.) You'll use the U.S. Supreme Court case, *Campbell*, if it's helpful to this particular issue. Next explain the law the Ninth Circuit has applied to this issue, focusing on the post-*Campbell* cases from the Ninth Circuit when you can. That may be all you need to do. But if you feel the need to give the reader a more complete picture, you might turn to pre-*Campbell* Ninth Circuit cases, other circuits, or to trial level opinions on your issue. And by now you have a pretty good handle on using weight of authority to help decide how to write strong analysis and how to organize the section of your memo where you describe the law.

EXAMPLES

Here are some examples requiring you to choose among authorities. For each example, choose the best answer. Explain to yourself why you've chosen that answer. Then read the explanations in the last section of this chapter to check your work.

Examples 4-1 and 4-2 are based on the following situation: *You're writing a memo on a state law question involving Ohio property law. The issue involves adverse possession and Ohio has a statute on point. Under the statute, adverse possession occurs when a landowner fails to prevent others from using his land. In that circumstance, the original owner loses title and the adverse possessor(s) become the lawful property owner. The constitutionality of Ohio's adverse possession statute is not at issue, which means this problem involves just state law.*

Consider the following sources and decide which sources would appear before others in your memo. Then answer the questions that follow.

A   a 1999 case on adverse possession from the intermediate appellate court in Ohio with similar facts to yours

B   a 2005 U.S. Supreme Court "takings" case on when the government can take land from private citizens for governmental purposes under the Fifth Amendment of the U.S. Constitution

C   a 2009 case on adverse possession from the Illinois Supreme Court with similar facts to yours

D   the most recent Ohio adverse possession statute

E   a 2008 case from the Ohio Supreme Court on a procedural issue but with similar facts to yours

F   a 2001 law review article from the *Ohio State Law Journal* on adverse possession

G   a 1975 case on adverse possession from the Ohio Supreme Court

Example 4-1

The best way to prioritize the sources listed is to start with . . .

    A. the U.S. Supreme Court case, and then follow with the 1975 Ohio Supreme Court case.

    B. the most recent Ohio adverse possession statute and then use the most recent Ohio case on adverse possession, the 1999 case from an Ohio intermediate appellate court with facts similar to yours.

    C. the Ohio adverse possession statute and then use the 1975 Ohio Supreme Court case.

    D. the Ohio adverse possession statute and then move to the most recent Ohio Supreme Court case: the 2008 Ohio Supreme Court case with similar facts but on a procedural issue. Next set out the 1975 Ohio Supreme Court case.

Example 4-2

Which of these statements reflect sound decisions about choosing sources for the previous problem? More than one answer might be correct.

    A. Use every source listed from Ohio.

    B. Use the Illinois Supreme Court case, but only if it adds something my analysis needed and it was based on an Illinois statute similar to the Ohio statute.

    C. Include the U.S. Supreme Court case because everyone must follow the U.S. Supreme Court. Even though takings and adverse possession are different claims, both are about taking property from private owners without paying for it.

    D. Do not use the *Ohio State Law Journal* article.

Example 4-3

This example is based on the following situation: *You're writing a brief that addresses the federal question of whether an employer in Boston, Massachusetts, has violated the Civil Rights Act of 1964 (42 U.S.C. § 2000 et seq.) by discriminating in hiring on the basis of race. The constitutionality of the act is not at issue. You're in the First Circuit, a federal intermediate appellate court. Consider the following sources and decide which sources would appear before others in your memo. Then answer the question that follows.*

A   a 2011 newspaper article on unemployment that states there are 500 qualified applicants for every position open in Massachusetts

B   a 2010 case with similar facts and on the same issue from the Third Circuit

C   Title VII of the Civil Rights Act, the applicable provision from the U.S. Code

D   a 2001 federal district court (trial level) case from Massachusetts with somewhat similar facts

E   a 1993 U.S. Supreme Court case that sets out the test for the relevant provision of Title VII

F   a 2007 Massachusetts Supreme Court case that interprets the Massachusetts state statute on employment discrimination

G   a 1995 First Circuit case that applies the test set out in the U.S. Supreme Court case above (E)

H   a 2004 First Circuit case that applies the test set out in the U.S. Supreme Court case above and adds a test to be applied in the First Circuit

Which answer best identifies which sources you would most likely use and best prioritizes those sources from the most weight to the least weight?

    A. Title VII of the Civil Rights Act; the 1993 U.S. Supreme Court case; the 2004 First Circuit case. I might also use the 1995 First Circuit case; the 2010 Third Circuit case; and the 2001 federal trial court case from Massachusetts. I would not use the Massachusetts Supreme Court case or the newspaper article.

    B. The U.S. Supreme Court case; Title VII of the Civil Rights Act; the 2007 Massachusetts Supreme Court case; the 2004 First Circuit case. I might also use the 1995 First Circuit case; the 2001 federal district court case from Massachusetts; the 2010 Third Circuit case; and the newspaper article.

    C. Title VII of the Civil Rights Act; the 1993 U.S. Supreme Court case; the 1995 First Circuit case; the 2004 First Circuit case; the Massachusetts Supreme Court case; the 2010 Third Circuit case; the 2001 federal trial court case from Massachusetts; the newspaper article.

    D. The 1993 U.S. Supreme Court case; Title VII of the Civil Rights Act; the 2004 First Circuit case; the 1995 First Circuit case; the 2010 federal trial court case. I might also use the 2010 Third Circuit case and the Massachusetts Supreme Court case. I would not use the newspaper article.

Example 4-4

Read the following statements and decide whether each makes a correct statement about using sources of law in a document. More than one answer may be correct.

    A. If you get all the sources into the document, it really doesn't matter what order you put them in. Choose the cases you like best first.

    B. Use primary sources when you can to support your arguments or analysis.

    C. It's always clear in exactly what order sources should appear in your document.

    D. It's not unusual for a document to contain only federal sources or only state sources.

Example 4-5

In the following excerpt, consider how the author uses authority. The excerpt comes from the beginning of a memo section that explains California law concerning "gifts in contemplation of marriage." To identify the court to which the author is citing, you need to know that "Cal." in the date parenthetical indicates the case is from the California Supreme Court and "Ct. App." in that parenthetical indicates a case is from an appellate court in California. Decide whether the statements that follow the example are correct.

According to the common law interpretation of the California "Gifts in Contemplation of Marriage" statute, there must be (1) a conditional statement (2) implied to the donee (3) during the transfer of the conditional gift. When determining whether a gift is conditional or not, courts in this jurisdiction search for unambiguous indicators of a condition.

For example, the court found that although a donor believed that the donee had accepted his marriage proposal, her true intentions were otherwise. *Steinback v. Halsey*, 115 Cal. Rptr. 2d 213, 255 (Ct. App. 1978). In that case, the court found the donee could retain some gifts because they were not made in contemplation of marriage. The *Steinback* donee retained gifts of perfume, luggage, clothing, and money, even though the court found her at fault for the breach of marriage promise. Similarly, in *Simon*, the donor's parents were present at the moment of the marriage proposal and on that occasion gave the donee a wristwatch with the explanation that "this is from dad and I." *Simon v. Marks*, 634 P.2d 259, 262 (Cal. 1969). The California Supreme Court in that case found that the words uttered during the transfer of the wristwatch were not conditional and therefore the wrist watch was a gift not in contemplation of marriage.

A problem with this excerpt is that . . . (note: more than one answer may be correct)

A. it doesn't quote and cite the statute it mentions.
B. all the cases it cites are from California.
C. it cites no authority for the statements it makes in the first paragraph.
D. it cites to intermediate appellate courts before it cites to the California Supreme Court, which is stronger authority.

EXPLANATIONS

Explanation 4-1

A is an easy mistake to make because most people think of the U.S. Supreme Court as the most powerful decision maker about the law. But here, the Supreme Court addresses a federal constitutional issue—takings—that has nothing to do with Ohio adverse possession law. This is a state law question and federal cases aren't likely to help. **B** is also wrong. Although it's important to start with the statute, and the factually similar case from an Ohio appellate court is a good case to use, you would most likely address the Ohio Supreme Court case before moving to the case from the Ohio intermediate appellate court. **C** is a good answer. The constitutionality of the Ohio adverse possession statute is not at issue, and thus the Ohio courts are bound by the statute's text. You'll start your analysis by quoting the state statute. Then you'll move to the highest court interpreting the statute, the Ohio Supreme Court case that addresses adverse possession specifically. This is true even though the case is 35 years old. In addition, you might then use the case from the Ohio intermediate appellate court. **D** is not as good as C because even though the 2008 Ohio Supreme Court case has similar facts and is much more recent than the 1975 case, the 2008 case was decided on a different issue and is not really relevant to your analysis.

Explanation 4-2

A is incorrect because although you want to concentrate on Ohio sources, your list includes Ohio sources that you would probably not use. The secondary source might be useful for you to read, but you probably wouldn't cite it. **B** is correct and illustrates the factors to consider when deciding to use a case from another jurisdiction. But you probably have adequate Ohio law to write your analysis here and you're not likely to cite the Illinois case. **C** is wrong. One of the important lessons of the first-year legal writing course is to keep the analysis for each type of claim separate. The U.S. Supreme Court has written much about "takings," but that is a completely different cause of action than adverse possession, which is usually a state law issue. The U.S. Supreme Court case is irrelevant. **D** is correct. Most professors believe it's efficient to use secondary sources to educate yourself about the law and to use the article's footnotes to find primary sources. They would not, however, be particularly impressed if you were to cite to a law review article instead of primary mandatory authority.

Explanation 4-3

A is the best answer. This question includes some tough judgment calls, but this answer starts with the text that binds the courts—the federal statute—and moves to the highest court in the federal system interpreting it, the U.S. Supreme Court. Because both of the First Circuit cases set out the test for courts in the First Circuit to follow, most writers would choose the most recent case next. These three binding sources are essential, but note that the First Circuit case comes after the statute and the U.S. Supreme Court case. The next group—cases you might use—starts with the older First Circuit case. If that case was very widely cited or its facts were closer to your case than the more recent First Circuit case, this case would be more important to include and might make the list of "essential" sources. You would then move to persuasive sources. Here the two most persuasive, because they have similar facts and are both from federal courts, are the Third Circuit case and the district court case. The Third Circuit case is usually considered more important than a district court case, even if the district is geographically within the same circuit as your problem. So the level of court within the federal system generally trumps both geographic location and date. Finally, most writers would not choose to go outside the law from the federal system to use the state court decision that is based on a different statute. Similarly most writers would ignore newspaper articles, regardless of their relevancy. **B** mistakenly puts the U.S. Supreme Court case before the federal statute that binds that Court. It also places the Massachusetts Supreme Court case in a position of importance. Remember that usually on federal issues you will not use state law cases. **C** again incorrectly uses the Massachusetts Supreme Court case and places it before other important federal system decisions. Finally, **D** is wrong because it starts with a case, albeit an important one, before the statute.

Explanation 4-4

A is a poor choice because the point of learning how legal readers weigh sources of law is to use that knowledge to prioritize authorities in your writing. Answer **B** is correct. Good legal writers almost always use secondary sources, if at all, after they have addressed primary authority. Remember, some legal writing professors ask first-year students not to cite secondary authority at all. **C** is wrong. Although the rules you've learned about weight of authority will guide you while deciding which sources to use and how to prioritize them, using authority is not an exact science. Sometimes authorities are close in weight, or you have other good reasons for choosing one authority over another. Those reasons might include unusual facts in your case or knowing your audience's specific preferences. **D** is also correct. If you're writing about a federal issue, it's not unusual for *all* the sources you use to be federal sources. Similarly, it would be typical for a document addressing a state law issue to contain only state law sources.

Explanation 4-5

A is correct. Generally speaking, start with your highest authority, and in this case that's the statute. Additionally, usually you'll quote the relevant part of the statute. With cases, on the other hand, you will most often paraphrase. **B** is wrong. When you have enough case law to present a convincing analysis, as you appear to here, there's no need to go outside your jurisdiction. **C** is correct. This chapter explains how important it is for the reader to know how much weight to give a statement about the law. If you don't provide a cite the reader will not know where the assertion comes from or how much deference to give to the assertion. **D** is also correct. Although occasionally there might be a good reason to deviate from ordering authority strictly according to weight, here there's no reason to explain what the lower courts did before explaining how the court resolved your issue.

CHAPTER 5

Interpreting Statutes

Is your first reaction when you see a statute quoted in a case or a casebook to skip it? If it is, you're like many readers. "After all," some readers rationalize, "the case will tell me about the important language. I don't need to parse it all out for myself." The trouble with that reaction is that learning to read statutes closely and to make arguments about them is one of the most important skills you'll learn in law school.

Terminology Notes: Some professors and textbooks speak of the "canons of construction." Others talk about the "rules of statutory interpretation." They mean the same thing. In addition, when talking about statutes, the terms "plain meaning" and "plain language" are used interchangeably.

WHAT YOU NEED TO KNOW ABOUT INTERPRETING STATUTES

Statutes require close reading. Outlining a statute to understand what the statute requires a party to prove often helps you understand what you're reading. In reading statutes, decide exactly what it requires you to prove or disprove for your client. Assume every word in the statute is there for a reason. Pay close attention to words like "and," "or," "except," "either," "unless," and "all." Often you'll need to outline more than one rule from just one statute. Once you've figured out what the statute requires a party to prove, then you'll know whether it applies to your problem.

As a primary source, you'll set out the statute in the section of your memo that states the rule and explains the law. Then you'll analyze the statute in the section that applies the law to your case. The statute is just like any other form of law you're applying to your facts. In fact, because it often tops your list of mandatory primary authority, you'll usually set it out first if it's on point for your issue.

Most legal readers prefer that you quote the relevant parts of the statute, even though the same reader often wants you to paraphrase a case. Although this can vary from professor to professor, the most common practice is to expect you to paraphrase what you've read in cases so that the reader can more easily move through your memo. The same idea applies to pruning the statute down to its most relevant parts by using ellipses or partial quotes. But because lawyers pay such close attention to the actual text of the statute, you'll want to quote those relevant sections. Paraphrase to explain a case's reasoning. Quote a statute's relevant words.

Statutory arguments are usually ordered according to the rules of statutory construction, also known as the canons of construction. The rules on how to interpret statutes are largely common to all jurisdictions. You'll find them in the cases from your jurisdiction. And like any other authority, you'll look for your jurisdiction's highest court's rules on how to interpret statutes in a particular legal issue.

There are too many canons to list, but here are a few examples:

- A statute should be read as a harmonious whole with its separate parts being interpreted in a manner that furthers the statutory purpose.
- All words in a statute should be given effect.
- A term used more than once in a statute should be given the same meaning throughout.

The canons are not always respected. In fact, scholars have sometimes criticized them for directing courts to treat statutes in inconsistent ways. Nevertheless, courts often use the canons in interpreting statutes.

One of the canons that courts most often honor is: "If the meaning of the statute is clear and unambiguous, the court will apply the plain meaning to the facts and look no farther." Thus, if the statutory language has only one meaning and is not ambiguous on its face, most lawyers will order statutory arguments in this way:

- First, analyze based on the "plain meaning" of the statute, including definitions or statements of purpose.
- Next, if the plain meaning of the statute doesn't favor your client, then you'll want the court to look beyond it. Your job will be to explain why the statute may have more than one meaning and thus is ambiguous,

which allows the court to look to courts' interpretations and legislative intent. Or to turn to other canons of construction that may apply.

- If one side can show the plain meaning of the statute is ambiguous, then both sides will look to cases interpreting the statute or cases interpreting similar statutes. Choose cases following the rules about weight of authority. (See Chapter 4.)
- Next, base your analysis about the statute on its legislative history.
- Finally, if none of the above helps much, consider citing secondary authority like law reviews or treatises to support your analysis about the statute.

HOW TO INTERPRET STATUTES

Using the cell phone manslaughter problem in Appendix A, we'll walk you through the process of developing statutory arguments.

Problem

> *Here is a quick overview of the cell phone manslaughter problem (for details see Appendix A).* Allison King used her wireless phone, without a hands-free device, while driving in dense fog on a winding road on the edge of an ocean cliff. King placed the call to warn her friends about the dangerous conditions, as they would be meeting later. While she was making the call, she hit and killed a bicyclist. The prosecution will attempt to convict King of vehicular manslaughter by showing that she drove while committing an illegal act (driving while using a wireless phone without a hands-free device) and with gross negligence. King will argue that her actions fit within the emergency exception to the wireless phone prohibition. She will also argue that she did not act with gross negligence.

Step 1: Read the statute closely, and decide which parts are most relevant for your problem by outlining a rule. As you read, ask yourself whether a change in your facts would make a difference to how this part of the statute would apply. If it would, then it's an important part of the statute for your problem.

Here is the first part of the statute:

Cal. Penal Code § 192. Manslaughter; voluntary, involuntary, and vehicular

Manslaughter is the unlawful killing of a human being without malice. It is of three kinds:

(a) Voluntary—upon a sudden quarrel or heat of passion.

(b) Involuntary—in the commission of an unlawful act, not amounting to felony; or in the commission of a lawful act which might produce death, in an unlawful manner, or without due caution and circumspection. This subdivision shall not apply to acts committed in the driving of a vehicle.

(c) Vehicular—

(1) Except as provided in subdivision (a) of Section 191.5, driving a vehicle in the commission of an unlawful act, not amounting to felony, and with gross negligence; or driving a vehicle in the commission of a lawful act which might produce death, in an unlawful manner, and with gross negligence.

This part will often be pretty easy. The state doesn't have to prove malice or intent. There are three kinds of manslaughter and to determine which part or parts apply, consider the facts, loosely interpreted. Your client was driving a car, suggesting that sub-section (c) is the applicable part. First you'd need to check to make sure the exception in Section 191.5(a) doesn't apply. Here, you'd see that section involves intoxication and doesn't apply to King's facts so it can be ignored. Next, it's clear that the state doesn't need to prove intent. It does have to prove your client was driving a vehicle with gross negligence AND either committing an unlawful act that does not need to be a felony OR a lawful act that might produce death in an unlawful manner.

So, your outline looks like this so far:

The state must prove that:
(1) King was driving with gross negligence
   AND
(2) committing either:
   (a) an unlawful act
      OR
   (b) a lawful act that might produce death in an unlawful manner.
(Note to self: The state does NOT have to prove intent or a felony.)

You now know that the state has two ways of convicting King. One way is to show that (1) she was driving with gross negligence and (2)(a) committing an unlawful act. The other is to show that (1) she was driving with gross negligence and (2)(b) committing a lawful act that might produce death in an unlawful manner. You consider our facts and decide that provision (2)(b) is unlikely to apply because the courts have never applied it in circumstances remotely similar to our case.

That leaves us with one way the state might convict King—if she was committing an unlawful act. Your research locates a statute concerning using a wireless telephone. These are the words of the statute:

Cal. Vehicle Code § 23123. Driving motor vehicle while using wireless telephone; penalty; exceptions

(a) A person shall not drive a motor vehicle while using a wireless telephone unless that telephone is specifically designed and configured to allow hands-free listening and talking, and is used in that manner while driving.

(b) A violation of this section is an infraction punishable by a base fine of twenty dollars ($20) for a first offense and fifty dollars ($50) for each subsequent offense.

(c) This section does not apply to a person using a wireless telephone for emergency purposes, including, but not limited to, an emergency call to a law enforcement agency, health care provider, fire department, or other emergency services agency or entity.

Let's outline and analyze this statute.

a. A person can use hands-free technology. (It appears that King may have violated this statute because she wasn't using her cell phone in a hands-free way. You should continue reading and outlining the statute.)

b. The punishment scheme. (We're unconcerned with this so far because at this point you're most concerned with determining whether King was driving while committing an unlawful act by making a cell phone call without a hands-free device.)

c. King will be excused for using the cell phone if she was making an emergency call. Qualifying emergency calls aren't limited to those listed, but the legislature did provide this list of examples:

    1. A law enforcement agency (no)
    2. A health care provider (no)
    3. A fire department (no)
    4. Another emergency services agency (no)

Adding this to the manslaughter statute, so far you know the state must prove that:

(1) King was driving with gross negligence
AND
(2)(a) she was committing an unlawful act by using a wireless telephone without hands-free technology while driving and not fitting the exception for making an "emergency call."

The state can show King was driving and that she was using her cell phone without a hands-free device. This means your reading of the relevant part of the statute boils down to two questions:

1. Can the state show her call was NOT for "emergency purposes"?
    AND
2. Can the state show she was grossly negligent?

Step 2: Quote the relevant parts of the statute in the section of the memo that sets out the applicable law. You'll need to address two issues that grow out of the statute. So first, you'll quote the parts of the statute that set up both issues early in the memo's Discussion section. Then, later in the Discussion section—at the beginning of each sub-section—you'll quote the relevant parts of the statute for that particular section. In each place, after quoting the statute's language, you'll discuss any cases that illuminate that part of the statute.

Step 3: Analyze how the statute applies to our facts in the corresponding application sections of the memo. Take a look at the order of arguments that lawyers usually follow when they make arguments about statutes and consider how they apply here. First come the "plain language" arguments. Here, the first issue is whether the exception to the prohibition against driving while using a wireless telephone applies to King because her call was for an "emergency."

King might make this plain meaning argument:

> Allison King was not committing an "unlawful act" when she used her wireless telephone without a hands-free device because she falls under the plain language of the exception that allows her to make calls in an "emergency" situation. It was an emergency because it was necessary for her to call her friends to prevent them from entering dangerous driving conditions. Under the plain language of the statute she was not driving unlawfully.

The state, in contrast, can argue:

> Allison King does not fall under the plain meaning of the exception to the statute that allows calls in an "emergency" because the plain language of the statute includes a list of circumstances that all involve calling an institution involved with public safety or health. The plain language does not include calling one's friends as an "emergency."

Next both sides might argue why, even if they don't prevail under the plain meaning, the statute is ambiguous. Then, each side will turn to cases for support.

King: Further, even if this court decides that the plain meaning of the statute does not include King's emergency, the plain language of the statute is ambiguous because it does not limit the use of the emergency exception to the list provided. In an emergency, imminent danger is present. *People v. Harris*, 104 Cal. Rptr. 3d 131, 133 (Ct. App. 2010). (The argument would continue from here, using fact-based or analogical analysis.)

State: Alternatively, the plain meaning of the statute is ambiguous because the courts have been left to define the meaning of "emergency." Thus, the court may turn to case law such as *People v. Harris* and *People v. Tompkins* for guidance about when an emergency exists. (The argument would continue from here, using fact-based or analogical analysis.)

Although many statutes lend themselves to plain meaning arguments, no strict rule requires lawyers to make this sort of argument. For instance, where courts have developed a lot of case law interpreting a statute, lawyers will typically start with arguments based on that case law rather than on the plain language of the statute.

EXAMPLES

Here are some examples that use statutes. For each example, more than one answer may be correct. Explain to yourself why you've chosen your answers. Then read the explanations in the last section of this chapter to check your work.

Example 5-1

Title IX of the Education Amendments of 1972 provides that "no person in the United States shall, on the basis of sex, be excluded from participation in, be denied the benefits of, or be subjected to discrimination under any education program or activity receiving federal financial assistance." Teenagers at Smithtown High School are bullying a team member, Jason Johnson, because he is gay. We know that Jason is a "person." What else does the statute require Jason to prove?

A. Jason must prove:
   1. he was excluded from an education program
   AND
   2. the education program was receiving federal financial assistance.
B. Jason must prove:
   1. one of the following occurred:
      a. he was effectively excluded from participation in an education program or activity on the basis of sex; or
      b. he was effectively denied the benefits of an education program or activity on the basis of sex; or
      c. he was effectively subjected to discrimination under an education program or activity on the basis of sex,
   AND
   2. one of the following is true:

        a. the education program received federal financial assistance; *or*

        b. the education activity received federal financial assistance.

C. Jason must prove:

    1. on the basis of sex one of the following is true:

        a. he was excluded from participation in an education program or activity; *or*

        b. he was denied the benefits of an education program or activity; *or*

        c. he was subjected to discrimination under an education program or activity,

  AND

    2. one of the following is true:

        a. the education program received federal financial assistance; *or*

        b. the education activity received federal financial assistance.

D. Jason must prove:

    1. because of his sexual orientation the school:

        a. excluded him from participation in an education program or activity; *or*

        b. denied him the benefits of an education program or activity; *or*

        c. subjected him to discrimination under an education program or activity,

  AND

    2. either:

        a. the education program received federal financial assistance; *or*

        b. the education activity received federal financial assistance.

Example 5-2

You represent the gay teenager, Jason Johnson, suing the school district under Title IX, the statute you outlined in Example 5-1. Review the following arguments and decide which ones would be effective.

  A. Argue that under the plain language of Title IX, Jason Johnson suffered discrimination "based on sex" because his teammates bullied him because of his sexual orientation.

  B. Argue that even if the statute does not mention sexual orientation, and no case law expands the word "sex" to include sexual orientation, Congress meant to include it because the statute uses the word "sex."

  C. Analogize to a Title VII case from the U.S. Supreme Court that held that bullying someone based on his sexual orientation is discrimination "based on sex."

D. Argue that if the statute is ambiguous, another canon applies that requires the court to interpret various provisions of the federal code in harmony with each other.

Example 5-3

New Mexico's negligent arson statute provides that negligent arson "consists of a person recklessly starting a fire or causing an explosion, whether on the person's property or the property of another person, and thereby directly causing the death or bodily injury of another person; or damaging or destroying a building or occupied structure of another person." Jessie Johnson threw a lit firecracker into a phone booth in Albuquerque, which cracked the glass of the phone booth. To convict Jessie of negligent arson, what must the prosecutor prove?

  A. The prosecutor must prove that Jessie:
  1. whether on a person's property or the property of another a person:
     a. recklessly started a fire; or
     b. recklessly caused an explosion,

  AND

  2. directly caused:
     a. the death of another person; or
     b. the bodily injury of another person; or
     c. damage to another person's building or occupied structure; or
     d. destruction to another person's building or occupied structure.
  B. The prosecutor must prove that Jessie recklessly caused an explosion and damaged a building of another person.
  C. The prosecutor must prove that Jessie:
  1. either:
     a. on the person's property; or
     b. on the property of another a person,

  AND

  2. either:
     a. recklessly started a fire; or
     b. recklessly caused an explosion,

  AND

  3. either:
     a. directly caused the death of another person or the bodily injury of another person; or

b. damaged a building or an occupied structure of another person.

D. The prosecutor must prove that Jessie was on another person's property and recklessly caused another person's death.

Example 5-4

New Mexico's negligent arson statute is quoted in Example 5-3. Jessie Johnson threw a lit firecracker into a phone booth in Albuquerque, which cracked the glass of the phone booth. You're the prosecutor. Assume that you have set out the rule by quoting the relevant parts of the negligent arson statute. You're writing a section on "damaging or destroying a building or occupied structure of another person," and have explained the law by describing mandatory authority that illustrates its application.

As you begin to apply the statute, you would start . . .

A. with a plain language argument because the statute is clear that it applies to buildings and all structures.

B. with a plain language argument because the word "building" normally has one meaning.

C. by arguing the legislature intended to include telephone booths because they are buildings.

D. by making arguments using either other canons of construction to clarify what the New Mexico Legislature intended when it wrote the statute or by making analogies to other cases about what "building" means.

EXPLANATIONS

Explanation 5-1

A is incorrect because it's incomplete. You may have identified one way the teenager could prove his claim, but the outline leaves out "on the basis of sex" and "or activity," both important parts of the statute. Every word counts! **B** is also incorrect. It identifies most of the elements of the statute, but it adds the word "effectively" to the statute. Although the case law interpreting the statute may add this concept, when working with statutes you can neither add nor subtract words from the statute. Lawyers will want to see the exact words of the statute. **C** illustrates one good way to outline the statute. You can easily see what the teenager has to prove. **D** is incorrect because, like B, it adds a concept to the statute—"sexual orientation" instead of "sex."

Explanation 5-2

A is correct. Lawyers often make arguments based on the plain language of the statute. The U.S. Supreme Court has held that if the language is clear and admits only one meaning, the Court will look no farther. **B** is incorrect. Most lawyers would reject that argument as too weak and unsupported to include in your analysis. Generally speaking, your analysis will focus on arguments each side can support with a cite to authority. **C** is correct. Analogizing to mandatory authority addressing a similarly worded statute is an argument most lawyers would be happy to make. **D** is also correct. There are many canons of construction and finding another that suggests that the court should interpret the statute in a way that is useful to your case is a good option.

Explanation 5-3

A is correct in that it's one of the possible ways you could outline the statute to figure out what the prosecutor has to prove. There isn't just one right way to outline the statute; the important thing is that you can see at a glance exactly what a prosecutor must prove. In the process of outlining, it's especially important to pay attention to modifiers and to discover whether the statute is ambiguous. **B** is also a correct answer although it's very brief and may be only one way of many that the prosecutor might bring his case. **C** is yet another correct answer because it's another way one might outline the statute without leaving out any relevant part. **D** is wrong. It not only leaves out relevant elements of the statute, but also chooses to include parts of the statute that don't apply to your facts.

Explanation 5-4

A is incorrect. The statutory language specifically limits applicability to buildings and *occupied* structures, not buildings and all structures. Although your facts might support a plain language argument that the telephone booth is a "building," the phrase "occupied structure" probably doesn't apply to your facts. **B** is a correct answer, although if your research had revealed many cases interpreting the word "building," you would no longer make the plain language argument. **C** is incorrect. Generally, move to a legislative intent argument only after you've argued the plain meaning or the case law interpreting the statute. **D** could be correct under certain circumstances. If your research had established that the word "building" is susceptible to several meanings, you would not make a plain language argument, but would indeed start by making arguments referring to the cases that interpret the word. Or perhaps your research has disclosed other canons of construction that courts typically apply in a case like yours. In that case, you might make arguments with another canon.

6

Organizing the Discussion

How should the Discussion section of your memo be organized? You might wonder whether the organization really matters much. The short answer is, "yes, it does." Professor Sheila Simon's lasagna metaphor demonstrates why. Lots of people like lasagna, and some don't. But we all expect it to be layered a certain way and to look "right." We expect meat (or vegetables), cheese, pasta, and sauce—and even though it's all in one casserole, we can still see (and taste) the distinct layers. Now imagine that the chef put the lasagna in a blender. Would we still like it? Probably not as well, even though all the parts are there. Somehow, the organization matters. The same is true for the Discussion section of a legal memo: the organization matters. Your reader expects the parts to be in a certain order, and she likely will be unhappy or confused if her expectations aren't met.

WHAT YOU NEED TO KNOW ABOUT ORGANIZING THE DISCUSSION

The analytical process that lawyers use to *think through* a legal problem is often referred to by the acronym "IRAC." Use IRAC to *plan* your work before you write, but the organization you actually write with will be slightly different, as we'll explain in a moment. Even though it sounds formulaic, IRAC (and each of its variations) is simply the structure of deductive reasoning. The IRAC letters stand for these parts:

I = issue
R = rule
A = application/analysis
C = conclusion

We'll go through each component in more detail in this chapter, with one modification (discussed in the next few paragraphs). And as this analytical structure implies, you'll organize your Discussion section around the issues rather than around the relevant authorities.

In a memo's Discussion section, use a variation on IRAC that begins with the conclusion you reach rather than a statement of the issue. Various terms are used in textbooks to express this structure, but they're all based on stating your conclusion first.

Your textbook might refer to CRAC, CREAC, CRuPAC, the organizational paradigm, or some other version of the IRAC structure that begins with a conclusion. Although you'll analyze a legal problem using IRAC, you'll communicate that analysis in writing—in the Discussion section of a memo—using CRAC or one of the other variations. All these variations begin with the conclusion on the issue (rather than the issue itself). Some variations explicitly include information that is implicitly presumed in IRAC's "Rule" component by including separate letters to represent explaining or proving the rule, which are introduced below and discussed in detail in Chapter 8. The following chart summarizes what these acronyms represent.

IRAC	CRAC	CREAC	CRuPAC (or the organizational paradigm)
I = Issue	C = Conclusion	C = Conclusion	C = Conclusion
R = Rule	R = Rule	R = Rule	Ru = Rule
		E = Explanation	P = Proof
A = Application/ Analysis	A = Application/ Analysis	A = Application/ Analysis	A = Application/ Analysis
C = Conclusion	C = Conclusion	C = Conclusion	C = Conclusion

In this chapter, we use the acronym CRAC, but CREAC and CRuPAC are not significantly different conceptually. When discussing organization with your teacher, it's a good idea to use the term your textbook or professor uses.

The "conclusion" is the answer to the legal question—the issue—your memo addresses. Why were you asked to write this memo? What problem does your client have? For instance, if you were writing a memo that addressed whether the court had personal jurisdiction over the defendant as well as whether the defendant was negligent, the conclusion on the first issue might be expressed this way: "The court likely has personal jurisdiction over the defendant." The conclusion on the second issue might be "The defendant was likely negligent." Notice how these conclusions are short; keep them to one short phrase or sentence, depending on your reader's expectations. You'll be able to express the conclusion more clearly after you've completed the analysis, so don't feel as though you have to draft a perfect conclusion for each issue at the beginning of the writing process. You can always go back and perfect your conclusions as you complete the Discussion section.

The "rule" is the law that resolves your issue. The rule can come from any type of authority—a constitution, a statute, an administrative regulation, or case law—or from some combination of them. If the rule comes from one source, your task is to articulate that rule and to break it into its parts, which are often elements or factors. For instance, if the issue is whether the statute of limitations has run in a negligence suit, the rule might be a state statute providing that all negligence suits must be filed within two years of the underlying incident giving rise to the claim. When the rule comes from more than one source, you need to synthesize a rule for the reader, as explained in Chapter 7 on Constructing a Rule. To support the rule in your writing, you should include a citation to the source for the rule and a discussion of the authorities that create the rule—often referred to as rule explanation or rule proof. See Chapter 8 on Stating and Explaining the Rule.

The "application/analysis" is where you apply the legal rule identified previously to the facts of your client's case. Notice this component is called both "application" and "analysis." Be sure to include counterarguments, and don't think of this step as simply mechanical. It's where you express your thought process and show your reader how the law and the facts fit together. In that sense, the application/analysis is a lot like eighth grade math. In math courses, even if you got the correct answer, you didn't get all the credit unless you "showed your work." In memo writing, the application/analysis section is where you "show your work"—and if you've done that well, the reader can reach her own conclusion and have confidence in your work product even if she disagrees with your conclusion. See Chapters 9-11 on Fact-Based Analysis, Analogical Analysis, and Policy Analysis.

The "conclusion" is where you briefly state the conclusion to your analysis on the issue. The conclusion should be explicit. You can hedge—"likely" and "probably" are fair game if it really is a close call—but you shouldn't just say "maybe." You were asked to write the memo because the reader wants your legal analysis, not to have to figure it all out for himself. The conclusion can usually be short, and is often a single sentence. It needs to be consistent with the answer you telegraph in the memo's Brief Answer section, but it can usually be much shorter. And it also has to be consistent with the conclusion you state at the beginning of the discussion of that issue.

If the memo addresses only one issue, though, many writers skip the final "conclusion" within the Discussion section's CRAC. Instead, they save that summation for the final Conclusion section of the memo, because it follows immediately after the Discussion section.

You should have one CRAC for each independent issue the memo addresses. It is much easier to follow one discussion at a time than to have a number of issues all mixed up together. So keep each independent issue separate, and analyze each issue in successive CRACs. If you have two independent issues, your Discussion section should have two CRACs, one after the other. This structure is much more effective than lumping the conclusions on the two issues together, then the two rules, then the two applications, and then both final conclusions. These two structures, in an outline format, would look like this:

GOOD EXAMPLE

DISCUSSION

Umbrella/roadmap section

Conclusion on Issue 1:   C
                             R
                             A
                             C

Conclusion on Issue 2:   C
                             R
                             A
                             C

BAD EXAMPLE

DISCUSSION

Umbrella/roadmap section

Conclusion on Issue 1 and Issue 2

                    C for Issue 1
                    C for Issue 2
                    R for Issue 1
                    R for Issue 2
                    A for Issue 1
                    A for Issue 2
                    C for Issue 1
                    C for Issue 2

Each separate issue—each CRAC—should have its own subheading within the Discussion section (unless the memo is extremely short, but even then headings are often helpful). When you're addressing more than one issue, you usually want a roadmap in the introduction or umbrella section to let the reader know there are a number of issues and to show how they relate to each other. If you have questions about how to write an umbrella section, see Chapter 12.

Sub-issues within a CRAC are usually organized into mini-CRACs within that main CRAC. Sub-issues are, after all, issues. They are just issues that fall under the umbrella of a larger issue. So you'll have a main CRAC to address the main issue, but you'll also organize the discussion of the sub-issues into mini-CRACs. How do you know whether you have sub-issues? If you have more than one contested element of a rule, you generally have sub-issues that need their own mini-CRACs.

These mini-CRACs fit in the "application/analysis" section of the main CRAC. Because they flow from the contested elements—which are part of the "rule"—they have to come in a part of the Discussion section that comes after the rule. That part is the application/analysis section, and the sub-issues follow each other the same way main CRACs would.

DISCUSSION

Umbrella/roadmap section

C	(conclusion on the main issue)
R	(main rule)
A	(umbrella paragraph identifying the sub-issues)

      Sub-issue 1:   c
                                   r
                                   a
                                   c

      Sub-issue 2:   c
                                   r
                                   a
                                   c

C   (main conclusion)

HOW TO ORGANIZE THE DISCUSSION

This section uses two scenarios to walk you through the process of organizing the Discussion: the cell phone manslaughter problem in Appendix A and a multi-issue problem that includes a civil battery issue and a statute of limitations issue. The section starts with the multi-issue problem involving civil battery and the statute of limitations. Then it will toggle back and forth between the two scenarios so you experience working on a problem with related issues under one claim, and working with a problem with more than one independent issue.

Problem

Here is a quick overview of the cell phone manslaughter problem (for details, see Appendix A). Allison King used her wireless phone, without a hands-free device, while driving in dense fog on a winding road on the edge of an ocean cliff. King placed the call to warn her friends about the dangerous conditions, as they would be meeting later. While she was making the call, she hit and killed a bicyclist. The prosecution will attempt to convict King of vehicular manslaughter by showing that she drove while committing an illegal act (driving while using a wireless phone without a hands-free device) and with gross negligence. King will argue that her actions fit within the emergency exception to the wireless phone prohibition. She will also argue that she did not act with gross negligence.

As with most writing questions, putting yourself in the reader's position will help shed some light on the answer.

Step 1: Articulate the conclusion on your issue, because the reader wants to know that first. Even if the conclusion wasn't clear to you when you started your memo, making the conclusion clear to the reader from the outset will make it much easier to follow your analysis. The conclusion can be as brief as *The Statute of Limitations Does Not Bar the Claim* or *The Defendant Is Likely Liable for Battery.* Most readers will think that more than this sentence heading is too much detail for this introductory conclusion. And some readers will expect just the issue here, rather than the conclusion. In those instances, the phrase *Statute of Limitations* or the term *Battery* would suffice. But absent a reason to think your particular reader expects that you simply state the issue, you're usually safest to start with your conclusion on that issue.

Imagine that your client has been sued for the tort of battery. The sole issue you're asked to address is whether the client will be held liable. Assume you conclude that she is not likely to be found liable for civil battery. You might articulate the opening conclusion within the Discussion section like this:

Liability for Civil Battery Is Unlikely.

In the same case, imagine that you have two issues: (1) whether the client is likely liable and (2) whether the statute of limitations has run (so that the plaintiff can't recover even if the client did commit battery). These issues are completely independent, so you need to organize your analysis of them in a separate CRAC for each. You know they're independent because they have separate rules, different relevant facts, and potentially separate outcomes. Because they are independent, you usually start with the procedural issue (statute of limitations). So your memo's Discussion section headings might look like this:

DISCUSSION

    I. The Statute of Limitations Is Not Likely a Bar.
    II. Liability for Civil Battery Is Unlikely.

Notice the roman numerals in front of these conclusions/headings. Keep the numbering in the Discussion section consistent with what you've used in the Questions Presented and Brief Answers. If you had two issues in the Questions Presented and labeled them "I" and "II," do the same thing with the conclusions on those CRACs in the Discussion section—and keep them in the same order. That way, if the reader wants to follow the discussion on one of the issues, he can find it easily.

Step 2: Next, the reader needs to know the rule. Rules come from a variety of sources. Frequently, you have to synthesize the rule from more than one source. Sometimes, this can be a complicated process. State the rule as simply as possible, breaking it into elements when possible and using the terms of art the legislature or courts use.

Turning to the cell phone manslaughter problem, the main rule might be stated as follows:

> "Manslaughter is the unlawful killing of a human being without malice." Cal. Penal Code § 192 (West 2008). Vehicular manslaughter is manslaughter that occurs when "driving a vehicle in the commission of an unlawful act, not amounting to felony, and with gross negligence." Cal. Penal Code § 192(c)(1) (West 2008).

From this rule, we can deduce four elements necessary to be convicted of vehicular manslaughter in California:

    (1) the unlawful killing of a human being;
    (2) while driving a vehicle;
    (3) committing an unlawful act; and
    (4) with gross negligence.

The analysis for each element, if in dispute, would be organized as a mini-CRAC within the Discussion. In the problem, it's clear the bike rider died, so the first element is not contested. It's also clear your client was driving a vehicle—her car—so the second element is also not contested. You'd point these facts out and demonstrate, not simply assert, that the first two elements were met. But because you could accomplish that in a few short sentences, you don't need mini-CRACs with complete headings for these uncontested elements. You could discuss those in the umbrella section, or address them very briefly at the beginning of the application. The third and fourth elements, though, are contested, so you'd address those two elements in mini-CRACs under the main CRAC of "vehicular manslaughter."

Returning to your client who was sued for civil battery, recall that you had two main issues: underlying liability for civil battery and a potential statute of limitations defense. Your jurisdiction follows the Restatement rule:[1] Civil battery occurs when the defendant (1) causes a harmful or offensive contact with the plaintiff, and the defendant (2) intends to cause harmful or offensive contact with the plaintiff or a third person.

Now let's add some facts. Your client, Ms. Johnson, was at a neighborhood park with her dog, Travis. Travis was on a long leash (about 15 feet), and he kept barking at a squirrel that had climbed up a tree. Ms. Johnson had been periodically pulling on the leash, but Travis kept ignoring her as he was far more interested in the squirrel. Travis' barking generally wasn't bothering Ms. Johnson, but she noticed a family with a sleeping baby approaching so she wanted Travis to stop barking. Rather than holler at Travis to get his attention—which was just as likely to wake the baby—she picked up a tennis ball she'd brought to the park and threw it at Travis' back legs to get him to turn and stop barking. Unfortunately, Ms. Johnson didn't have very good aim, and the tennis ball rolled under the foot of a nearby runner, causing him to trip. As a result of being tripped, he fell into a cement bench and broke his right arm.

Of course the commotion caused an even greater disturbance than Travis' original barking, and Ms. Johnson felt terrible. But she felt even worse when the runner filed suit for civil battery. With the elements outlined previously, the first element is clear; Ms. Johnson caused a "harmful or offensive contact" with the runner. But the second element requires intent, and that is questionable in two respects: First, did Ms. Johnson intend to cause any "harmful or offensive" contact? Second, even if hitting Travis in the back legs with a tennis ball would have been harmful or offensive, because she didn't intend to cause a harmful or offensive contact with the runner, does Travis qualify as a "third person"?

In outline format, the CRAC up to this point—so including the "C" and the "R"—for a memo in that case might look like this:

---

1. Restatement (2d) of Torts § 13 (1965).

DISCUSSION

Umbrella/roadmap section

C(onclusion on Issue 1) R	I. The Statute of Limitations Is Not Likely a Bar. rule for statute of limitations rule explanation for statute of limitations * * *
C(onclusion on Issue 2) R	II. Liability for Civil Battery Is Unlikely. rule for civil battery rule explanation for civil battery
(mini-CRAC Conclusion)	1. Likely Intent to Cause a Harmful/Offensive Contact
(mini-CRAC Rule)	rule for h/o contact rule explanation for h/o contact * * *
(mini-CRAC Conclusion) (mini-CRAC Rule)	2. Likely No Intent Regarding a "Third Person" rule for third person rule explanation for third person * * *

Step 3: Next, the reader needs to know how the facts apply to the rule — the "application/analysis." As always, try to help the reader as much as possible. Starting the application/analysis section with a transition like "here" or "in our case" tells the reader you're moving from the rule section to your facts.

What facts do you include? Include any fact that is relevant, meaning it could, at least potentially, change the outcome. Even if you thought about a fact and ultimately decided it would not change the result, you should still address that fact in the application/analysis. The reader may wonder about the same fact, and if you haven't explained why it doesn't change the result, the reader may have less confidence in your final conclusion. You can't completely know which facts are relevant until you understand the law, and additional facts themselves can make a fact relevant that might otherwise be insignificant. But if you think the reader might wonder about a fact, you should include it.

Consider the relevant facts in the cell phone manslaughter problem, included in Appendix A. We'll address the sub-issue noted previously from the fourth element of the main rule: whether King acted with "gross negligence." Imagine that you formulated your basic gross negligence rule as follows (which would be followed with more detail and facts from the relevant cases):

> "'Gross negligence' is the exercise of so slight a degree of care as to raise a presumption of conscious indifference to the consequences." *People v. Harris*, 104 Cal. Rptr. 3d 131, 133 (Ct. App. 2010). Courts apply the standard objectively. *Id.* If a "reasonable person in the defendant's position would have been aware of the risk involved," the law presumes the defendant was aware of the risk and he acted with gross negligence, even if he in fact was unaware of the risk. *Id.* Gross negligence depends on the circumstances of each case. *People v. Newton*, 104 Cal. Rptr. 3d 138, 141 (Ct. App. 2010). However, at least one California court held that, as a general matter, a defendant "knew or should have known that driving while talking on his cell phone was endangering the lives of others." *People v. Tompkins*, 89 Cal. Rptr. 3d 904, 909 (Ct. App. 2009).

Once you understand the rule and the relevant cases, you'd likely conclude that the following facts are relevant to the gross negligence sub-issue:

- King dialed her cell phone while driving
- the road was a winding two-lane road
- the road was on the edge of a cliff with the sea below
- there was dense fog; "near whiteout conditions"
- driving conditions were even more hazardous than usual
- King was driving slowly

If, on the other hand, the issue you were concerned with was whether King was entitled to the "emergency purpose" defense, which is a sub-issue under the third main element—committing an act that is not a felony (driving while talking on her cell phone)—the relevant facts might include these:

- the road offers very few places to pull over
- King was concerned for the safety of several friends and others on the road
- King planned to warn her friends to refrain from driving until road conditions improved and it was safer

Notice how the relevant facts change depending on the issue; the facts necessary to resolve the "gross negligence" element are different from the facts necessary to resolve the "emergency purposes" defense.

Once you've determined which facts are relevant, your task in this part is to connect those facts to the rule. You need to use the key terms of art and compare or contrast—in legal writing terms "analogize" or "distinguish"—your facts with the facts in the precedent cases. (See Chapter 10.)

Step 4: Finally, remind the reader of your conclusion. You began your CRAC with your conclusion. And after reading the rule and application/analysis, the conclusion ought to be obvious. But you still need to restate it. Do so at the end, usually in just a sentence at the end of the application section. And just as signal words help in the application/analysis section, signaling this conclusion with words like "therefore" or "in conclusion" makes your organization easier for the reader to follow. Finally, few legal questions are a slam-dunk, so don't be afraid to qualify your projections with "probably" or "likely."

In the civil battery case used earlier, the final conclusion on the statute of limitations CRAC might read like this:

> Therefore, the Plaintiff's civil battery suit will not likely be barred by the statute of limitations.

And now, if you wanted to see an outline of the CRAC structure for the Discussion section of a memo in Ms. Johnson's civil battery case, it might look like this:

DISCUSSION

Umbrella/roadmap section

C	I. The Statute of Limitations Is Not Likely a Bar.
R	rule for statute of limitations
	rule explanation for statute of limitations
A	application for statute of limitations
C	conclusion for statute of limitations
C	II. Liability for Civil Battery Is Unlikely.
R	rule for civil battery
	rule explanation for civil battery
A (mini-CRAC Con.)	1. Likely Intent to Cause a Harmful/Offensive Contact
(mini-CRAC Rule)	rule for h/o contact
	rule explanation for h/o contact
(mini-CRAC App.)	application for h/o contact
(mini-CRAC Con.)	conclusion for h/o contact
(mini-CRAC Con.)	2. Likely No Intent Regarding a "Third Person"
(mini-CRAC Rule)	rule for third person
	rule explanation for third person
(mini-CRAC App.)	application for third person
(mini-CRAC Con.)	conclusion for third person
C	conclusion for civil battery

EXAMPLES

Here are some examples of the organization for a memo's Discussion section. As with many of the illustrations provided in this chapter, these examples are in bullet format so you can quickly see the organizational structure rather than the details within each component. Some, but not all, come from the cell phone manslaughter problem in Appendix A. For each example, choose the best answer. Explain to yourself why you have chosen that answer. Then read the explanations in the last section of this chapter to check your work.

Example 6-1

DISCUSSION

- Vehicular Manslaughter Is Likely.

- *Harris*—arguably similar (a reasonable person would realize making a cell phone call while driving, especially with road conditions King faced, was dangerous), so probably gross negligence, but probably more of an emergency, so maybe not an unlawful act.

- *Tompkins*—arguably similar (a reasonable person would realize making a cell phone call while driving, especially with road conditions King faced, was dangerous), so probably gross negligence, and probably similar regarding whether an emergency, so likely an unlawful act.

- *Newton*—arguably distinguishable on gross negligence because the circumstances weren't as extreme of an emergency; similarly, arguably not as strong in terms of an emergency, so likely an unlawful act.

- It is therefore likely King committed vehicular manslaughter.

This is an . . .

   A. effective organization for the memo's Discussion section because the conclusion on the main issue is clearly identified, all of the relevant authorities are analogized or distinguished from your case, and it ends with the conclusion.
   B. effective organization for the main issue of vehicular manslaughter because it includes all the components of deductive reasoning.
   C. ineffective organization for the memo's Discussion section because it's organized around the authorities rather than the issues.
   D. ineffective organization for the main issue but an effective organization of the two sub-issues.

Example 6-2

DISCUSSION

- King Did Not Likely Commit an "Unlawful Act."
- King's case is like *Newton*, where the call to the obstetrician satisfied the "emergency purposes" exemption, and not like *Harris* or *Tompkins*.
- Although cell phone calls while driving are generally prohibited, that prohibition "does not apply to a person using a wireless telephone for emergency purposes." Cal. Vehicle Code § 23123 (West Supp. 2011).
- King probably did not commit an unlawful act by talking on her cell phone while driving because she likely made the call for "emergency purposes."

This is an . . .

A. effective organization for the "unlawful act" sub-issue because it follows the CRAC format.

B. effective organization for the "unlawful act" sub-issue because it includes all of the components necessary to answer the legal issue.

C. ineffective organization for the "unlawful act" sub-issue because although it includes the sub-rule for unlawful act, it does not quote the main rule governing vehicular manslaughter.

D. ineffective organization for the "unlawful act" sub-issue because the rule should come before the application/analysis.

Example 6-3

DISCUSSION

- "No Gross Negligence"
- "[T]he exercise of so slight a degree of care as to raise a presumption of conscious indifference to the consequences"
- Discuss cases that consider gross negligence
- Analogize/distinguish King's facts with case facts

This is an . . .

A. effective organization for the "gross negligence" sub-issue because it follows the CRAC format.

B. effective organization for the "gross negligence" sub-issue because a final conclusion is not necessary for a sub-issue; the conclusion can be included in the overall Conclusion section of the memo.

C. effective organization for the "gross negligence" sub-issue because it includes the four parts of deductive reasoning.

D. incomplete organization for the "gross negligence" sub-issue because it omits the final conclusion.

Example 6-4

DISCUSSION

- Conclusion = King Is Likely Guilty of Vehicular Manslaughter.

- Rule = quote and cite Cal. Penal Code § 192(c)(1) (West 2008); elements =
  1) the unlawful killing of a human being;
  2) while driving a vehicle;
  3) committing an unlawful act that is not a felony; and
  4) with gross negligence.

- Application/Analysis = first two elements met (explain why very briefly); final two elements contested (mini-CRACs)

  A. C = King Likely Committed an Unlawful Act.
      R = quote/cite Cal. Vehicle Code § 23123 (West Supp. 2011). Statute has an exception when call is for "emergency purposes." Discuss cases (*Harris*, *Tompkins*, *Newton*) with regard to the "emergency" element—facts, issue, holding.
      A = analogize/distinguish King's facts from facts in each of the cases on this issue.
      C = King's call likely not made for an "emergency purpose."

  B. C = King Likely Acted with Gross Negligence.
      R = synthesized rule from the cases (good language in *Harris*). Then discuss cases on the gross negligence issue—facts, issue, holding.
      A = analogize/distinguish King's facts from facts in each of the cases on this issue.
      C = King likely acted with gross negligence.

- Conclusion = because all four elements are met, including unlawful act (because probably not an "emergency purpose") and gross negligence, King is likely guilty of vehicular manslaughter.

This is an . . .

A. effective organization for the Discussion section because it follows the CRAC format.
B. ineffective organization because the application/analysis section is too long.
C. ineffective organization because the sub-issues can be better addressed together rather than separating them.
D. ineffective organization for the reasons stated in both B and C.

EXPLANATIONS

Explanation 6-1

A is incorrect. Although the conclusion on the main issue is articulated, it anticipates analogizing and distinguishing the relevant authorities, and it ends with the conclusion; this organization is ineffective. This outline organizes the Discussion around the relevant cases rather than the better approach of organizing by the issues—which in this case are (1) whether King committed an unlawful act and (2) whether she acted with gross negligence. **B** is also wrong. First, simply including all the components of deductive reasoning does not ensure they are organized effectively. Second, this example does not include all of the parts; the main rule (the statute that defines vehicular manslaughter) is absent, and without that, the reader has no basis to determine whether King is guilty. **C** is correct. As noted in answer A, this outline is organized by the cases rather than the better approach of organizing by relevant sub-issues. In CRAC terms, the organization of this outline would be difficult for a reader to follow: C*R*A*R*A*R*A*C. When analysis is organized by cases instead of sub-issues, the reader has to jump back and forth to figure out the synthesized rule and analysis for each sub-issue instead of having the writer do that work for the reader. In addition, as noted in answer B, the main rule is missing. **D** is wrong. The sub-issues should be divided into mini-CRACs allowing the reader to follow the analytical process for each issue independently. Mixing them together will only confuse the reader.

Explanation 6-2

A is wrong. This outline starts with the conclusion on the sub-issue and ends with the conclusion, as the CRAC structure suggests. But the application/ analysis section should not come before the rule, and in this example, the writer has started analogizing and distinguishing cases before telling the reader about the governing statute, which creates the rule, or the cases that interpret that statute. This structure is ineffective because the reader expects to read about the legal rule before reading your analysis of how that rule applies to the facts at hand. Keep the rule and application separate from each other and in the correct order. **B** is also wrong. The order of the components matters, and here, the order is ineffective for the reasons noted in answer A. Furthermore, the cases should be discussed before they are applied to your case. **C** is incorrect. The organization is ineffective for the reasons noted in answer A. In addition, within a mini-CRAC, readers seldom expect the main rule to be quoted again. Remember that this section is just one part of a larger Discussion section: The main CRAC would cover the vehicular manslaughter requirements and quote the relevant portions of the statute. Within a mini-CRAC, the reader only needs to understand the answer to that smaller question. Hence, the main rule might (or might not) be referred to, but is usually not quoted even when it's included. **D** is the correct answer, as noted in answer A. The rule section should also include information about the cases, as noted in answer B.

Explanation 6-3

A is incorrect. The outline for the sub-issue has no final conclusion; it ends with the application/analysis. The reader expects an explicit conclusion at the end of the analysis for a sub-issue—even if it's a close case, even if it follows logically from the application/analysis section, even if the reader can figure out how you would have concluded, and even though you have already stated your ultimate conclusion in the heading. **B** is also incorrect. Although it's true that some writers omit the final "C" within a Discussion section's CRAC because the memo's Conclusion section will immediately follow the Discussion, that should only be the case when you are writing a single-issue memo. An explicit conclusion at the end of each mini-CRAC is necessary for sub-issues. **C** is incorrect for the reasons listed in answer A. The final conclusion is missing, and although the rule and the rule explanation are explicitly broken apart in this outline, it still represents only three of the four CRAC steps. **D** is correct for the reasons listed in the explanations for A, B, and C.

Explanation 6-4

A is correct. This example follows the CRAC format well. It is organized around issues rather than authorities and the sub-issues are addressed in separate mini-CRACs. The headings are logical—labeling the sub-issues "A" and "B" helps keep them separate—and the sub-issues are properly within the application/analysis section of the main CRAC. **B** is incorrect. When a memo addresses sub-issues, the application/analysis section will likely be relatively long. That section includes the mini-CRACs for the sub-issues, so it's often the longest part of a memo with sub-issues. **C** is also incorrect. Combining sub-issues will make the memo harder, not easier, to follow. They have separate rules and the facts relevant to each sub-issue vary. Therefore, breaking them apart, as done in this example, into separate mini-CRACs is generally the most effective organization for sub-issues. **D** is incorrect. Because both answers B and C are wrong, answer D cannot be correct.

Constructing a Rule

In law, what is a rule? You know about lots of rules from daily life—such as "No trespassing," "No parking here between 8 am and 6 pm," and "All drivers must wear seatbelts." In the context of law a rule is a principle that governs actions. It can also be thought of as the legal test that a court applies to resolve an issue.

Understanding the applicable rule is important. It's a foundational building block for an office memo's legal analysis and the argument in a persuasive brief. Indeed, one of the first things a reader wants to know is what rule will apply to your set of facts. This chapter explains how to identify the rule that a court applies in a case and how to synthesize multiple cases or sources of law to determine the governing rule of law.

Terminology Notes: This interpretive process of reading and understanding various sources of applicable law is what we mean by "rule synthesis" or "constructing" a rule.

WHAT YOU NEED TO KNOW ABOUT CONSTRUCTING A RULE

In law, you'll see common rule types and structures over and over again. A rule can require action (e.g., "shall," "must"), prohibit action (e.g., "shall not," "is prohibited"), authorize action (e.g., "may," "at its discretion"), or declare something to be true (e.g., "Any person who . . . is guilty of . . ."). And rules can be structured in various ways, for instance requiring that certain elements be met or listing factors for a court to consider in making a determination. Don't worry about memorizing these rule structures or their names. But it might be helpful to know as you're reading authorities such as statutes and case law that there are common rule structures. Pay attention to words like "and," "or," and "must" that will help you understand how a rule works. Also, the rule structure will guide your large-scale organization choices, as you learned in Chapter 6.

Here are some common rule structures and an idea of how they might appear:

A *conjunctive test* (also known as an *elements test*): a rule that has a list of required elements.

X results if these elements are met: 1, 2, *and* 3.

A *disjunctive test*: a rule that is structured by an "either/or" test.

X results if either A *or* B is met.

A *defeasible rule*: a rule with an exception or exceptions.

X results where . . . *unless* . . . occurs or exists.

A *factors test*: a rule that provides multiple factors or criteria for determining whether a certain standard is met.

To determine whether X results, *consider* A, B, C, and D.

A *balancing test*: a rule that weighs various considerations against each other, often using factors to measure the considerations.

X results where A *outweighs* B.

Sometimes a rule will have more than one of these structures, in a nested fashion. For instance, a rule might be a conjunctive test with a list of required elements, and one of the elements might use a factors test for determining whether it's met.

X results if these elements are met:
1. –,
2. –, and
3. –.
To determine whether element 3 is met, consider the following factors:
A,
B,
C, and
D.

When you have a single relevant opinion, understanding the rule is simply a matter of reading and analyzing the opinion to figure out the legal test the court applied and how it works. You've probably done this when briefing a case. Note that the rule is different than the case holding. The rule is the legal test that the court applied to resolve the issue. The holding is the court's conclusion after applying that rule to the specific facts of the case. When you're looking for the rule, you're looking to find out what test a court would likely apply to the next case that comes along after the one you're reading.

To figure out what the rule means and how it works, first break the rule down into its parts and diagram or outline it (i.e., list and number the elements or factors in the test).

Pay careful attention to the opinion itself, for example noting whether the rule's language uses words like "must," which suggests a mandatory rule, or "may," which suggests a discretionary rule. Also pay attention to how the case defines the element or factors, how many factors or elements are in the rule, whether a piece of the analysis is an exception, etc. Once you've diagrammed the rule into its parts, examine each part separately and figure out its meaning. Then put the rule back together in your mind by mentally walking yourself through how it works, or by jotting it down as a flowchart and running through how the rule would apply to a hypothetical set of facts.

When you have more than one relevant opinion or source of law, you've got to synthesize them to construct the rule. Synthesis means a conceptual combining of several cases or sources of law into a statement of a legal rule. To do this, first read each authority, and then figure out how they fit together. In this analytical step, abstract a rule that explains all authorities together and forms the legal test that a court looking to those authorities would apply.

Synthesizing authorities doesn't mean creating a catalog in which you describe them one after another. For instance, you aren't synthesizing authorities if you simply say, "Section 123 of the ABC Act provides: . . . . In *Jones*, the court held . . . . In *Woods*, the court held . . . . In *Meyers*, the court held. . . ." That sounds like a list of holdings rather than a rule. Instead, to synthesize authorities you must analyze what they have in common, how they relate to each other, and from that you abstract what rule they stand for together, to be applied to the next case that comes along. This requires reading authorities carefully, reading cases actively and grappling with which facts were important to the result, what the result was, the court's reasoning for reaching that result, and how those aspects of the case compare and relate to the other cases. Sometimes it helps to create a chart or take notes. We'll explain how to do this for one of the examples that follows. You'll also need to consider the weight of authority and the dates of the cases. Sometimes not all of the cases are binding authority, or you may find two seemingly conflicting cases but one is more recent and may have implicitly overruled the earlier case.

This is usually a process of inductive reasoning, as you'll work with the details of the authorities until you see the larger common threads that create a synthesized rule. Sometimes you'll find that a recent decision from a binding court in your jurisdiction has explicitly stated a synthesized legal rule. In that instance, you can just restate that rule if it applies. More often, you have to do the analytical work of figuring out how the authorities fit together to create the governing law.

When you move from figuring out the legal rule to writing about it, you'll want to start by writing about the synthesized rule rather than focusing on the individual authorities. This is the opposite of the inductive reasoning that you did when figuring out how to synthesize the rule. When writing, start by stating your broader synthesis and then explain that rule with narrower detail from the authorities, usually precedent cases. This gives the reader what she wants: a statement of the rule and some explanation of what the rule means and how it works by using explanatory detail from the precedent cases that you used to construct the rule. The next chapter addresses this in more detail.

When the relevant cases don't explicitly state a rule, constructing the rule is a subjective, analytical process. Keep in mind that constructing the rule is more a craft than a science and it's often possible to construct the rule in slightly varying yet still accurate ways. The rule can be formulated narrowly or broadly. You'll want to be aware of this choice and align it with the purpose of your writing, whether that's objective analysis or persuasive argument. For instance, a plaintiff might argue that the court should interpret some case law broadly, to apply to the defendant, while the defendant might argue that the court should construe the case law as setting out a narrow rule that applied to the facts in the precedent case but not to the defendant at hand. In an objective office memo, you'd want to construct the rule neutrally: in the way you think a court would likely view it.

HOW TO CONSTRUCT A RULE

Using the copyright and fair use problem in Appendix B, we'll walk you through the process of constructing a rule.

Problem

> *Here is a quick overview of the copyright and fair use problem (for details, see Appendix B).* Young is suing Olds for violating the Copyright Act when Olds wrote a song based on Young's original, "Rockin' in the Free World." Olds' song uses the structure and many lyrics of the original but changes the original song's political message. The music of the two songs is not at issue, only the lyrics. Young expects that Olds will argue that his song is a parody that falls under the fair use exception to the Copyright Act. The court will consider the relevant factors set out in the fair use statute, 17 U.S.C. § 107 (2006): whether the copy was transformative and targeted the original; whether it took more than necessary of the original; and whether it will interfere with the original's market.

A preliminary note: This process can be hard. Learning to read and understand law, particularly when you've got many authorities, requires some intellectual heavy-lifting. Sometimes you have to read the authorities multiple times, consult legal dictionaries or other resources, and work through the details of the law like a puzzle. And there isn't a trick that always works for this analytical process. Sometimes it helps to make a chart of the cases. Sometimes you'll find a recent case that provides a thorough, comprehensive statement and explanation of the synthesized rule. Other times you need to slog through the authorities, closely reading them in search of a pattern or way of understanding them as a synthesized rule or finding gaps in the law.

Step 1: Identify the relevant authorities. This usually requires legal research. For your legal writing class, your professor may provide authorities to use for your assignment.

Assume that you're working on the copyright and fair use problem and have the authorities in Appendix B: federal copyright statutes regarding exclusive rights in copyrighted works and a "fair use" limitation to those exclusive rights, 17 U.S.C. §§ 106 & 107, and case law interpreting those sections. The case law includes: *Campbell v. Acuff-Rose Music, Inc.*, 510 U.S. 569 (1994), *Dr. Seuss Enterprises, L.P. v. Penguin Books USA, Inc.*, 109 F.3d 1394 (9th Cir. 1997), and *Mattel, Inc. v. Walking Mountain Productions*, 353 F.3d 792 (9th Cir. 2003).

At this point you might mentally order these in terms of their weight of authority: the federal statutes trump the case law interpreting them and the U.S. Supreme Court case trumps the Ninth Circuit cases. If you need a refresher on the basic concepts of weight of authority, see Chapter 4.

Step 2: Read the authorities and try to figure out how they relate to each other in terms of a legal rule. Look for the legal test set out in each of the authorities and then see how each compares with the others. Carefully read language that states a legal test, noting words like *must* or *shall*, suggesting a mandatory rule, or *may*, suggesting a discretionary rule. Also note the structure of the rule, how the case defines the elements or factors, etc.

In the copyright and fair use problem, you're trying to figure out the rule that would determine whether Olds infringed Young's copyrighted lyrics and whether Olds has a viable defense. Start with the statutory authority in Appendix B. Section 106 provides that the owner of a copyright has certain exclusive rights. And § 107 sets out a limitation on the exclusive rights, called "fair use." It provides that "fair use of a copyrighted work . . . for purposes such as criticism, comment, news reporting . . . is not an infringement of a copyright." This language sounds like a defense to copyright infringement. If the use is a "fair use" then there's no copyright infringement.

How do you know if a use is a "fair use"? The next line of the statute tells us: "In determining whether the use made of a work in any particular case is a fair use the factors to be considered shall include . . ." and then lists four factors. Notice that the statute calls the four items "factors" and notes that they "shall" "be considered." This tells us that they're not required elements that all have to be met, but that a court must consider these four factors in making its decision about fair use. You might wonder at this point how to interpret those factors and how courts have decided the case when some of the factors weigh against fair use. Look to the case law to better understand this statutory rule.

It often makes sense to read the case law by starting with the most recent binding authority, which for the copyright and fair use problem is *Mattel, Inc. v. Walking Mountain Productions*, 353 F.3d 792 (9th 2003), or with the case from the highest authority, which is *Campbell v. Acuff-Rose Music, Inc.*, 510 U.S. 569 (1994). From these cases, a picture starts to emerge about how courts interpret the four-factor fair use test. This leads us to our next step.

Step 3: Fully synthesize the authorities to determine the specific rule of law. After you've gotten a basic sense of how the authorities relate to each other with respect to a legal rule, you've got to get a more specific understanding. This usually requires fully synthesizing the case law to a detailed level. As noted previously, there's no special trick for this. You've got to closely read the authorities in search of a pattern or way of understanding them as a synthesized rule.

Continuing on with the sample of our copyright and fair use problem, you need to synthesize the case law to figure out how courts have interpreted the four statutory factors for fair use and applied these factors in precedent cases. Start by reading *Campbell* because it's the only Supreme Court case in our set of authorities and thus carries the greatest weight of authority. We are reading closely and pulling out what looks like important information about how the Supreme Court interprets the statutory factors as a legal test.

Imagine that you take the following notes on *Campbell*. You could put them in a chart format or just jot them down. Do whatever works best for you to process the information.

	17 U.S.C. § 107 (the fair use statute)	***Campbell v. Acuff-Rose Music, Inc.*, 510 U.S. 569 (1994)**
General	"In determining whether the use made of a work in any particular case is a fair use the factors to be considered shall include—[the statutory factors]"	To determine whether an alleged infringing act falls within the fair use exception, courts engage in a case-by-case analysis and do not treat the four statutory factors in isolation, rather the "results [are] weighed together, in light of the purposes of copyright."
First Fair Use Factor	"the purpose and character of the use, including whether such use is of a commercial nature or is for nonprofit educational purposes"	The inquiry here is "whether and to what extent the new work is 'transformative.'" A "transformative use is not absolutely necessary for a finding of fair use, [but] the goal of copyright, [is] to promote science and the arts . . ." Parody has transformative value when it has "critical bearing on the substance or style of the original composition" and its "parodic character may reasonably be perceived."
Second Fair Use Factor	"the nature of the copyrighted work"	This factor is not likely to help make the fair use determination in cases involving parodies "since parodies almost invariably copy publicly known, expressive works."
Third Fair Use Factor	"the amount and substantiality of the portion used in relation to the copyrighted work as a whole"	Courts consider whether "the amount and substantiality of the portion used in relation to the copyrighted work as a whole . . . [is] reasonable in relation to the purpose of the copying." "[T]he extent of permissible copying varies with the purpose and character of the use." A parody "must be able to 'conjure up' at least enough of the original

	17 U.S.C. § 107 (the fair use statute)	Campbell v. Acuff-Rose Music, Inc., 510 U.S. 569 (1994)
		to make the object of its critical wit recognizable," but "how much more is reasonable will depend . . . on the extent to which the song's overriding purpose and character is to parody the original or, in contrast, the likelihood that the parody may serve as a market substitute for the original."
Fourth Fair Use Factor	"the effect of the use upon the potential market for or value of the copyrighted work"	Courts must consider "the extent of market harm caused by the particular actions of the alleged infringer" and "whether unrestricted widespread conduct of the sort engaged in by the defendant . . . would result in a substantially adverse impact on the potential market for the original."

You might also take notes on the key facts of *Campbell* and how the Court applied the test to those facts. Next, you might read *Mattel*, the most recent Ninth Circuit case in our set of authorities. You'd read it with a critical eye toward reconciling it with *Campbell*. Does it add or change anything in the rule?

Comparing *Mattel* to *Campbell*, the general rule about applying the statutory factors appears the same. The *Mattel* court in fact cited *Campbell* in explaining the case-by-case analysis that uses a "flexible balancing" of the statutory factors. And the *Mattel* court seems to explain each of the statutory factors in the same way, often quoting and citing *Campbell*. If you were to add a column for *Mattel* in our chart, you wouldn't have much to say other than that it basically said the same thing about the factors as *Campbell*.

Before finalizing our understanding of the synthesized rule, you'd want to carefully read the rest of *Mattel* to see whether the *Mattel* court did anything notable in applying the test set out in *Campbell*. You'd also want to read the rest of our authorities, bearing in mind the weight of the authorities. After doing that, you'd find that *Campbell* set out the rule regarding the fair use statutory factors and that the Ninth Circuit has followed it. Therefore, the Supreme Court's statement of the rule in *Campbell*, as reflected in our chart, represents a view of the synthesized rule. The next chapter addresses how to turn your rule construction into a written rule statement and explanation for the Discussion section of your office memo.

EXAMPLES

Here are some examples of rule construction, based on the cell phone manslaughter problem in Appendix A. For each example, choose the best answer. Explain to yourself why you have chosen that answer. Then read the explanations in the last section of this chapter to check your work.

Example 7-1

Read the following three statutory sections for the hypothetical cell phone problem: California Penal Code §§ 192 and 191.5 and California Vehicle Code § 23123.

Cal. Penal Code § 192. Manslaughter; voluntary, involuntary, and vehicular

Manslaughter is the unlawful killing of a human being without malice. It is of three kinds:

(a) Voluntary—upon a sudden quarrel or heat of passion.

(b) Involuntary—in the commission of an unlawful act, not amounting to felony; or in the commission of a lawful act which might produce death, in an unlawful manner, or without due caution and circumspection. This subdivision shall not apply to acts committed in the driving of a vehicle.

(c) Vehicular—

(1) Except as provided in subdivision (a) of Section 191.5, driving a vehicle in the commission of an unlawful act, not amounting to felony, and with gross negligence; or driving a vehicle in the commission of a lawful act which might produce death, in an unlawful manner, and with gross negligence.

Cal. Penal Code § 191.5. Gross vehicular manslaughter while intoxicated

(a) Gross vehicular manslaughter while intoxicated is the unlawful killing of a human being without malice aforethought, in the driving of a vehicle, where the driving was in violation of Section 23140, 23152, or 23153 of the Vehicle Code, and the killing was either the proximate result of the commission of an unlawful act, not amounting to a felony, and with gross negligence, or the proximate result of the commission of a lawful act that might produce death, in an unlawful manner, and with gross negligence.

Cal. Vehicle Code § 23123. Driving motor vehicle while using wireless telephone; penalty; exceptions

(a) A person shall not drive a motor vehicle while using a wireless telephone unless that telephone is specifically designed and configured to allow hands-free listening and talking, and is used in that manner while driving.

(b) A violation of this section is an infraction punishable by a base fine of twenty dollars ($20) for a first offense and fifty dollars ($50) for each subsequent offense.

(c) This section does not apply to a person using a wireless telephone for emergency purposes, including, but not limited to, an emergency call to a law enforcement agency, health care provider, fire department, or other emergency services agency or entity.

Synthesize these into a rule that would apply to Allison King. She has been charged with vehicular manslaughter after hitting and killing a cyclist while driving in the fog on a highway located on a narrow, winding cliff. When she hit the cyclist, she was making a cell phone call, without a hands-free device, to warn a friend of the hazardous conditions. Which of the following choices best synthesizes the statutory sections for our own analytical purposes (although not necessarily phrased in the exact language you would use when drafting a memo or brief)?

A. A person commits vehicular manslaughter by unlawfully killing a human being while driving a vehicle with gross negligence and using a wireless telephone, unless the telephone was used "hands-free" or for "emergency purposes."

B. Vehicular manslaughter is "the unlawful killing of a human being without malice." There are three kinds: voluntary, involuntary, and vehicular. The California Penal Code has a separate section for gross vehicular manslaughter while intoxicated. That is one type of vehicular manslaughter. It would also be vehicular manslaughter if the person were driving "in the commission of an unlawful act" that was not a felony and with gross negligence or if driving "in the commission of a lawful act which might produce death, in an unlawful manner," and with gross negligence. One unlawful act would be driving while using a wireless telephone unless used in a "hands-free" manner or for "emergency purposes."

C. It is vehicular manslaughter when someone kills someone else while driving and using their cell phone, unless used "hands-free" or for "emergency purposes."

D. A person commits vehicular manslaughter by driving a vehicle with gross negligence and using a wireless telephone, unless used "hands-free" or for "emergency purposes."

Example 7-2

After reading the statutory sections in Example 7.1, you understand the statutory rule that a court would apply to King. The statute doesn't, however, explain what constitutes "gross negligence" or what qualifies as using a cell phone for "emergency purposes." (The statute provides that "emergency purposes, includ[es], but [is] not limited to, an emergency call to a law enforcement agency, health care provider, fire department, or other emergency services agency or entity." So you know the listed instances would qualify, but because the list isn't exclusive, you don't know what else would qualify as an "emergency purpose.")

You'd look to case law to understand these terms better. Read the following three cases: *People v. Harris*, *People v. Tompkins*, and *People v. Newton*.

Case 1: *People v. Harris,* 104 Cal. Rptr. 3d 131 (Ct. App. 2010)

On May 14, 2009, Harris was driving his car at approximately the speed limit, 45 mph. The vehicle in front of Harris was driven by Colter; Colter was preparing to turn right, and his turn signal was on. A pedestrian was crossing in the crosswalk, however, and Colter therefore had to stop before he could turn. Harris struck the back of Colter's car and Colter was killed. Skid marks at the scene reveal that Harris did not apply his brakes until his car was only three feet from Colter's vehicle. Harris was convicted of vehicular manslaughter under Cal. Penal Code § 192(c)(1) (West 2008), and he now appeals that conviction.

At the time of the accident, Harris was talking on a cellular phone without the benefit of a "hands-free" device. Harris admitted that he was aware it was a violation of California law to use a cellular phone while driving, but makes two contentions: 1) that he fits into the cell phone statute's exception for "emergencies"; and 2) that his actions did not constitute "gross negligence" under the manslaughter statute.

First, we hold that calling to inform a wedding party that the best man, Harris, would be late is not an "emergency" within the meaning of Cal. Vehicle Code § 23123(c) (West Supp. 2011). Harris' contention that pulling over to call would make him even later does not elevate the nature of the call to emergency status.

Second, as for whether the act was "gross negligence" under Cal. Penal Code § 192(c)(1) (West 2008), a reasonable person in Harris' position would have realized the risk involved in making the phone call while driving. "Gross negligence" is the exercise of so slight a degree of care as to raise a presumption of conscious indifference to the consequences. The test is objective: whether a reasonable person in the defendant's position would have been aware of the risk involved. If a *reasonable person* in defendant's position would have been aware of the risk involved, then defendant is presumed to have had such an awareness. The defendant's *lack* of such awareness does not preclude a finding of gross negligence if a reasonable person would have been so aware.

The fact that Harris was from Nevada and that the state of Nevada allows drivers to use cell phones while driving does not mitigate the risk. Harris' subjective belief in the safety of his act does not mitigate the fact that he should have known the danger involved. Therefore, we affirm Harris' vehicular manslaughter conviction.

Case 2: *People v. Tompkins,* 89 Cal. Rptr. 3d 904 (Ct. App. 2009)

In the case before us today, Mr. Tompkins was convicted of vehicular manslaughter for causing the death of Jordan Smith while driving and simultaneously talking on his cell phone. To be guilty of vehicular manslaughter the state must show the defendant was "driving a vehicle in the commission of an unlawful act, not amounting to felony, and with gross negligence." Cal. Penal Code § 192(c)(1) (West 2008). In this case, the unlawful act was the violation of Cal. Vehicle Code § 23123(a) (West Supp. 2011), driving a motor vehicle while using a wireless telephone that is not configured to allow hands-free listening and talking.

It is undisputed that Mr. Tompkins was driving and simultaneously speaking on his cell phone without a hands-free device when he struck and killed Mr. Smith. Tompkins contends, however, that the exception permitting use of a cell phone in case of an emergency, Cal. Vehicle Code § 23123(c) (West Supp. 2011), applies. Mr. Tompkins was driving from San Francisco to Los Angeles when he learned from a radio newscast that an earthquake measuring 6.9 on the Richter scale had struck the Bay Area. He called home to reassure himself that his wife and children were safe.

We hold that these facts do not constitute an emergency. An emergency implies imminent danger. Any danger to either Mr. Tompkins or his family had passed before the time of Tompkins' phone call. Further, as to the issue of gross negligence, Tompkins knew or should have known that driving while talking on his cell phone was endangering the lives of others. Therefore, we affirm the trial court's decision finding the defendant guilty of vehicular manslaughter.

Case 3: *People v. Newton*, 104 Cal. Rptr. 3d 138 (Ct. App. 2010)

On December 20, 2009, Roger Newton was driving on Interstate 15 near San Bernardino, California. He was accompanied by his wife, Annette, who was seven months pregnant. Annette Newton had experienced several problems in the pregnancy, but had been free of problems for the previous three weeks. Suddenly, Mrs. Newton moaned in pain and announced she could "feel the baby coming." Mr. Newton immediately altered his course to head to St. Thomas Hospital in San Bernardino. He also used his cellular phone to call Mrs. Newton's obstetrician, hoping the doctor would meet the couple at the hospital. While on the phone, Newton did not see Julie Wolfe, who was jogging on the side of the road. The Newtons' car struck Ms. Wolfe and she died from injuries suffered in the accident. The Newtons' baby was born at the site of the accident.

Roger Newton was convicted of vehicular manslaughter. The trial court rejected his claim that calling his wife's doctor was an "emergency," stating that he could have pulled over to make the call. Further, the trial court explained that although the statute contemplates calls for emergency medical help, Newton was not calling doctors to the scene of an emergency; furthermore, there would be doctors at the hospital when the couple arrived.

We reverse Newton's vehicular manslaughter conviction because a genuine emergency existed and a reasonable person in Newton's shoes would have wanted the physician most familiar with his wife's pregnancy to meet the couple at the hospital. Gross negligence depends on the nature of the circumstances and was not present here.

Synthesize these cases into a rule explaining what constitutes "gross negligence." (The next example asks you to synthesize a rule about "emergency purposes.") Which of the following choices best synthesizes the case law on the rule for gross negligence?

A. Gross negligence depends on the defendant's belief about the danger involved and awareness of the risk of driving while talking on a cell phone.

B. It is grossly negligent to drive and make a phone call to check on your family after an emergency or to tell a wedding party that the best man will be late because driving while talking on a cell phone endangers the lives of others.

C. The test for gross negligence is objective: whether a reasonable person in the defendant's circumstances would have realized the risk involved and refrained from doing the act.

D. It is grossly negligent to drive and make a phone call that is not for emergency purposes.

Example 7-3

Continuing from Example 7-2, which of the following best synthesizes the case law on the rule for using a cell phone for "emergency purposes"?

A. Calling a wife's obstetrician when she goes into early labor and has pregnancy difficulties constitutes using a cell phone for emergency purposes.

B. The "emergency purposes" exception permits using a phone to deal with urgent circumstances.

C. A genuine emergency exists when a passenger goes into early labor, but not when a best man is late for a wedding or an earthquake has already occurred and a family member calls to check on his family.

D. A call is for "emergency purposes" if to an emergency services agency, to someone who is in imminent danger, or from someone who is in imminent danger to someone who is specially suited to assist the caller.

EXPLANATIONS

Explanation 7-1

A is correct. This nicely synthesizes the statutory rule that would apply to Allison King. Remember, at this point, you're just working on the analysis you'd want to figure out before writing. When writing your memo or brief you'd want to quote more of the key statutory language, but at this stage you're just trying to figure out a synthesized rule and how it works. The prosecution would have to show that she killed someone while driving a car, that she was driving with gross negligence, that she was using a cell phone that she hadn't configured and used in the "hands-free" mode, and that she hadn't been using the phone for emergency purposes. Since you know that she was driving a vehicle and she hit and killed the cyclist when using a cell phone held up to her ear, the issues will be whether she was driving with "gross negligence" and whether calling her friend to warn her of the hazardous driving conditions was an "emergency purpose." **B** is not the best choice. It reflects correct analytical steps, but because it's not fully synthesized into the specific rule that would apply to King this isn't the best choice. **C** is wrong because it omits the gross negligence requirement. Synthesizing authorities can be like working a puzzle. Be careful not to leave out an important piece. **D** is wrong because it omits the part of the rule about killing a human being. It's not vehicular manslaughter unless there's an "unlawful killing of a human being without malice."

Explanation 7-2

Now that you're synthesizing the rule from multiple cases interpreting gross negligence (and "emergency purposes" in the next example), it'd be a good idea to make a chart, outline, or some other kind of diagram or notes to help us puzzle this out. Here's what one might look like for this problem:

	Key Facts	Using Cell Phone for "Emergency Purpose"?	Gross Negligence?	Result: Vehicular Manslaughter?
People v. Harris	Harris hit and killed Colter when Colter had on his turn signal, but had to stop for a pedestrian in the crosswalk. Harris didn't apply his brakes until his car was only 3 feet	No. Calling to tell a wedding party that the best man will be late is not an emergency.	Yes. A reasonable person in Harris' position would've realized the risk involved.	Yes.

Key Facts	Using Cell Phone for "Emergency Purpose"?	Gross Negli-gence?	Result: Vehicular Man-slaughter?
from Colter's car. Harris was talking on a cell phone (without a "hands-free" device) to inform a wedding party that he, the best man, was late.			
People v. Tompkins — Tompkins killed someone while driving. He was on his cell phone without a "hands-free" device, driving from San Francisco to Los Angeles, calling home to assure himself that his wife and children were safe after a 6.9 earthquake had struck the San Francisco Bay Area.	No. There was no imminent danger to Tompkins or his family at the time of his phone call.	Yes. Tompkins knew or should have known the risk involved.	Yes.
People v. Newton — Newton's pregnant wife started to go into early labor and Newton used his cell phone while driving to call his wife's obstetrician, who had helped with earlier difficulties in the pregnancy. Newton struck and killed a jogger on the side of the road while on the phone.	Yes. A genuine emergency existed on these facts.	No. A reasonable person in those circumstances would have wanted the obstetrician familiar with the wife's pregnancy to meet them at the hospital.	No.

This chart helps us sort out the rule on what gross negligence means. To make it, just list the case names down the left and then across the top write "key facts," whatever elements, factors, or considerations the courts analyze, and the result on the ultimate issue (here, vehicular manslaughter). After a preliminary first or second read of the cases, you'll fill in the chart by consulting each case again. Charts like these are often helpful when you've got fact-intensive precedents and several factors or considerations the courts analyze.

Looking at this completed chart, and reflecting on the cases you read, you see that courts use an objective test for gross negligence that asks what a reasonable person would have done in the defendant's circumstances. **A** is therefore wrong. The test doesn't consider what the defendant thought. It considers whether a reasonable person in the same circumstances would've been aware of the risk involved. **B** is a good start on the rule synthesis, but it's not the best choice because it focuses on the details of the cases like a catalog instead of focusing on the more general rule that the cases provide. So B is wrong. **C** is correct. This choice reflects what the gross negligence column on our chart reflects, which is that all of the case law provides an objective test for gross negligence. **D** is not the best choice. Looking at our completed chart, and reflecting on the cases you read, it indeed seems that there's a relationship between gross negligence and whether the person's phone call was for emergency purposes. In both cases where the courts found vehicular manslaughter, the courts concluded the defendant had acted with gross negligence and made a phone call that was not for emergency purposes. C is a better choice than D, however, because the question asks for the best synthesis of the case law on the rule for gross negligence, which the cases interpret as C expresses.

Explanation 7-3

A is not the best choice. It's a good summary of facts that a court held constituted "emergency purposes," and it provides good explanation of the rule, which the next chapter discusses. But it's not the best choice of a synthesized rule because it simply asserts the result in one of the relevant cases. **B** is not the best choice. The first part of the sentence "The 'emergency purposes' exception permits using a phone to . . ." is off to a great start. It's phrased like a synthesized rule. But the end of the sentence "to deal with urgent circumstances" doesn't tell the reader anything about the rule from the case law. Unlike A, choice B moved in the right direction of abstracting a rule from the multiple relevant cases, but it went too far into abstraction. "Urgent circumstances" doesn't tell the reader much more than "emergency purposes" itself, and so B is not the best choice. **C** is not the best choice. It's a good summary of facts and it provides good explanation of the rule. But it's not the best choice of a synthesized rule because it's focused more on the results in particular precedent cases and not phrased as a synthesized rule that would apply to the next case that comes along. **D** is correct. It's the best choice of a synthesized rule on what constitutes "emergency purposes." It accurately reflects the case law, meshes the statutory example of a call to an emergency services agency, and is phrased as a rule that would apply to the next case that comes along. If you were stating and explaining the rule in the Discussion section of a memo or brief, it'd be good to explain this rule with key facts from the precedent cases. C does a nice job of this and would follow well after D. The next chapter covers the topic of writing your rule construction.

CHAPTER 8

Stating and Explaining the Rule

Do you remember math classes in which you would get the right answer but not all of the available points because you didn't "show all your work"? It never worked to ask the teacher "How did I know the answer was 67.32179 if I didn't follow the steps correctly?" You had to write each of those steps on paper. The fact that you followed them correctly in your head didn't matter. The writing that lawyers do is a lot like those math classes. If you don't show how you got to your conclusion, you won't get all the points—in legal writing courses, on exams, or in the practice of law.

In the law, you "show your work" by providing a detailed legal analysis because the reader needs to understand the foundations of your analysis fully to decide whether she agrees with your ultimate conclusion. In this chapter, we'll talk about "showing your work" in terms of explaining why the rule is in fact the rule and describing its parameters. (Chapters 9-11 explain how to "show your work" in terms of applying the rule to your facts.) This "rule explanation" shows how courts in the past have applied the rule, which will, in turn, help the reader understand how the rule is likely to apply in your case.

The first step in showing your work is explaining the rule. Even though you've figured out—and clearly articulated—the rule that's likely to govern your client's case, the reader needs more than just the statement of the rule. She also needs you to "explain"[1] (sometimes called "prove"[2]) the rule. If

---

1. For instance, Linda Edwards refers to this process as "Rule Explanation." Linda H. Edwards, *Legal Writing: Process, Analysis, and Organization* 81 (5th ed. 2010).
2. Richard Neumann refers to this concept as "rule proof or rule proof and explanation." Richard K. Neumann, Jr., *Legal Reasoning and Legal Writing: Structure, Strategy, and Style* 94 (6th ed. 2009).

you're still having trouble articulating your rule, review Chapter 7 on Constructing a Rule. Once you've constructed the rule, you're ready to think about stating and explaining that rule.

WHAT YOU NEED TO KNOW ABOUT STATING AND EXPLAINING A RULE

"Stating the rule" means to clearly articulate the legal standard that applies in your client's situation. Chapter 7 discusses how to construct a rule. Often you'll have to synthesize the rule from a number of sources. Once you have the rule, the task is to state it in clear and simple terms for the reader. Quote key statutory language and generally quote sparingly from cases.

"Explaining the rule" means citing to, and discussing, the authorities that create the rule. Immediately after stating the rule (or each part of the rule), cite the authority that supports it. If you've had to synthesize a number of sources to create a rule, you'd cite those key sources here. Then, right after the citation(s), discuss precedents that show how courts have previously applied that rule as well as any authority that doesn't obviously support the rule.

Rule explanation helps the reader believe that the rule is actually what you say it is. Citing and discussing the authorities that support your rule statement makes it more likely that you didn't just make up the rule, or even misstate the rule. Provide enough information so the reader can understand why you formulated the rule as you did. Legal readers are skeptical readers!

Even if the reader is inclined to believe your analysis, rule explanation helps her check to be sure you're right. Think of rule explanation as a way to educate the reader. Your analysis might be correct without it, but the reader won't have enough information to be sure. With the citations and discussion of the supporting authorities, the reader can, for himself, judge whether your formulation of the rule is sound.

Rule explanation also allows the reader to understand what the rule means—its contours—and understand how it has been applied in precedent cases. The statement of a rule in the abstract is one thing. Understanding how that rule has affected the outcome in real cases is another, and the latter is often what makes the difference in predicting how the rule will affect your client's case. In addition to creating a more complete picture of the rule, discussing the precedent cases here allows you to compare and contrast, or in legal terms, "analogize and distinguish," your client's facts with the facts in the precedent cases.

In addition, address any other likely formulations of the rule.

The appropriate depth for any rule explanation depends on three things: (1) the type of authority; (2) how controversial the rule is; and (3) how central the rule is to your analysis. Sometimes an entire rule explanation can fit into an explanatory parenthetical at the end of a case citation. Usually, though, a longer explanation is more effective. In longer memos, it's not unusual for the rule explanation alone to span several pages of your Discussion section.

(1) *The type of authority*: With constitutional provisions, statutes, and administrative regulations, quoting the relevant language suffices for stating the rule. In those instances, adding a citation to the authority constitutes the rule explanation. Sometimes you'll need to go into legislative history to help interpret particular provisions, but that comes later, after you've stated the rule interpreting that particular provision. When it comes to the rule itself, simply quote the statutory language and add the citation.

When case law is part of the rule, though—as often happens even when a statute or other authority applies—the reader needs more than simply a citation to the case to understand your statement of the rule. The reader needs to understand how the case law has interpreted and applied the statute. To this end, it's helpful to explain the facts, issue, and holding of the precedent case. The court's reasoning is also helpful if it isn't explicit in your statement of the issue or holding. This information allows the reader to independently judge your formulation of the rule. And keep in mind that when the rule comes from a case (or series of cases), what the court *did* is key. What happened in the trial court? Was the defendant convicted? Did the plaintiff win on a motion for summary judgment? Next, what was the outcome in the appellate court? Discussing these outcomes helps narrow down the actual issue the court faced and helps ensure your rule formulation is accurate.

On a related note, although you should quote statutory language, quote sparingly from cases. Sometimes the court provides a clear, logical formulation of the rule. Often, though, you need to work through several cases and synthesize the rule. In those instances, it's often difficult to find a concise passage that accurately sums up the rule and you should paraphrase the synthesized rule. Overreliance on quotations makes it more likely you're taking statements out of context.

(2) *How controversial the rule (or its parameters) is*: When the rule is settled, not much rule explanation is necessary. When the rule itself could be the subject of debate, though, more is needed. For instance, if you were challenging the admissibility of a defendant's confession, you would likely start your rule with the relevant constitutional provision (the Fifth Amendment), and then with the rule that emerged from the seminal Supreme Court case, *Miranda v. Arizona*. Your rule statement might be very basic: Custodial interrogations are admissible only when the defendant has been advised of his right to remain silent and has voluntarily waived that right. *Miranda* stands for that

proposition, so you would cite the case. You wouldn't expect anyone to disagree with that statement because it comes from a Supreme Court decision that courts have long followed, and so a parenthetical explanation of *Miranda* would be enough here. But if the parties disputed the more specific issue of whether the interrogation occurred while the defendant was "in custody," you would need to explain in more detail any applicable cases that establish what "in custody" means.

(3) How central the rule is to your analysis: If the rule is not very essential to your analysis, a parenthetical explanation may be sufficient. But if the rule you state is key to your conclusion, then the rule explanation needs to be longer. It may be a paragraph, or a page, or even numerous pages. As with all depth questions, use your best judgment, but consider how important the rule is before you decide how much explanation to include.

HOW TO STATE AND EXPLAIN A RULE

Using the cell phone manslaughter problem in Appendix A, we'll walk you through the process of stating and explaining a rule.

Problem

> *Here is a quick overview of the cell phone manslaughter problem (for details, see Appendix A).* Allison King used her wireless phone, without a hands-free device, while driving in dense fog on a winding road on the edge of an ocean cliff. King placed the call to warn her friends about the dangerous conditions, as they would be meeting later. While she was making the call, she hit and killed a bicyclist. The prosecution will attempt to convict King of vehicular manslaughter by showing that she drove while committing an illegal act (driving while using a wireless phone without a hands-free device) and with gross negligence. King will argue that her actions fit within the emergency exception to the wireless phone prohibition. She will also argue that she did not act with gross negligence.

Step 1: Clearly articulate your rule. If you need help with this step, review Chapter 7. With the cell phone manslaughter problem, you'd probably identify your main rule like this:

> Vehicular manslaughter is manslaughter—"the unlawful killing of a human being without malice"—that occurs when "driving a vehicle in the commission of an unlawful act, not amounting to felony, and with gross negligence."

Step 2: Add citations to support each component of the rule. For the main rule in the cell phone manslaughter problem, you'd add the citation to the statute, so your rule explanation would simply be this:

Cal. Penal Code § 192 (West 2008).

Put together, the rule and rule explanation might look like this:

Vehicular manslaughter is manslaughter—"the unlawful killing of a human being without malice"—that occurs when "driving a vehicle in the commission of an unlawful act, not amounting to felony, and with gross negligence." Cal. Penal Code § 192 (West 2008).

If your main rule came from a case, you'd have a longer rule explanation because you'd need to explain the case and show why it stands for the rule. But with a statutory rule, the explanation for that particular rule—the statute itself—is short because it's just the statutory citation. Of course, you'd likely have interpretive case law to address as well, and that would lengthen the ultimate rule explanation.

If a disputed issue in your case involved the element of gross negligence, you might phrase the "gross negligence" sub-rule like this:

"'Gross negligence' is the exercise of so slight a degree of care as to raise a presumption of conscious indifference to the consequences." Gross negligence depends on the circumstances of each case. Courts apply the standard objectively. If a "reasonable person in the defendant's position would have been aware of the risk involved," the law presumes that the defendant was aware of the risk and acted with gross negligence, even if he in fact was unaware of the risk. At least one California court held that a defendant "knew or should have known that driving while talking on his cell phone was endangering the lives of others."

Note that this rule contains several principles. Each of them needs support from authority.

You'd start your rule explanation in the same way you did with the main rule: by adding citations. That rule, with the citations, might look like this:

"'Gross negligence' is the exercise of so slight a degree of care as to raise a presumption of conscious indifference to the consequences." *People v. Harris*, 104 Cal. Rptr. 3d 131, 133 (Ct. App. 2010). Gross negligence depends on the circumstances of each case. *People v. Newton*, 104 Cal. Rptr. 3d 138, 141 (Ct. App. 2010). Courts apply the standard objectively. *Id.* If a "reasonable person in the defendant's position would have been aware of the risk involved," the law presumes that the defendant was aware of the risk and acted with gross negligence, even if he in fact was unaware of the risk. *Id.* At least one California court held that a defendant "knew or should have known that driving while talking on his cell phone was endangering the lives of others." *People v. Tompkins*, 89 Cal. Rptr. 3d 904, 909 (Ct. App. 2009).

Notice that for each rule explanation, the citation comes after the rule. Unless the supporting source is especially significant, you don't need to preface your rule statement with a reference to the authority. For instance, you don't need to preface your general rule with language like this: "California's Penal Code, in section 192, defines vehicular manslaughter as follows . . . ." The reader wants to know the rule, and will see where the rule comes from by looking at the citation that follows. Always provide a pinpoint citation to the smallest possible portion of the authority that supports the rule—the statutory section or sub-section, and with case law, to the exact page or pages where the relevant material appears.

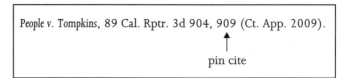

People v. Tompkins, 89 Cal. Rptr. 3d 904, 909 (Ct. App. 2009).

pin cite

Step 3: Discuss the authorities that support the rule. Most often, you'll be discussing cases here. But you might also be discussing legislative history or some other source, like the "purposes" section in a statutory scheme that sets out the policy objectives of the statute, to support your formulation of the rule. Either way, your goal is to provide enough detail to explain—to the skeptical reader—how the authority supports your rule.

For instance, imagine that for the act prohibiting driving while talking on a cell phone without a "hands-free" device, the purposes section of the statute states the following:

> Drivers on California's roads and highways have caused thousands of deaths and injuries by talking on their cell phones without using a "hands-free" device. This problem is especially severe on some of our State's winding, inherently dangerous roads. The goal of this Act is to protect the lives of our citizens by eliminating the use of cell phones by drivers except when used in a hands-free mode.

The policy behind the statute is helpful. Understanding California's concern about "winding, inherently dangerous roads" can help the reader determine which violations of the statute are committed with gross negligence and which aren't. Sometimes policy comes from the legislature, and sometimes courts discuss it. Either way, it's often helpful to include.

When case law helps explain the rule, you'll need to educate the reader about those cases. In your paragraph on "gross negligence" in Step 2, you've stated the rule and you've begun your rule explanation by providing citations to the relevant cases. But you haven't yet fully explained the rule. You do that by describing the facts, issues, and holdings (and, as noted earlier, the rationales if not implicit in the holdings) of the relevant cases. Often, your rule explanation will consist of one paragraph per case. That paragraph usually begins with the case's rule followed by the case's facts/issue/holding/rationale, as the following paragraph demonstrates:

> A defendant's subjective belief that his actions are safe does not prevent a court from finding gross negligence. *Harris*, 104 Cal. Rptr. 3d at 134. In *Harris*, the defendant struck the back of a car that was waiting for a pedestrian to exit the crosswalk before turning right. *Id.* at 132. The defendant was travelling 45 miles per hour and applied the brakes only three feet before he hit the car, killing its driver. *Id.* The court determined that Harris acted with gross negligence by talking on his cell phone without a hands-free device even though he subjectively thought he was behaving safely. *Id.* at 135. His actions were illegal in California, and even though Harris' home state of Nevada had no such restriction, Harris should have known of the danger posed by using his cell phone while driving. *Id.*

Following this same pattern, the next two paragraphs could explain the other two cases relevant to the statute's gross negligence rule:

> Talking on a cell phone while driving may be enough to demonstrate gross negligence. *Tompkins*, 89 Cal. Rptr. 3d at 908. In *Tompkins*, the court held the defendant acted with gross negligence when he called home while driving to check on his family's safety after hearing a news broadcast about an earthquake; during that call, the defendant hit and killed Mr. Smith. *Id.* The defendant was driving from San Francisco to Los Angeles, and the court concluded, without providing facts about the road conditions or other details, that the defendant "should have known" that talking on his cell phone while driving was "endangering the lives of others." *Id.* at 909.
>
> On the other hand, all of the surrounding circumstances are relevant, and those circumstances can suggest the absence of gross negligence for making a cell phone call while driving. *See Newton*, 104 Cal. Rptr. 3d at 141. In *Newton*, the defendant's wife went into labor while he was driving on Interstate 15 near San Bernardino. *Id.* at 139. His wife was only seven months pregnant and had previous complications. *Id.* The defendant altered his course to drive to the hospital and called his wife's obstetrician from his cell phone without a hands-free device. *Id.* at 140. While on the phone, the defendant hit and killed a jogger. *Id.* The court held the defendant did not act with gross negligence under these circumstances. *Id.* at 141. A reasonable person whose wife was in labor at seven months would want the doctor who had been treating his wife and understood her prior complications to be present at the hospital. *Id.*

Your rule explanation for cases won't always be one paragraph per case. Recall that sometimes the entire rule explanation for a case can fit into a parenthetical following that case's citation. For example, in the following paragraph, a number of cases are used to explain one noncontroversial rule:

> Evidence that flows from information obtained during an illegal arrest is inadmissible. *Wong Sun v. United States*, 371 U.S. 471, 487-88 (1963) (holding that narcotics discovered because of a statement given during an illegal search were inadmissible). Based on this exclusionary rule, the Court has reversed criminal convictions in a number of contexts. *See, e.g.*, *id.* (narcotics case); *Brown v. Illinois*, 422 U.S. 590, 604 (1975) (murder case); *Taylor v. Alabama*, 457 U.S. 687, 694 (1982) (robbery case).

At other times, you'll need a page or more to fully discuss a key case. And recall that courts might also indicate the policies that certain rules promote. When you glean those policy rationales from the cases, add them to the rule explanation.

Note also that you haven't included the client's facts as you explain each case. Keep your rule statement and explanation separate from the application of that rule. The goal here is to convince the reader that your rule formulation is correct. Later, you'll apply the rule to your facts and analogize (or distinguish) your facts with the facts in the precedent cases. But for now, just explain the cases without reference to your client.

Step 4: Address alternative formulations of the rule. The rule isn't always crystal clear. In fact, if someone has bothered to ask you to write a memo, there's a decent chance the rule isn't clear. That means some other rule formulation has some merit, even if you discount it in the end. Rather than ignoring that competing formulation, address it head-on and explain why a court is less likely to adopt that formulation than your formulation.

EXAMPLES

Here are some examples of stating and explaining the rule. For each example, choose the best answer. Explain to yourself why you have chosen that answer. Then read the explanations in the last section of this chapter to check your work.

Example 8-1

"A person commits robbery if in the course of taking any property of another from his person or immediate presence and against his will, such person threatens or uses force against any person with intent either to coerce surrender of property or to prevent resistance to such person taking or retaining property." Ariz. Rev. Stat. Ann. § 13-1902(A) (2010).

A. This cite to the quoted statute is an insufficient rule explanation for statutory language because all it consists of is the statute's citation.

B. This is an insufficient rule explanation for statutory language because the complete legislative history is always necessary.

C. This rule explanation is sufficient because it's short, and being concise is always preferred.

D. This rule explanation is sufficient because statutory language, once properly quoted, is explained with a citation to the statute.

Example 8-2

The second factor in the fair use exception to copyright protection, "the nature of the copyrighted work," is of minimal significance in the context of a parody. *Campbell v. Acuff-Rose Music, Inc.*, 510 U.S. 569, 586 (1994) (reversing a finding of no fair use and stating that the second factor was "not much help" because "parodies almost invariably copy publicly known, expressive works"); *Mattel Inc. v. Walking Mountain Prods.*, 353 F.3d 792, 803 (9th Cir. 2003) (holding an artist's parody of Mattel's Barbie doll was permitted by fair use, noting the second factor is not "terribly useful" and quoting *Campbell*).

A. This is an insufficient rule explanation because each case always needs a full paragraph of discussion.

B. This is an insufficient rule explanation because it does not include the issues the cases addressed.

C. This rule explanation is sufficient because when the issue is not likely to be contested, a parenthetical explanation can be enough.

D. This rule explanation is sufficient even if the issue was contested because it includes the facts, issues, and holdings of each case.

Example 8-3

Under the fourth fair use factor, "the effect of the use upon the potential market for or value of the copyrighted work," parodies present a unique situation. 17 U.S.C. § 107(4) (2006). "[W]hen a lethal parody, like a scathing theater review, kills demand for the original, it does not produce a harm cognizable under the Copyright Act." *Campbell v. Acuff-Rose Music, Inc.*, 510 U.S. 569, 591-92 (1994).

A. This is an insufficient rule explanation because when a rule that is central to the analysis comes from a case, the reader needs to know the case's facts, issue, and holding to understand why the case stands for that proposition.

B. This is an insufficient rule explanation because the policy behind a statute should always be included.

C. This rule explanation is sufficient because it cites both the quoted statutory language and the quoted Supreme Court case.

D. This rule explanation is sufficient because it includes pinpoint citations to the relevant sub-section of the fair use statute and the page number within the case where the language can be found.

Example 8-4

An "unlawful killing" for purposes of California's vehicular manslaughter statute, California Penal Code § 192 (West 2008), requires that the defendant's actions contributed to the victim's death, even if another factor also contributed. *People v. Matthews*, 89 Cal. Rptr. 3d 1027 (Ct. App. 2009). In *Matthews*, the victim did not die immediately after being struck by the defendant's car. Instead, she died two days after being released from the hospital. The cause of death was "acute subdural hematoma," which is a collection of blood on the surface of the brain. *Id.* at 1029. The hematoma was caused by the accident, but the hospital failed to diagnose it and released the victim. Had it been properly diagnosed, there was a 98 percent chance that she would have survived. *Id.*

A. This is an insufficient rule explanation because more of the *Matthews* facts need to be included.

B. This is an insufficient rule explanation because although the *Matthews* facts are included, the reader is not told what the issue or holding was in the *Matthews* case.

C. This rule explanation is sufficient because it includes a pinpoint citation to the relevant pages in *Matthews*.

D. This rule explanation is sufficient because it cites both the governing statute and the relevant case.

Example 8-5

Title VII's prohibition on discrimination "because of sex" includes discrimination based on an employee's transgender status. *See, e.g.,* Barnes v. City of Cincinnati, 401 F.3d 729, 737 (6th Cir. 2005). In *Barnes*, the Sixth Circuit upheld a jury verdict finding that the city violated Title VII when it demoted a transgender plaintiff for his failure to conform to sex stereotypes. *Id.* at 747. Although some cases hold the opposite, their reasoning is flawed.

A. This paragraph is a sufficient rule explanation for the stated rule because it includes *Barnes'* facts, issue, and holding and cites to them.
B. This paragraph is a sufficient rule explanation for the stated rule because in addition to describing *Barnes*, it advises the reader of contrary authority.
C. This paragraph is an insufficient rule explanation because Title VII's remedies should be included when discussing the *Barnes* case.
D. This rule explanation is insufficient because the reader needs more information about the "cases holding the opposite."

EXPLANATIONS

Explanation 8-1

A is incorrect. Because this rule comes from a statute and it is properly quoted, the statutory citation here, including a citation to the relevant subsection, is sufficient. **B** is also incorrect. Legislative history can be helpful, but it isn't always so. Furthermore, although other statutory sections, like an act's purpose section, might be helpful, they are not always useful either. **C** is incorrect. Rule explanations vary in length, depending on the type of authority, how controversial the rule is, and how central the rule is to your analysis. Although a short rule explanation is appropriate in some cases, it isn't always. **D** is correct for the reasons A is incorrect. If case law interprets that statutory language, though, you would also add discussion of that case law to the extent relevant.

Explanation 8-2

A is incorrect. Although many rule explanations for cases are a paragraph or more, if the point is not controversial or central to the analysis, the rule explanation can be condensed into a parenthetical. Here, that is the case because in *Campbell*, the Supreme Court stated that the second statutory factor was largely irrelevant in parody cases. *B* is also incorrect. The two parenthetical explanations address the global issue (fair use) as well as the specific question here (the second factor in the fair use test). *C* is correct. As stated in A, the length of rule explanations varies. Here, if the issue is not contested, these parenthetical explanations provide enough information for the reader to understand the rule and agree with the writer's formulation. *D* is incorrect. Although these parentheticals include the cases' basic facts, issues, and holdings, this bare information would likely be insufficient if the issue were contested.

Explanation 8-3

A is correct. Because the issue is central to the analysis, simply quoting one line from a case and adding a citation is probably not enough to explain the rule to the skeptical reader. Even though this quote is from the Supreme Court, so it carries more weight, an effective rule explanation would add the case's facts, issue, and holding to show how the case stands for the quoted proposition. *B* is incorrect. Although it's true that sometimes the policy behind a particular statute is helpful, that isn't always the case. *C* is incorrect for the reasons listed in A. *D* is also incorrect. Although rule explanations should include pinpoint citations for both statutes and cases, those citations are usually not enough. The writer needs to go further and add the case explanation.

Explanation 8-4

A is incorrect. Plenty of the *Matthews* facts are included. What is lacking is the issue and holding. Without those, the reader has no idea what effect these particular facts have on the rule. *B* is correct for the reasons A is incorrect. *C* is incorrect. This example does not include the pinpoint citation to the main rule. Although it includes the pinpoint citation at the end of the paragraph, the reader needs the pinpoint citation for the rule. Furthermore, pinpoint citations alone are insufficient to create an effective rule explanation. They are necessary, but not sufficient. *D* is also incorrect. Simply citing a case is not enough for an effective rule explanation. Unless the issue is uncontested and the law is firmly established, adding a parenthetical or a discussion of the facts, issue, and holding of a case is usually needed to explain how the case illustrates the rule or how a court has applied the rule.

Explanation 8-5

A is incorrect. Although the paragraph does include the basic facts, issue, and holding of *Barnes* (and citations), the cases that "hold the opposite" need to be addressed. Furthermore, because there's contrary authority, additional information from *Barnes*, such as the court's reasoning, would be helpful to the reader trying to decide which rule formulation was more likely to be accepted. *B* is also incorrect. It is true that readers should be advised of opposing authority. But it's not helpful to simply state that those authorities exist without citing to or discussing them. *C* is incorrect. The rule this paragraph is explaining is whether Title VII prohibits a particular type of discrimination, not what the available remedies might be. *D* is correct for the reasons A and B are wrong. The reader needs to know more about *Barnes* and know about the cases that reach the opposite result. This rule explanation fails to provide that information.

Applying the Law: Fact-Based Analysis

"Just the facts, ma'am," is a favorite admonishment of police officers and prosecutors in many crime stories. And most people think of facts in that way—as fixed and unchanging. Lawyers, on the other hand, know that within certain constraints, facts are what you make of them. And when lawyers apply the law to the facts of a problem, fact-based analysis is one of the most basic skills in the toolbox.

Terminology Notes: Some textbooks will call analysis based on the law and just the facts of your assignment as "rule-based reasoning" or a "factual argument based on the plain language of the rule." This fact-based analysis is distinct from analysis based on facts of precedent or on policy.

WHAT YOU NEED TO KNOW ABOUT FACT-BASED ANALYSIS

Understand the difference between a fact and an inference. "Kay was driving 120 mph" is a fact. "Kay was driving too fast" or "Kay was breaking the speed limit" are inferences. Sometimes an inference is so commonplace that we forget it's an inference. "When the light turned red, John stopped" is a fact. "John stopped because the light turned red" is an inference. When you argue based on the facts, you want the inferences you draw to seem so natural that your audience will accept your version of what happened without question.

Depending on the inferences you make, the same fact can often work to help both sides. Once you have some practice with fact-based analysis, you'll be amazed at how many times you can "flip" a fact to work for either side. Here's one example:[1]

> Fact: the car accident happened while a father was driving with children in the car.

> First inference: children in a car can be distracting and thus the accident was the father's fault because he was distracted.

> Second inference: parents drive more carefully when they have children in the car and thus the accident was not the father's fault because he was driving carefully.

Connect the fact to the statute or rule to show why the fact is legally significant. Remember that the best legal analysis mixes law and facts. A sentence that just restates a fact without telling the reader why you think that fact is important in this part of the analysis is a waste of time. **Specify the connection between the fact or factual inference and the law. One way to do this is by using the word "because" or its synonyms.** Explain to the reader why you've singled out these particular facts as important. Make your reasoning explicit.

To help you plan, you might make a chart that sorts the facts of the problem with the various parts of the rule. If you're a visual thinker, charts can be helpful. (See Chapter 7, Constructing a Rule, for a chart that helps you connect a case to a part of a statute.) Here, with fact-based analysis, you can design a chart that will help you visually connect facts with parts of the rule.

HOW TO WRITE FACT-BASED ANALYSIS

Using the copyright and fair use problem in Appendix B, we'll walk you through the process of writing fact-based analysis.

---

1. *See* Albert J. Moore, *Inferential Streams: The Articulation and Illustration of the Advocate's Evidentiary Intuition*, 34 UCLA L. Rev. 611 (1987).

Problem

> *Here is a quick overview of the copyright and fair use problem (for details see Appendix B).* Young is suing Olds for violating the Copyright Act when Olds wrote a song based on Young's original, "Rockin' in the Free World." Olds' song uses the structure and many lyrics of the original but changes the original song's political message. The music of the two songs is not at issue, only the lyrics. Young expects that Olds will argue that his song is a parody that falls under the fair use exception to the Copyright Act. The court will consider the relevant factors set out in the fair use statute, 17 U.S.C. § 107 (2006): whether the copy was transformative and targeted the original; whether it took more than necessary of the original; and whether it will interfere with the original's market.

Step 1. Sort the facts, deciding which facts support each side (or, in some instances, both sides). You may wish to make notes to yourself in a more casual fashion, but you can also make a chart that states the rule and connects facts to the rule. For instance, pick out a few facts related to the fourth factor of the fair use test: "the effect of the use upon the potential market for or value of the copyrighted work."

Fact Related to Fourth Factor (the effect of the copy on the possible market for original)	Inference That Favors Young	Inference That Favors Olds
Young's song is very famous.	It is more likely that Olds is trying to capture some of the big market for the song.	It is more likely that buyers will know the original and know the copy is not the original.
Both songs make a political statement about America.	This is precisely the same market — rock fans that like political statements.	The political statements are so different that the buyers are unlikely to confuse the songs.
Both songs are rock music.	The copy is a direct assault on the same market as the original.	The specialized rock music audience is more likely to know the original and realize the copy is a parody.

Fact Related to Fourth Factor (the effect of the copy on the possible market for original)	Inference That Favors Young	Inference That Favors Olds
Young's song has been played at patriotic rallies.	Despite the purported difference in message, both songs serve as positive patriotic songs and thus Olds' song will cut into that part of Young's market.	No inferences favor Olds on this fact at first look.
Olds' song uses images of good things in America.	No inferences favor Young on this fact at first look.	The images in the songs are so different that buyers will not be confused.

Step 2. Review the fact-based inferences you've generated and choose the strongest one or two. Suppose you're writing for Young, the copyright holder. You'll want to choose the fact-based inference that the alleged infringer, Olds, either can't argue another way, or if he can, it will be a weak response. Here, also choose one more fact-based inference just to get more practice. The other inferences seem pretty well balanced, so perhaps you just choose one you like, such as that both songs are in the rock genre and therefore easy for buyers to confuse.

Step 3. Write sentences that tie together the fact and the law's text. You want both in the same sentence when possible. Start with the law's text:

> Olds' song is likely to produce an "effect on the market of the original."

And then you'll add the facts to the same sentence and use "because" to explain how the facts and the law combine:

> Olds' song is likely to produce an "effect on the market of the original" because Young's original song has been played at patriotic rallies and despite the purported change in message, Olds' song also appeals to the market of those looking for a patriotic song.

You've woven together the facts and law in this fact-based analysis. For the second fact-based rationale, the process is the same. This time start with facts:

> Both songs are in the same genre.

And add law and inference:

> Both songs are in the same genre and thus the copy is likely to affect the original's market because the copy is a direct assault on the market of the original, rock music fans who like songs with a political message.

Step 4. Check to make sure you've told the reader explicitly how the facts and law are connected. Remember that the word "because" is handy here. Both of your fact-based analyses use the word "because" to make the connection explicit.

EXAMPLES

Here are some examples of fact-based analyses. Most, but not all, are based on the copyright and fair use problem in Appendix B. For each example, choose the correct answer or answers, noting that more than one answer may be correct. Explain to yourself why you have chosen the answer or answers you selected. Then read the explanations in the last section of this chapter to check your work.

Example 9-1

The third factor of the fair use test requires the court to weigh the "amount and substantiality of the portion used in relation to the copyrighted work as a whole." The rule includes a test where the author of a parody may take "the heart of the original." Here is a fact-based analysis on this third factor:

> While a parody may use the heart of the copyrighted work, Olds has used over half of Young's work to make his song, which comprises more than just the heart of the original, so the court will likely rule against his fair use claim.

A. This fact-based analysis successfully ties the facts to the law.
B. This fact-based analysis would be better if it used the word "because" to tether the facts to the law.
C. "Olds has used over half of Young's work" is an inference rather than a fact.
D. The amount taken "comprises more than just the heart of the original" is an inference rather than a fact.

Example 9-2

Continuing to address the third factor, consider this analysis:

> Olds started his phrases in the same way as Young's phrases and then Olds changed the meaning so that the listener would feel the contrast between his message affirming how America is and Young's message for change in America.

A. This fact-based analysis is successful because it implies a connection to the factor that addresses the amount taken and uses the facts in a clever way.

B. This fact-based analysis should be more explicitly tied to the law.

C. This fact-based analysis is strong because it could apply to either factor three about the amount taken or to factor four about interfering with the original's market.

D. This analysis is based on fact not inference.

Example 9-3

Continuing to address the third factor, consider this analysis:

> The amount and substantiality Olds took was too great for fair use because he copied nearly 65 percent of the original lyrics and the form of twenty-four lines. Further, Olds nearly duplicated the chorus.

A. This is a good fact-based based analysis because it connects the facts to the law.

B. This fact-based analysis uses the facts to create an inference that 65 percent is too much to take of the original.

C. This fact-based analysis would be stronger if it connected the law and the facts.

D. This fact-based analysis is weak because it doesn't state the outcome the author wants.

Example 9-4

Here is an example from a sexual harassment claim. The rule requires the harassment to be "severe or pervasive." Consider this analysis:

> The alleged harassment Jennifer Jones experienced was not "severe or pervasive" considering that her coworkers did not call her names every day but only sporadically over almost a year.

A. This fact-based analysis is weak because it's based on inference not facts.

B. This fact-based analysis would be stronger if it used the word "because."

C. This is not fact-based analysis because it refers to a rule.

D. This is good fact-based analysis because it explicitly tells the reader the legal significance of the facts.

Example 9-5

Here is an example from a sexual harassment claim. The rule requires the harassment to be "based on sex." Consider this analysis:

> Although Jennifer Jones was a transsexual, the alleged harassment she suffered is not actionable because it was not "based on sex" as the statute requires. None of the federal appellate courts have recognized such a claim, nor has the Supreme Court recognized it.

A. This is not fact-based analysis because it focuses on how courts have interpreted the statute and not on analyzing how the rule applies to the facts of the case.

B. This fact-based analysis is strong because it uses the word "because" to connect to the law.

C. This fact-based analysis is strong because it mentions that the best authority, the U.S. Supreme Court, has not yet recognized this claim.

D. This fact-based analysis is weak because it includes only one fact: that Jennifer Jones was a transsexual.

EXPLANATIONS

Explanation 9-1

A is incorrect. This analysis is good in that it has a fact and an inference drawn from the fact. But instead of tying the fact explicitly to the text of the factor, it simply says that Olds would lose. Because the conclusion is not specific to the factor, it is weaker than it could be. *B* is correct. The answer would be better if it used the word "because" to tie the fact to the text of the factor. It could say "Olds used an amount too great in relation to the whole of the work because he used more than half of the original lyrics, which was more than the 'heart of the work.'" Using the word "because" is not strictly required, but it often works well for constructing sentences that clearly link law and fact. **C** is correct because whether Olds used more than half of the lyrics is a measurable fact and not an inference or conclusion of law. **D** is correct. Whether one who has taken more than half has indeed taken "the heart" of something is a judgment call, or an inference.

Explanation 9-2

A is incorrect. Fact-based analysis is stronger when it is connected explicitly to the law. Although you don't always need to connect the facts and law in one sentence, the connection must be more explicit than the implication here. **B** is correct. Fact-based analysis is stronger when it is connected explicitly to the law. Here, the author might have continued the analysis by saying: "Thus, Olds needed to copy as much as he did to parody the original, and the third factor allows him to copy this amount." **C** is incorrect. The author should analyze one factor at a time. Tying the fact-based analysis to the text of a factor will help you refrain from running your arguments together. **D** is incorrect. The inference here is about what Olds intended and what an audience will draw from the song.

Explanation 9-3

A is correct. The example starts with the law and tells the reader how the facts relate to the law. **B** is also correct. Although the inference is not explicit, the author leads the reader to that conclusion. This inference works well for Olds. **C** is incorrect. As explained for answer A, the example starts with the law and tells the reader how the facts relate to the law. **D** is incorrect. Not every fact-based analysis will include something about the outcome you want the court to reach. You can choose to include it, but there is no rule requiring you to identify an outcome.

Explanation 9-4

A is incorrect. The example includes facts. Even if it were based on an inference, it might still be good fact-based analysis as long as the inference is strong and tied to the law. **B** is incorrect. Although it's a great idea to use the word "because," the word "considering" is a synonym for "because" here and the sentence connects facts and law. No strict rule requires using the word "because." **C** is incorrect. Fact-based analysis *should* refer to a legal text, such as a rule or a statute. **D** is correct. This is good fact-based analysis, tying the facts to the law.

Explanation 9-5

A is correct. Although you could say that explaining that courts have not recognized a certain claim is a "fact," fact-based analysis usually explains how a rule applies to the facts of the case you're analyzing. **B** is wrong. Even though we encourage you to use the word "because" to connect facts to law, just adding the word "because" won't automatically make the analysis strong or indicate that it's fact-based analysis. **C** is also wrong. The analysis is not fact-based and a cite to the Supreme Court doesn't make it fact-based. **D** is only partially correct. If this is fact-based analysis at all, it's very weak. Including one fact does not make it into fact-based analysis. The analysis still focuses on the state of the law, and not on how the law applies to facts in this case.

Applying the Law:
Analogical Analysis

You've undoubtedly been reasoning by analogy since before you could read. Any game that asked you to sort objects into categories asked you to reason by analogy. And just as you tried then to figure out which shared characteristics were important enough to group objects together and label them as alike, now as a lawyer you'll analyze by trying to figure out which shared facts and concepts in similar cases are important enough to group cases together and label them with similar outcomes. (Did you notice that the last sentence was a good example of an analogy?)

Analogical reasoning is important because it's a key way that courts make decisions in a common law system. Courts generally want to treat similar cases alike. Thus, courts will reason by analogy in deciding cases, and lawyers will accordingly argue that their case is like or unlike a precedent. Indeed, when lawyers say that an argument is "well-supported" they usually mean that the argument is based on, or connected to, a text to which the relevant court would defer. When you reason or argue by analogy, that text is a case. And you support your analysis or argument by explaining how your case is the same or different from a precedent case.

Terminology Notes: Lawyers talk about "analogizing to or distinguishing from" a precedent case. When you "distinguish a case," you tell the reader how your case is different from the precedent and therefore requires a different response or outcome. Distinguishing a case is also sometimes called "counter-analogical reasoning."

WHAT YOU NEED TO KNOW ABOUT ANALOGICAL REASONING

It's not enough to say that your case is like or unlike a precedent case. Explain *how* they're alike or different. Sometimes you may feel as though you're stating the obvious, but when making analogies or distinctions, it's best to make your analysis explicit. For instance, instead of just saying Olds' work is like the defendant's work in *Mattel*, explain that they are both transformative and describe the facts in *Mattel* and in your case that show the work is transformative.

Compare or contrast facts that are *relevant* to the precise issue you're addressing. That your case and a precedent are similar or different in some respect is not what matters; you could find something similar or different about any two cases in the world. Rather, the comparison or distinction needs to be about something that is relevant to the issue—typically, that your case is similar or different with respect to a fact that mattered to the outcome in the precedent.

If you're having a hard time deciding whether a fact is relevant, remove the fact from the narrative and ask yourself whether your analysis would change. If removing a fact would change the analysis, then it's a relevant fact.

You can phrase analogical reasoning effectively in many different ways. The keys are to write clearly, make the connections explicit, and keep the structure parallel so that you compare apples to apples. For instance, if you're analogizing the defendant in your case to the defendant in a precedent, make sure to keep a parallel structure—defendant to defendant.

> Like the defendant in *Poehlen*, the defendant here also robbed a convenience store at gunpoint.
> Not:
> Like *Poehlen*, the defendant robbed a convenience store at gunpoint.

Here are templates that provide phrasing lawyers might use for analogizing and distinguishing. Where you see brackets, you would insert material from your assignment and the precedent you're discussing.

> **Like the** [defendant/plaintiff/victim/etc.] **in** [Precedent]**, here the** [defendant/plaintiff/victim/etc.] **similarly** [relevant facts that are alike]**.**

> Like the defendant in *Jones*, who had a long record of criminal activity, here the defendant also has a long record of criminal activity.

As the [—] in [*Precedent*], here also [—].

As the defendant in *Fisher* targeted the same genre of music as the original, here also Olds targeted the same genre of music as Young's original.

In [*Precedent*], [—]. Likewise, here [—]. Thus, in both [*Precedent*] and the instant case [similar relevant facts], and [—] should result.

In *Jones*, the defendant used more than 50 percent of the original's lyrics and the court found no fair use. Likewise, here Olds used more than 50 percent of Young's "Rockin' in the Free World" lyrics. Thus, in both *Jones* and the instant case the defendants used more than 50 percent of the lyrics and no finding of fair use should result.

Although in [*Precedent*] [the precedent's facts or reasoning or both-], here [your facts, etc.].

Although in *Campbell* the copy used only four bars of the original to create the parody, our case is distinguishable because here Olds' copy used over twenty bars of the original.

Similar to [*Precedent*], in which [relevant precedent facts], here [corresponding similar facts in case at hand].

Similar to *Mattel*, in which the defendant copied part of the original to deliver a social message, here Olds copied part of Young's song to deliver a social message.

Unlike in [*Precedent*], where [relevant precedent facts], here [corresponding differing facts in case at hand].

Unlike in *Jones*, where the defendant was calling a public health official, here King was calling her friends.

In [*Precedent*], [—]. In contrast, here [—]. Thus, as [—], it does not follow that [—] should result.

In *Jones*, the defendant received *Miranda* warnings as soon as she was in custody. In contrast, here the defendant was in custody for several hours before receiving the *Miranda* warnings. Thus, as the defendant in our case did not know of his right to a lawyer in a timely fashion, it does not follow that his confession should be admissible.

HOW TO ANALOGIZE AND DISTINGUISH

Using the copyright and fair use problem in Appendix B, we'll walk you through the process of analogizing and distinguishing.

Problem

> Here is a quick overview of the copyright and fair use problem (for details see Appendix B). Young is suing Olds for violating the Copyright Act when Olds wrote a song based on Young's original, "Rockin' in the Free World." Olds' song uses the structure and many lyrics of the original but changes the original song's political message. The music of the two songs is not at issue, only the lyrics. Young expects that Olds will argue that his song is a parody that falls under the fair use exception to the Copyright Act. The court will consider the relevant factors set out in the fair use statute, 17 U.S.C. § 107 (2006): whether the copy was transformative and targeted the original; whether it took more than necessary of the original; and whether it will interfere with the original's market.

Let's start with analogizing to precedents concerning the first factor of the fair use test—"the purpose and character of the work"—that looks at whether the work in question is "transformative." Making analogies and distinguishing cases can be tricky with this copyright and fair use problem because in addition to comparing the problem's facts to precedent (as usual with analogical reasoning), the reader will also be comparing the two songs in the problem's facts (the original song and the parody). Nevertheless, the problem provides a good chance to look at how to make analogies and how to distinguish cases.

Step 1: Read the cases and consider the facts of the precedents and the facts of your assignment, looking primarily for facts that are about the precise issue you're addressing. In the copyright and fair use problem, courts consider whether a work is "transformative" when deciding the first fair use factor. A work is transformative when it "adds something new, with a further purpose or different character altering the first with new expression, meaning, or message." *Campbell v. Acuff-Rose Music, Inc.*, 510 U.S. 569, 579 (1994). Read the cases, looking for facts and outcomes we can make comparisons to. In each of two cases, *Mattel v. Walking Mountain Productions*, 353 F.3d 792, 806 (9th Cir. 2003), and *Campbell v. Acuff-Rose Music, Inc.*, 510 U.S. 569, 589 (1994), a court that creates binding precedent for your problem decided that a work was "transformative."

These facts seem relevant to the issue of whether a work is transformative:

Mattel:
- The manufacturing company, Mattel, had established its doll, Barbie, as "the ideal American woman."

- Mattel's advertisements show the dolls dressed in various outfits, leading glamorous lifestyles and engaged in exciting activities.

- To sell its product, Mattel used associations of beauty, wealth, and glamour.

- The defendant in that case developed different associations with his use of Barbie in his photography. In some of his photos, Barbie is about to be destroyed or harmed by domestic life in the form of kitchen appliances. In other photos, the defendant conveys a sexualized perspective of Barbie by showing the nude doll in sexually suggestive contexts.

- The defendant's commentary intends to show the harm that he perceived in Barbie's influence on gender roles and the position of women in society.

Campbell:
- The defendants used the recognizable starting lyrics of Roy Orbison's song "Oh, Pretty Woman" to form a connection to the original.

- The original song romanticized prostitution.

- The original song was in the rock genre.

- The defendant's song was in the rap genre.

- The structure of the defendant's song was different from the structure of the original.

- The original song portrayed a romanticized story of an encounter with a prostitute.

- The defendant's song was a modern, gritty approach to prostitution.

- The original song is full of restraint and innuendo.

- The defendant's song takes a direct insulting approach.

Step 2: Choose the facts from your assignment that may be relevant to the particular legal test that applies to your issue. Here, that means choosing facts that address whether the new work is "transformative," that is to say, whether it "adds something new, with a further purpose or different character, altering the first with new expression, meaning, or message." Look for facts, both positive and negative, that show how the defendant Olds' song is the same or different from the plaintiff Young's song.

We find these facts in the copyright and fair use problem.

- Young's song sends a message that America has faults and points out weaknesses in certain aspects of American life.

- The chorus of Young's song sends the message that we should be empowered to change faults and not lose sight of reasons to be proud of America.

- Young's song became a symbol of American patriotism after the attack on New York on September 11, 2001.

- Olds' song is not critical of America at all.

- Olds' song sends a message of pride in America with lyrics like "there's a bright light on the road ahead."

- Young's song is in the rock genre.

- Olds' song is in the rock genre.

- Young's song speaks of an unsure America, disliked worldwide.

- Young's song has images of a drug-addicted mother who abandons her child.

- Young's song ends with a negative statement on conflict and consumerism.

- Olds' song refers to an idyllic American family.

- Olds' song praises American consumerism.

- Olds' song is proud of America's position in the world and its involvement in conflict.

Step 3: Pick out the key facts from an analogous case, being careful to articulate exactly *how* and *why* the two cases are similar or different. Here are some possible comparisons that you might make. Only a few of the many possible comparisons can be illustrated here.

- Unlike the songs in *Campbell*, where the genre of the songs were different, here the genre is the same because Young's song and Olds' song are both in the rock music genre.

- Olds' song is different from Young's in the way that the parody was different from the original in *Campbell*. In *Campbell* one song was a criticism of society and the other presented a romanticized view of society. Here also, Young's song is a criticism of society and Olds' song presents a romanticized view of the same society.

- Similar to *Campbell*, where the lyrics of the parody differed greatly from the lyrics of the original, here the lyrics of the two songs differ greatly.

- Unlike in *Campbell*, where the structure of the defendant's song differed greatly from the original, here the defendant's song uses the exact same structure of chorus and verse.

Finally, notice that the extent to which facts are generalized can change their effect. A difference can be framed as a similarity, and vice versa, if you zoom far enough in or out. In objective writing it's a good idea to take a neutral approach, as you would expect a court to do. In persuasive writing, be aware of the importance of these framing choices, while being careful not to stretch too far.

Here is an analogy that stretches the comparison in an acceptable way:

- Similar to *Mattel*, where the defendant's purpose was to criticize the viewpoint of the original work about women in society, here also the defendant's purpose was to criticize Young's view of America and change it to Olds' message of complete pride in America.

Here is an analogy that might go too far:

- Unlike in *Mattel*, where the copy's purpose was to challenge the way the original doll represented women in society, here the purpose of Olds' work is identical to that of Young's, to make a comment on America.

EXAMPLES

Here are some examples of analogical reasoning. Some are based on the copyright and fair use problem in Appendix B. For each example, more than one answer may be correct. Explain to yourself why you've chosen your answers. Then read the explanations in the last section of this chapter to check your work.

Example 10-1

In the copyright and fair use case at hand, just as in *Campbell*, it was fair use because it was transformative.

This is a . . .

    A. strong analogy because it says they are both transformative.

    B. strong analogy because it refers to *Campbell*, which was decided by the U.S. Supreme Court.

    C. weak analogy because it doesn't explain how the facts in the precedent and in the problem are alike.

    D. weak analogy because although it uses an important word from the rule, it doesn't explain its conclusion.

Example 10-2

Like the defendants in *Campbell* who set up an expectation by using the lyrics and opening bars of the original but shattered it with a different message, Olds uses the music, structure, and lyrics of the original to set up an expectation that he shatters with his different message.

This is a . . .

    A. strong analogy because it compares the facts of the precedent to the facts of the copyright and fair use problem.

    B. strong analogy because it uses the same words for both cases.

    C. weak analogy because it goes on and on about something the reader can figure out without explanation.

    D. weak analogy because it's repetitive.

Example 10-3

Unlike *Mattel*, Olds failed to substantially transform his work in order to convey his message. The verse and chorus pattern in Olds' parody is the exact pattern used in Young's song.

    A. This author strongly distinguishes the *Mattel* case because the author uses facts to support the conclusion.

    B. This successfully distinguishes the problem from *Mattel* because it compares the facts of the copyright and fair use problem to *Mattel*.

    C. This unsuccessfully distinguishes the problem from *Mattel* because it doesn't say why copying a verse and chorus pattern is important.

    D. This unsuccessfully distinguishes the problem from *Mattel* because it does not tell the reader which facts in *Mattel* are different from the facts of the copyright and fair use problem.

Example 10-4

This example doesn't use the copyright and fair use problem. Instead, consider these three examples from a different case:

Example (4)1:   Under *Daniels*, falling is not a danger that fills this rule. Therefore the plaintiff cannot win.

Example (4)2:   Falling from the height of the boat was a danger a child would understand in *Daniels*. Falling from the height of the ladder and hayloft in our case is also an understandable danger. In both cases the danger of falling from a height is a danger immature minds can comprehend.

Example (4)3:   Jack fell from the ladder in the same manner that the plaintiff in *Daniels* fell from the stationary boat. Jack is also a year or two older than the plaintiff in *Daniels*, strengthening the argument that he should be aware of the danger of falling.

Choose a good observation about these examples:

    A. Example (4)1 is better than Example (4)2 because it tells what is the same about both cases.

    B. Example (4)2 is better than Example (4)1 because it uses the facts of the precedent case to show how the facts in the case at hand are stronger.

    C. Example (4)1 is not as strong as the others but it's a good analogy using the same case.

    D. All of the examples are poor because they use more than one sentence to make the analogies.

EXPLANATIONS

Explanation 10-1

A is insufficient. **B** makes a good point for weight of authority questions, but it doesn't help much for analogical reasoning. **C** is probably the best description of why it's a weak analogy, because A does not explain why or how the two cases are similar. The author does not compare facts. **D** is also a good answer and it names a common problem first-year students experience: simply using an important word from the test without explaining how it applies. On law school exams, a professor would call this kind of answer "conclusory." It states a conclusion without the reason for it.

Explanation 10-2

This example is a strong analogy. *A* is the best description of why it's strong. The analogy here is very specific, telling the reader how the view was different in each case. **B** is also good. It's fine to repeat phrases to make your point. You may have learned elsewhere to vary your language to keep a reader interested. In law, readers want information they can grasp quickly without doing much work. You're unlikely to be graded down for using the same words to describe similarities. **C** is problematic. Remember to explain the links for the reader as specifically as you can. This is especially true in a first-year class when you are learning to make clear analogies. **D** is incorrect. Although the example repeats certain words and repeats concepts that you explained, this is new information for the reader—how and why the precedent case supports a similar finding.

Explanation 10-3

A is incorrect. You might have seen facts and assumed they were factual comparisons between the case at hand and the precedent. Instead the comparisons are between the two songs in the problem. **B** is incorrect. It assumes that mentioning a case name is enough. We know that it's not. **C** is correct. The comparison doesn't really explain much about how the two cases are different. In addition, the structure is not parallel. **D** is the best characterization of the difficulty here. Reread the example. Is there anything in it about the facts in the precedent case? No. So although the author is thinking about ways the two cases are different, she has not provided an explanation. The only facts we see are from the copyright and fair use problem itself. No facts are from the precedent.

Explanation 10-4

Here it is interesting to see how informative good examples are when you have no background about a case. Examples (4)2 and (4)3 are taken directly from first-year student papers and show you how much you can learn about an issue merely by reading a couple of sentences of good analysis. Although the student undoubtedly explained more about the precedent earlier in the paper, notice that you quickly learn how the precedent case illustrated the rule that requires a danger to be understandable by an immature mind. And then, almost as quickly, you see how the facts of the problem compare to the precedent.

A is not correct. Example (4)1 tells little about what facts are similar in both cases. **B** is correct, for the opposite reason. Example (4)2 does explain how the facts are alike. **C** is incorrect. Example (4)1 does not contain an analogy. It merely refers to an appropriate precedent case. **D** is also incorrect. It's fine to use more than one sentence to make an analogy. Sometimes it makes an analogy very strong to fit it all into one sentence. But if putting it all in one sentence is unwieldy, it's fine to use as many sentences as you need.

Applying the Law: Policy Analysis

Law professors are fond of policy rationales. Your Contracts or Property professor probably spends considerable time helping the class see the societal interests served by a rule of law. In practice and when you're learning to write practice documents, it's sometimes a different story. Both sides to a dispute can make sweeping statements about how the outcome each wants will help society. If these sweeping statements are not substantiated by solid analysis, they will seldom convince. In this chapter, we explain how to make specific, well-supported policy arguments that can be quite important in practice documents.

Terminology Notes: When professors use the term "normative argument," they mean an argument about what *should* happen for the benefit of society. It's a synonym for "policy argument."

WHAT YOU NEED TO KNOW ABOUT POLICY ANALYSIS

"Analyzing policy" means explaining how an outcome will benefit or disadvantage society. Because both sides of an issue can generate reasons why society would be better off if their side won, think of generating policy rationales as looking for the strongest policy reasons that benefit a particular side, rather than looking for the "right answer" or the one "correct" policy.[1]

Make your policy analysis specific to your assignment. Identify exactly how your position will benefit society. Most readers understand that anyone can make broad sweeping policy rationales to benefit either side. Those abstract generalities are rarely important unless the writer also explains specifically and concretely how an outcome will affect society.

Like any other analysis, policy analysis is stronger when supported by citations to mandatory primary authority. Look for authority in a couple of places. Often statutes will begin with a section that states the purpose or goals of the statute—the policy behind the statute. Courts also address the policy behind decisions in opinions.

Policy rationales can show the reader why your analogical analysis or fact-based analysis is important. With analogies or fact-based rationales you're asking the court to put the facts of your case in a certain category. (For example, you might argue that certain facts fall in the "burglary category," or that your case is just like the precedent case where the court held that an allegedly infringing use was "fair use.") The policy analysis tells the court why it's important to categorize your case your way.

Think about your audience while deciding how much to emphasize policy. The highest court in a jurisdiction will find policy considerations important when deciding a case because the high court's decision will probably affect more subsequent cases and affect a broader section of society. A trial court and intermediate appellate court are less likely to decide a case based primarily on policy reasons. Any court, however, will consider policy when addressing a case of first impression or a case that presents new arguments.

HOW TO GENERATE POLICY RATIONALES

Using the copyright and fair use problem in Appendix B, we'll walk you through the process of generating policy rationales.

---

1. For more detailed information on making policy arguments, see Ellie Margolis, *Closing the Floodgates: Making Persuasive Policy Arguments in Appellate Briefs*, 62 Mont. L. Rev. 59 (2001).

Problem

> Here is a quick overview of the copyright and fair use problem (for details see Appendix B). Young is suing Olds for violating the Copyright Act when Olds wrote a song based on Young's original, "Rockin' in the Free World." Olds' song uses the structure and many lyrics of the original but changes the original song's political message. The music of the two songs is not at issue, only the lyrics. Young expects that Olds will argue that his song is a parody that falls under the fair use exception to the Copyright Act. The court will consider the relevant factors set out in the fair use statute, 17 U.S.C. § 107 (2006): whether the copy was transformative and targeted the original; whether it took more than necessary of the original; and whether it will interfere with the original's market.

Step 1: Generate a list of policy rationales. You need policies that legislatures and courts have already recognized as societal interests. The logical place to start is to check primary, mandatory authority to find policy statements or arguments that might be helpful to your analysis. Because you're working with a statute, first look at the statute's introductory section to see whether it includes a policy statement. Or you might look at the first section of a title or other subdivision of a larger enactment. For example, at the beginning of a state code's section on criminal law, there may be general policy statements about criminal law in that jurisdiction. At the beginning of the Copyright Act, however, you'll find definitions but no statement of policy or of Congress's intention when it adopted the Act.

Next turn to cases, looking first at cases from the courts of last resort as a likely place to find policy. Cases from a high court will also provide the best authority for policy. After evaluating cases from the highest courts, you may consider looking for policy in lower court decisions.

Here, looking at the highest court for your jurisdiction, you see that *Campbell*, a U.S. Supreme Court case, states that:

> The fair use doctrine thus "permits [and requires] courts to avoid rigid application of the copyright statute when, on occasion, it would stifle the very creativity which that law is designed to foster." *Campbell v. Acuff-Rose Music, Inc.*, 510 U.S. 569, 577 (1994) (quoting *Stewart v. Abend*, 495 U.S. 207, 236 (1990)).

Or looking at a lower court, you find this statement:

> The primary intent of fair use is to weigh the rights of the original owner against the benefit that the secondary use provides to society. *Mattel, Inc. v. Walking Mountain Prods.*, 353 F.3d 792, 806 (9th Cir. 2003).

So, your list of policies looks like this:

- the purpose of the Copyright Act is to encourage creativity
- the court should not stifle creativity
- the court will balance the rights of the original owner with the benefit the copy makes to society

Step 2: If you don't find policy in the primary sources for your assignment, generate a list of ideas and then look for authority to support those ideas. If you find nothing about policy in your statutes or cases, think through the effects of a potential ruling. The analysis will still be stronger with a citation to some kind of authority, so you'll want to look for the authority after you've come up with the idea. If you can't find authority in primary sources, try citing secondary sources or social science outside of legal sources.

To generate the list, think of the consequences, both direct and indirect, of your desired outcome. Some consequences might be moral, economic, or practical. They might implicate our institutions of government such as which branch of government is best situated to make a decision or whether the decision will affect the integrity of the justice system.

Here, the copyright and fair use problem includes an interesting twist in the facts. Olds' song criticizes the politics expressed in Young's original. So when you think of other policies that might help persuade a decision maker to Olds' side, you can say that his copy is a form of political speech. The problem doesn't include a First Amendment claim, which requires an entirely different analysis, but the facts arguably involve political speech, a highly protected form of speech.

Thus, you can look at First Amendment cases for policy statements that help, even though they are not part of copyright law. A useful statement about the importance of political speech appears in a Supreme Court case:

> "Freedom of speech is 'indispensable to the discovery and spread of political truth,' and 'the best test of truth is the power of the thought to get itself accepted in the competition of the market.'" *Consol. Edison Co. of N.Y., Inc. v. Pub. Serv. Comm'n of N.Y.*, 447 U.S. 530, 534 (1980) (internal citations omitted).

We might make this more concrete and take it out of the First Amendment analysis by considering the consequences of a precedent a court would establish by deciding the controversy between Young and Olds. So you might add to your list that political parody is valuable to society and future artists may hesitate to critique political statements, which would mean the general public would lose the chance to hear both sides of an issue.

Step 3: Craft an argument that is specific to your assignment. A common mistake for beginners is to make a broad, sweeping statement of policy without following through to tell the reader how it applies in your assignment. Remember, the more specific the rationale, and the better supported by authority, the stronger the policy analysis.

Because the court's policy statements are a part of the law, you'll put those in the section of the paper that describes, explains, or proves the law. Then in the application or analysis section you'll apply that statement to your assignment. So take a look at these policy statements and the arguments you make with them.

Policy statement #1:	The fair use doctrine thus "permits [and requires] courts to avoid rigid application of the copyright statute when, on occasion, it would stifle the very creativity which that law is designed to foster." *Campbell v. Acuff-Rose Music, Inc.,* 510 U.S. 569, 577 (1994) (quoting *Stewart v. Abend,* 495 U.S. 207, 236 (1990)).
Policy rationale #1:	If the court finds that Olds' song is not fair use, it will be counter to the policy of encouraging creativity because artists will refrain from creating a new work of art that comments on the message of an earlier work of art for fear of litigation.
Policy statement #2:	The primary intent of fair use is to weigh the rights of the original owner against the benefit that the secondary use provides to society. *Mattel, Inc. v. Walking Mountain Prods.,* 353 F.3d 792, 806 (9th Cir. 2003). The "freedom of speech is 'indispensable to the discovery and spread of political truth.'" *Consol. Edison Co. of N.Y., Inc. v. Pub. Serv. Comm'n of N.Y.,* 447 U.S. 530, 534 (1980) (internal citations omitted).
Policy rationale #2:	Here the benefit to society of free and open critique of an earlier political song outweighs the rights of the original artist because a democratic society is more informed and better able to make choices when artists freely exchange opposing ideas. This exchange is "indispensable" in a democratic society. *Consol. Edison Co. of N.Y., Inc. v. Pub. Serv. Comm'n of N.Y.,* 447 U.S. 530, 534 (1980).

EXAMPLES

Here are some examples of policy analysis. Some are based on the copyright and fair use problem in Appendix B. For each example, more than one answer may be correct. Explain to yourself why you've chosen your answers. Then read the explanations in the last section of this chapter to check your work.

Example 11-1

It would be against the public policy interest in safety to convict Allison King of vehicular manslaughter.

This is a . . .

A. weak public policy analysis because it's not supported by a reference to mandatory authority stating that the state has an interest in safety.
B. strong public policy analysis because it correctly identifies that the state has a strong interest in the safety of its citizens.
C. weak public policy analysis because it doesn't specify how the outcome the author advocates would further the state's interest in safety.

Example 11-2

Courts recognize adverse possession as a doctrine that "encourages land be put to its most productive and highest use." *Jones v. Jones*, 116 N.E.2d 1235, 1237 (Mass. 1945). Here, Calvin Kolb was an absentee owner. If the law fails to punish absentee owners, there will be more absentee owners whose land is unused.

This is a . . .

A. good policy analysis because it cites primary authority and is specific about Calvin Kolb being an absentee owner.
B. good policy analysis because it includes how the outcome may influence future cases.
C. poor policy analysis because the analysis relies on an assumption the author hasn't stated. The assumption is that all absentee owners fail to put land to its highest and best use. Hence, even though the answer uses specific facts and speculates about how the outcome will influence future cases, it focuses on where the owner lives and not on whether the land is well used. The author could make it better by

stating the assumption: "Here Calvin Kolb was an absentee owner and did not put his land to its highest and best use."

Example 11-3

"The purpose of copyright is to create incentives for creative effort." *Sony Corp. of Am. v. Universal City Studios, Inc.*, 464 U.S. 417, 450 (1984). Here, artists, like Young, will lose the incentive to create new works if they are likely to lose profits to copyists, like Olds, who copy so closely that consumers are likely to confuse the two works. Future artists will hesitate to expend creative effort if they will fail to reap the reward.

    A. This policy analysis is weak in that it connects the abstract generality with specific and concrete effects the desired ruling will produce and it talks about the future.

    B. This is good policy analysis because it cites good authority and makes concrete and practical arguments about how a contrary decision would affect society.

    C. This analysis will work only if the case is in the U.S. Supreme Court.

Example 11-4

Courts recognize that the criminal code protects the safety of the people. *State v. Smith*, 592 N.W.2d 1303, 1306 (Minn. 1999). Our case is similar to *Smith*, because both cases are burglary cases. Thus, it is important to convict Harrison of burglary so that the people will be safe.

This is a . . .

    A. good policy analysis because it shows the reader why the analogy to *Smith* is important.

    B. good policy analysis because it tells the reader why it's important to society to convict the defendant.

    C. poor policy analysis because it is so broad that it could be used in any criminal case.

    D. poor policy analysis because it cites to primary authority.

EXPLANATIONS

Explanation 11-1

A is correct because public policy analysis is most effective if you have laid the groundwork by citing good authority for the proposition that your jurisdiction cares about the policy in the section of the paper where you explain the law. *B* is incorrect because this is not strong policy analysis. In fact, both sides could make this argument to the court. In addition, it does not specifically explain how the outcome the author advocates or predicts would further the state's interest in safety. *C* is correct. The analysis would be much stronger if the author told the reader that excusing King's cell phone use would promote safety because citizens could warn others of dangerous road conditions without fear of prosecution.

Explanation 11-2

A is partially true because it correctly states that citing to high authority is important in strong policy analysis. But it incorrectly states that being specific about where the land's owner lives is a concrete policy consideration. *B* is also partially correct because good policy analysis often does connect the current problem to future results. But it's incorrect because this particular example doesn't do a good job of connecting the current problem to future results. It refers to absentee ownership, which may be relevant, but is not the same as failure to put the land to its best use, which is the policy behind adverse possession. *C* correctly identifies that problem.

Explanation 11-3

A is wrong because this policy analysis connects the abstract idea of giving artists incentives to create new works with the artists' fear of losing money when their work is copied. This is exactly the kind of concrete, practical policy analysis that is effective. Further, good policy analysis usually addresses the future. *B* is correct because not only is the analysis specific, it also cites good authority for the general proposition upon which it's based. *C* is wrong. Although the highest courts are more likely to consider policy, all courts might be influenced by it.

Explanation 11-4

A is wrong because the analogy to *Smith* has nothing to do with policy. Noting that the criminal charge in both cases was the same does not support the idea that safety is an important policy. Further, the analogy itself is weak. If you'd like to know more about making a strong analogy, see Chapter 10. **B** is only partially correct. It is good to tell the reader why an outcome is important to society, but in this example, the author needs to be more specific about how finding the defendant guilty will further a societal interest. **C** is correct. This rationale is so broad that it would apply in any criminal case and that means it's so broad it fails to convince. **D** is wrong. Although the answer correctly identifies the example as a poor policy rationale, providing a cite to authority for a policy rationale is good to do.

CHAPTER 12

Writing the Introduction to the Discussion (or Argument)

In the part of this book that covers memo writing, why does the chapter on writing the introduction to the Discussion or Argument come near the end? It's because the introduction will include the points you think are most important and only after you've written the bulk of the analysis contained in the Discussion section or Argument section will you know how it should be introduced.

The same principles that apply to the introduction to the Discussion or Argument section will apply whenever you write the introductory paragraph for each issue or sub-issue of the Discussion section. Each section will have an introductory section and you'll put the same bits of information into short introductions, or introductory paragraphs, throughout the memo or brief.

Terminology Notes: Terminology about this section of your document is varied and rich. Your textbook or teacher may call the introductory section of a document or a section of a document an "introduction," "thesis paragraph," "rule paragraph," "umbrella paragraph," or "umbrella rule paragraph." Although these labels may emphasize different components of an introductory paragraph, the components of a good introductory section or paragraph will be the same. Some will use "roadmap" to refer to the entire introduction, while others will use that term to mean only the part of the introduction that tells the reader the sequence in which you'll address the issues and sub-issues. Finally, some may use "claim" as synonym for "thesis statement."

WHAT YOU NEED TO KNOW ABOUT WRITING INTRODUCTIONS

Write or revise an introduction only after you've identified the points that are most important to your analysis in the Discussion section of a memo or the Argument section of a brief. An introduction should contain the points you think are most essential for the reader to know before you discuss the details. Although people often imagine writing to be organizing your thoughts and then pouring them perfectly onto the page from start to end, you've probably realized by now that you actually work through your ideas as you write. Writing is thinking. Often you won't know the most important points on each side until you've written the Discussion section. So revise the introductory section of the Discussion or Argument as the last drafting task before you begin the final editing and proofreading to make sure your paper is perfect.

A good introduction to the Discussion section will include:

- *A thesis statement:* A thesis statement is an assertion or series of assertions about how a court will decide the issue or issues you're writing about—the outcome. Some think of a thesis statement as your conclusion put up front. In fact, some teachers will call the entire introduction to the memo a general "thesis paragraph."
- *The rule or rules the court will apply to your issue:* Usually the introduction includes only the main rule that applies to the issue, and not the rules that apply to the sub-issues that make up this larger rule. Some teachers will call this the "umbrella rule," or the rule that "covers" the whole issue. Those teachers may call the introduction "the umbrella rule paragraph."
- *A statement about those parts of the rule that will not be at issue, along with a very brief explanation of why not:* Note that when more than one rule, or more than one part of the rule, applies, of course your Discussion section will address everything the parties are likely to contest. Even if you decide the plaintiff can't prove an essential part of the rule, you'll still need to analyze every part that a plaintiff could make arguments about, in case you're wrong about the plaintiff ultimately losing on another point. The only time you can omit an issue from the Discussion section is when you decide a party has no valid arguments to make on the issue. In that situation, your introduction should note the issue that is not likely to be in dispute and explicitly explain why it won't be "at issue."
- *A roadmap of the memo:* A roadmap is a sentence or paragraph that outlines the organization of the discussion that follows for the reader. Legal

readers want to know exactly where they are going, without surprises. Usually setting out the rule and explaining which parts of it are at issue acts as the "roadmap" of your paper because the reader will assume that you will proceed in your Discussion section in the same order. But sometimes the organization is more complex and you will need to spell out the order in which you'll address each issue or sub-issue.

Unless your teacher has specified a sequence she finds most effective, you can put these pieces together in the introduction in any order that makes sense to you. The last piece will often include a sentence that provides a transition from the introductory section to where you begin to analyze the first issue. For more on CRAC and organizational paradigms, see Chapter 6.

You can also include other statements that apply to the issue generally rather than to one particular section. For instance, perhaps the statute or key case identifies policies served by the rule. General policy statements are not usually dispositive, and sometimes have limited persuasive value, but it may make sense to include them in the introduction if they are noteworthy and you can't find a way to weave them into your detailed analysis.

One of the difficulties you'll run into is how much detail to include in stating rules or in a roadmap. If you give too little detail, the reader will miss the links that connect the information you've presented, and the introduction won't make much sense. If you give too much detail, the reader will be bogged down with information that is not immediately usable. Readers get frustrated if you clutter up their short-term memory with details they can't immediately use. So the key is really to give readers enough to understand what is going on and what to expect from the memo, but not a bit more.

Finally, writing the introduction may make later sections seem repetitive to you. Remember that the reader may read only parts of your memo rather than reading it like a book from start to finish. Each section has to stand on its own. Don't repeat within a section, but don't worry about repeating something from the introduction in another part of the memo.

HOW TO WRITE INTRODUCTIONS

Using the copyright and fair use problem in Appendix B, we'll walk you through the process of writing introductions and introductory paragraphs.

Problem

> *Here is a quick overview of the copyright and fair use problem (for details see Appendix B).* Young is suing Olds for violating the Copyright Act when Olds wrote a song based on Young's original, "Rockin' in the Free World." Olds' song uses the structure and many lyrics of the original but changes the original song's political message. The music of the two songs is not at issue, only the lyrics. Young expects that Olds will argue that his song is a parody that falls under the fair use exception to the Copyright Act. The court will consider the relevant factors set out in the fair use statute, 17 U.S.C. § 107 (2006): whether the copy was transformative and targeted the original; whether it took more than necessary of the original; and whether it will interfere with the original's market.

Step 1: Plan. Develop a thesis, a rule statement, an explanation of why neither side is likely to dispute some part of the rule, if that's true, and a roadmap.

Step 2: Write a thesis statement. Remember that the thesis statement is your conclusion stated up front. When you can identify one primary reason for your conclusion, include that in your thesis sentence. Sometimes there won't be just one primary reason for your conclusion. Then you can write a general thesis statement.

Using the copyright case, you could have come to several conclusions, because you have to decide whether Olds violated the Copyright Act and whether the fair use exception will work for him. Let's write several thesis sentences that cover most of the possibilities.

For instance, you could decide that Olds violated the Copyright Act and won't be able to prove the fair use exception:

> The court will most likely hold that Olds violated the Copyright Act and Olds cannot prove that his use falls under the fair use exception because he used more of the original than needed for his parody.

Put another way with less detail: Young can successfully show that Olds is liable for violating the Copyright Act and that the fair use exception is not available to him.

Or your analysis might show that Olds did the things that would normally constitute a copyright violation, but you might believe he can avoid liability through the fair use exception:

> Although Young can show Olds infringed upon Young's copyright, Olds can successfully assert the fair use exception as a defense because the court

is likely to find the transformative nature of the parody outweighed other factors.

Put another way with less detail: The court will find that Olds violated the Copyright Act but that he can escape liability under the fair use exception.

Or you could decide that Olds didn't violate the Copyright Act, and that in any case, he could successfully use the fair use exception:

> Olds will successfully defend the claim of infringement because he did not violate the Copyright Act and even if he did, he can prove the fair use exception because he used only what he needed to make a parody, his work had a different message than the original, and it was a different genre of music that was not likely to intrude on the original's market.

Put another way, with less detail: Young cannot prove Olds infringed his copyright and even if he could, Olds can prove his use falls under the fair use exception.

Some legal writing textbooks suggest putting the relevant thesis statement as the heading that announces that particular section of the paper. The heading will be an assertion about the outcome of the analysis in that section.

Step 3: State the rule or rules that govern overall. It's important to include enough for the reader to understand which rules apply overall to the problem. This is especially true because the structure of the rule that applies overall will most often form the structure of your analysis and provide an organization for you to follow. That's also why the rule statement so often serves as the roadmap for your paper. But do more than just cut and paste the rule into your paper. Although the reader will expect you to quote statutes or the test that the court sets out, edit the statute or rule to make it easy for the reader to see what the parties need to prove. Too much detail will clutter the introduction and just burden the reader with more than he needs to start.

Sometimes you'll need to make a judgment call on how much context you need to give. The copyright and fair use problem provides a good example. You have choices about which rules to include in your introduction. You can start with the rights given to Young by the Copyright Act, or you can start with the rules for the fair use exception that Olds will assert. Let's look at how they both would work.

If the reader would need some background to understand the Copyright Act section that gives Young the right to sue Olds over using his song, you might write something like this:

> Among the exclusive rights that the Copyright Act, 17 U.S.C. § 106 (2006), provides copyright holders are the rights to perform, copy, distribute, and make derivatives of the copyrighted work. These rights are subject to exceptions for

fair use, which includes "purposes such as criticism" and "comment." 17 U.S.C. § 107 (2006). The statute provides four factors that courts can use to determine whether there is a fair use exception to the infringement:

(1) the purpose and character of the use, including whether such use is of a commercial nature or is for nonprofit educational purposes;

(2) the nature of the copyrighted work;

(3) the amount and substantiality of the portion used in relation to the copyrighted work as a whole; and

(4) the effect of the use upon the potential market for or value of the copyrighted work.

Id.

Or, if you decide that the general principles of copyright are so well known to your audience that you don't need to set them out, you could go right to the rules that govern your analysis in this memo:

Olds is likely to answer a claim of copyright infringement by asserting that he falls under the fair use exception to the Copyright Act. Fair use includes "purposes such as criticism" and "comment." 17 U.S.C. § 107 (2006). The statute provides four factors that the courts can use to determine whether there is a fair use exception to infringement:

(1) the purpose and character of the use, including whether such use is of a commercial nature or is for nonprofit educational purposes;

(2) the nature of the copyrighted work;

(3) the amount and substantiality of the portion used in relation to the copyrighted work as a whole; and

(4) the effect of the use upon the potential market for or value of the copyrighted work.

Id.

Decide how much information is necessary and useful for the ordinary legal reader. This may be difficult for you as a first-year law student, but it will become second nature to you as you become more experienced as a legal reader and a legal writer. For now, it's not wrong to give a fuller context than necessary for the rules you apply; but it can be a time-waster for the reader and use up valuable words if you're under a strict word count or page limit. In those cases, you may decide to go right to the rules that most apply in your analysis.

Step 4: Tell the reader which parts, if any, the parties are not likely to dispute. If one of the issues in your assignment so clearly falls to one party that the other party has no good arguments to make about it, you should dismiss those issues or sub-issues in the introduction.

In the copyright and fair use problem, the U.S. Supreme Court has held that the second factor is not likely to weigh in cases involving a parody. Thus, you would include a couple of sentences like these:

In our case, the second factor, the nature of the copyrighted work, is relatively insignificant in a parody case because parodies "almost invariably copy publicly known, expressive works," and this factor has been largely disregarded by the courts in such cases. *Campbell v. Acuff-Rose Music, Inc.*, 510 U.S. 569, 586 (1994). Thus, because the court is not likely to weigh this factor, the parties are not likely to dispute it.

Or

The second factor, the nature of the copyrighted work, is not likely to be in dispute because the Supreme Court has stated that courts disregard this factor in cases like ours involving parody. *Campbell v. Acuff-Rose Music, Inc.*, 510 U.S. 569, 586 (1994).

Step 5: Make sure you have a roadmap. Most often the rule will act as your roadmap. Usually, your Discussion section will address the issues in the same order that the source of the rule does. For instance, if your rule comes from a statute, you'll address the elements or factors in the same order as the statute does. Or if you're using a rule or test delineated in a case, address each part of the rule in the same order the court did. In these cases, once you state the large-scale rule in your introduction you don't need to add a separate roadmap.

Sometimes, however, you'll have a good reason for departing from ordering the issues in the same way the rule does. Perhaps one part of the rule is more important to your case. If you're writing a persuasive brief, you might order your arguments by their strength and indicate this order in the introduction to your argument. Or perhaps you're applying more than one rule and no statute or case suggests an order to use for more than one rule. In those cases, you'll add a simple sentence or two, setting out the organization your memo will follow. For instance:

In our case, the court will probably weigh the third factor, "the amount and substantiality of the portion used in relation to the copyrighted work as a whole," more heavily than the others. Thus, this memo will focus first on that factor before turning to the purpose and character of the use, and the potential effect on markets.

Step 6: Put it all together. Here are a couple of ways you could put together an introduction section to your sample memo:

Introduction

The court will most likely hold that Olds violated the Copyright Act and that his work does not fall under the fair use exception because he used more of the original work than needed for his parody. Olds is likely to answer a claim of copyright infringement by asserting that his use falls under the fair use exception to the Copyright Act. Fair use includes "purposes such as criticism" and "comment." 17 U.S.C. § 107 (2006). The statute provides four factors that courts use to determine whether there is a fair use exception to infringement:

> (1) the purpose and character of the use, including whether such use is of a commercial nature or is for nonprofit educational purposes;
>
> (2) the nature of the copyrighted work;
>
> (3) the amount and substantiality of the portion used in relation to the copyrighted work as a whole; and
>
> (4) the effect of the use upon the potential market for or value of the copyrighted work.

Id. The second factor, the nature of the copyrighted work, is not likely to be in dispute because the Supreme Court has stated that courts disregard this factor in cases like ours involving parody. *Campbell v. Acuff-Rose Music, Inc.,* 510 U.S. 569, 586 (1994).

In our case, the court will probably weigh the third factor, "the amount and substantiality of the portion used in relation to the copyrighted work as a whole," more heavily than the others. Thus, this memo will focus first on that factor before turning to the purpose and character of the use, and the potential effect on markets.

Or you might write this instead:

Introduction

Among the exclusive rights that the Copyright Act, 17 U.S.C. § 106 (2006), provides copyright holders are the rights to perform, copy, distribute, and make derivatives of the work. These rights, however, are subject to exceptions for fair use. 17 U.S.C. § 107 (2006).

Fair use includes "purposes such as criticism" and "comment." *Id.* The statute provides four factors that courts use to determine whether there is a fair use exception to the infringement:

> (1) the purpose and character of the use, including whether such use is of a commercial nature or is for nonprofit educational purposes;
>
> (2) the nature of the copyrighted work;
>
> (3) the amount and substantiality of the portion used in relation to the copyrighted work as a whole; and
>
> (4) the effect of the use upon the potential market for or value of the copyrighted work.

Id.

In our case, the second factor, the nature of the copyrighted work, is relatively insignificant in a parody case because parodies "almost invariably copy publicly known, expressive works," and thus this factor has been largely disregarded by the courts in such cases. *Campbell v. Acuff-Rose Music, Inc.,* 510 U.S. 569, 586 (1994). Thus, because the court is not likely to weigh this factor, the parties are not likely to dispute it. Although Young can show Olds infringed upon Young's copyright, the court is likely to find Olds' use falls under the fair use exception because the transformative nature of the parody outweighed other factors.

EXAMPLES

Here are some examples of introductions—or as your professor may call them, "umbrella rule paragraphs" or "thesis paragraphs." Most, but not all, are based on the copyright and fair use problem in Appendix B. For each example, choose the best answer or answers, noting that more than one answer may be correct. Explain to yourself why you've chosen that answer or answers. Then read the explanations in the last section of this chapter to check your work.

Example 12-1

Introduction

ISSUE: Copyright law grants specific privileges for copyrighted material under Title 17 U.S.C. § 106 (2006). Congress's intention in creating a copyright monopoly of protected uses is grounded in the larger context of societal advancement. Congress recognized elements where society would be better served by allowing "fair use" of copyrighted material and codified this in Title 17 U.S.C. § 107 (2006). In that section Congress created four elements that courts should use to weigh when deciding whether a work is "fair use" of copyrighted material. In light of this the case law recognizes there is "fair use" of copyrighted materials that would otherwise violate copyright holder's rights. Specifically, courts have clearly recognized parody as a potential fair use of copyrighted material.

RULE: To determine whether Phil Olds' song "Stop Knockin' the Free World" is a "fair use," we must weigh the four factors using the facts of the case. *Campbell v. Acuff-Rose Music, Inc.*, 510 U.S. 578 (1994). The first and arguably the most important factor, the character of use, will show Mr. Olds' song is transformative enough to be "fair use." The second factor regarding the nature of the work will not likely be in dispute because the nature of parody requires significant copying of the original and thus both sides would agree on that factor. *Id.* at 586. The third factor, substantial use, will show that an excessive amount of the copyrighted work was not used. Finally the fourth factor, market effect, will show that there is potential for market substitution barring "fair use."

THESIS: Considering the balance of the four factors as a whole, it is highly unlikely that Mr. Young can have an injunction served against Mr. Olds to stop him from using Mr. Young's lyrics.

A. This rule statement in this introduction works well because it personalizes the statute and saves the reader the trouble of reading it. This makes the introduction flow well.

135

B. This introduction works well because it labels the components so that the teacher can see the student included everything.

C. This introduction should not include the Copyright Act, because the analysis really focuses on the fair use exception.

D. One of the things this introduction does well is explain what is not in dispute.

Example 12-2

Introduction

To prove fair use of copyrighted material, four elements must be considered. 17 U.S.C. § 107 (2006). The first element assesses whether the material is for a commercial purpose and what its character is. The second element assesses if the nature of the material is covered under copyright law. The third element assesses the amount of the copyrighted work that was copied and borrowed in relation to the entire copyrighted work. The fourth element determines whether the new song has an economic impact on the copyrighted song.

The first element is partially disputed. That Olds intended his song to be used for commercial purposes is not under dispute. Olds asserts that his song is a parody and is legal under fair use. Here, there is no argument that both the original and the new work are in the same genre and similar lyrical composition so the work's nature is not in dispute. Young is disputing that Olds' song is a parody. The second factor is not in dispute because by definition a parody will copy or mimic the original work. In addition, Olds recognizes that Young copyrighted his song. Olds' song was played on the radio. The substantiality of the amount used in reference to the whole will be the last factor addressed. Finally, since these are factors and not elements, the last section will weigh the factors.

A. A weakness of this introduction is that it does not contain a thesis statement and, like the first example, it does not quote the statute.

B. This introduction is strong because it repeats facts to give the reader context for its analysis.

C. A weakness of this introduction is that it uses the words "element" and "factor" as synonyms.

D. A strength of this introduction is that it tells the reader how the court will decide each factor.

Example 12-3

Introduction

To decide whether the defendant's parody falls under the fair use exception to the Copyright Act, the court will weigh the four factors of the fair use statute. 17 U.S.C. § 107 (2006). The statute provides:

Notwithstanding the provisions of sections 106 and 106A, the fair use of a copyrighted work, including such use by reproduction in copies or photographic records or by any other means specified by that section, for purposes such as criticism, comment, news reporting, teaching (including multiple copies for classroom use), scholarship, or research, is not an infringement of copyright. In determining whether the use made of a work in any particular case is a fair use the factors to be considered shall include:

(1) the purpose and character of the use, including whether such use is of a commercial nature or is for non-profit educational purposes;

(2) the nature of the copyrighted work;

(3) the amount and substantiality of the portion used in relation to the copyrighted work as a whole; and

(4) the effect of the use upon the potential market for or value of the copyrighted work.

Id.

The fact that a work is unpublished shall not itself bar a finding of fair use if such finding is made upon consideration of all the above factors. Id.

In this case, the defendant has the greatest burden of proof because fair use is an affirmative defense. Campbell v. Acuff-Rose Music, Inc., 510 U.S. 569, 590 (1994). The court has established that the plaintiff is the owner of a copyright, and as such, is entitled to protect his work against copyright infringement. 17 U.S.C. § 106 (2006). Consequently, the issue of exclusive rights of copyrighted works is beyond the scope of this discussion. Id. The court will likely find that Phil Olds' song violates the Copyright Act and that his song does not fall within the fair use exception because three of the four factors weigh against the defendant. The "character and purpose" factor weighs in favor of Olds, but none of the other factors do.

Which of the following statements about this introduction are true? Which are false?

A. This introduction contains a thesis statement.

B. Although this introduction quotes the statute, it quotes so much that the reader will find it hard to see the test the court will apply.

C. This introduction lets the reader know whether the parties are unlikely to dispute any of the factors.

D. This introduction correctly orders the components of a good introduction.

Example 12-4

Introduction

To revoke a gift given in contemplation of marriage, California Civil Code § 1590 requires donors seeking to recover the gift to first show that they indeed gave the gift in contemplation of marriage. A donor gives a gift in contemplation of marriage if the plaintiff can prove the following elements. First, the donor "makes a gift of money or property to the other." Cal. Civ. Code § 1590 (West 2007). Neither party disputes that the facts of this case fulfill this requirement. Second, the donor gives the gift "on the basis or assumption that the marriage will take place." Id. The parties are in dispute over this element.

If a gift is given in contemplation of marriage, to recover the gift, the plaintiff must establish that either "the donee refuses to enter into the marriage as contemplated" or the marriage is "given up by mutual consent." Id. Then "the donor may recover such gift or such part of its value as may, under all of the circumstances of the case, be found by a court or jury to be just." Id.

The court will likely find that defendant Norton can keep the painting because the donor did not give that particular gift in contemplation of marriage, but rather as a token of love. California Civil Code section 1148 governs and provides, "A gift, other than a gift in view of impending death, cannot be revoked by the giver." Cal. Civ. Code § 1148 (West 2007). Norton can also keep the ring her fiancé gave her, even though he gave it in contemplation of marriage, because courts have construed a fiancée's unforeseen death as "mutual consent" to end the engagement and not the fault of either party.

Which of the following statements about this introduction are true? Which are false?

A. This introduction is too complicated and has too many rules to be a good introduction.

B. Some of these rules could be described in another order and the introduction/memo would still be successful.

C. The readers need more facts to understand this introduction.

D. This introduction ends with good thesis statements.

EXPLANATIONS

Explanation 12-1

A is incorrect. It's fine to personalize a rule, and some textbooks teach students to do that. But when a statute is involved, even when personalizing the rule, readers will want to know the exact language of the statute. Generally, quote statutes or the precise tests set forth by cases. (When discussing cases in your analysis, you're often encouraged to paraphrase the intricate language the court uses in its rationale so that it's shorter and easily understood by readers.) Here, the author did not give readers the precise language of the statute. And what looks like an effort to make the introduction "flow" is actually a dense writing style. **B** is incorrect. Although you might attach these labels internally, the reader will find it amateurish and distracting to find these labels in the text. The same convention applies to exams. Most professors believe all the components should be there (what the issue is, the rule, your analysis, and conclusion), but they also believe the components should not be labeled. **C** is incorrect. It's fine to include a rule statement about the Copyright Act as context for the fair use exception. It's also fine to include policy statements about the Copyright Act, although this author mistakenly neglected to provide a citation for those statements. Policy analysis is always stronger if supported by mandatory authority. How much context to provide is a judgment call, without a specific answer. Provide as much as the reader needs, without overburdening the reader. **D** is correct. The author tells us which factor will not be in dispute, and tells us why not. Further, she gives us a citation to mandatory authority telling us that courts disregard this factor in cases such as this one.

Explanation 12-2

A is correct. This introduction gives the reader no idea how the author predicts the court will rule. Further, like the first example, it doesn't quote the statute. You can probably see even more clearly here that failure to use the statute's exact words can be very confusing for the readers. **B** is incorrect. Your professor has probably told you that each section of the Discussion section of a memo should "stand alone," enabling a reader to read just that section and understand what is going on. You can assume, however, that readers either are familiar with the facts or will read the Facts section of the memo before reading the analysis. Don't repeat facts in the introduction. **C** is correct. The words *element* and *factor* are terms of art for legal readers. Each has a specific meaning and they are not interchangeable. An element is a part of the rule that a plaintiff must prove to win on that issue. The plaintiff must prove all of the elements to win. A factor, on the other hand, is a part of a rule that a court weighs against other factors to come to a decision. (See Chapter 7.) Courts may weigh factors equally or with varying levels of importance depending on the applicable law and circumstances of the case. Thus, if a plaintiff fails to prove an element, she will fail to prove her ultimate claim. But if she loses on a factor, it is not dispositive and another factor may be so strong that she can still ultimately prove her claim. **D** is incorrect. It's not always wrong to tell the reader how you predict that a court will decide each element or factor. But it's not necessary and clutters up the introduction. And to simply announce that a factor will be "at issue" wastes words. Legal readers will assume that both sides have arguments to make about every factor unless you have told them the parties will not dispute it and why.

Explanation 12-3

A is correct. The last two sentences form a thesis statement that gives readers a clear idea of the predicted outcome. **B** is also correct. Even though it's a good idea to quote a statute, you probably need to do more than cut and paste the whole statute into your paper. It is important to edit the statute so that all the critical language is there, but it's in a form easy for readers to absorb. Here, the author should include the precise language of the four factors courts apply. But much of the rest of the statute can be discarded. **C** is incorrect. The author neglected to let the reader know that courts in parody cases usually disregard the second factor. **D** is incorrect. There is no universally accepted way to order the components of a good introduction. Your own professor may suggest an order for you to follow and of course you should follow those individual instructions. But most texts want you to include the components of a good introduction without demanding that you put those components in a certain order.

Explanation 12-4

A is incorrect. Sometimes the law is complicated and you'll need to untangle how several rules will apply. This introduction does a good job of leading the reader through the relevant rules. **B** is correct. The author has made it relatively easy for readers to follow a complex series of rules. Other ways could be just as successful. For example, you could place the rule about ordinary gifts being irrevocable, California Civil Code § 1148, in the first paragraph, which explains how courts decide whether a gift is given in contemplation of marriage. **C** is incorrect. Chances are good that you understood enough about the law to begin reading this analysis. In any case, legal writing convention requires laying out a Facts section to familiarize readers with the relevant facts of the case. **D** is correct. The author has done a good job with the thesis statement.

Writing the Question Presented (Objective)

Throughout law school, you're asked to answer difficult questions. This section of the memo lets you be the one to ask the question. So even if the issue—the disputed legal question—is provided to you, your task as a writer is to craft a useful "Question Presented." The Question Presented poses the legal question the memo resolves. It identifies the governing authority, tells the reader the precise legal question, and includes the key facts that control the outcome.

Terminology Notes: Sometimes the Question Presented is called the "Issue," and sometimes it's referred to by its acronym, "QP."

WHAT YOU NEED TO KNOW ABOUT AN OFFICE MEMO'S QUESTION PRESENTED

A Question Presented includes three parts: (a) the applicable law, (b) the legal question, and (c) the determinative facts. Writers sometimes use a shorthand formula, called "Under/Does/When," to express all three of these parts:

Under: the applicable law

Does: the legal question

When: the determinative facts

Using this structure, the Question Presented is framed like this: "Under (*the applicable law*), does (*the legal question*) when (*the determinative facts*)?" The three parts aren't always in this order. Any logical order is fine as long as the Question Presented contains all three components. The "under/does/when" format and other formats are discussed more fully later in this chapter.

A Question Presented should generally be one complete sentence, phrased as a question. Readers need to quickly grasp the issue your memo addresses. Most writers therefore draft the Question Presented as one sentence, although some writers use two or more sentences. Also, the Question Presented is usually a complete sentence (rather than a phrase). The "under/does/when" formula is inherently a question and whether you use that formula or not, the Question Presented is generally just that—a question.

Try to phrase the Question Presented so that the answer would be either "yes" or "no" or a qualified "yes" or "no" (such as "likely yes" or "probably no"). The reader needs to see, as quickly as possible, what your bottom-line answer is. As we explain in Chapter 14 on Brief Answers, you'll add a little more explanation soon after the Question Presented. But the Question itself should be framed so the answer can be a simple yes or no.

Generally include only main issues in the Questions Presented. For instance, when you have two main issues—such as whether the plaintiff can prevail on a breach of contract claim and whether she can prevail on a tort claim alleging intentional interference with a contractual relationship—you would have two Questions Presented.

If you have more than one issue, call this section "Questions Presented" (or "Issues") and number them. As suggested previously, each separate issue addressed should be a separate Question Presented. If you have three main issues (as opposed to one issue with two sub-issues, which would mean you have only one issue), you should have three Questions Presented. Number them 1, 2, and 3, and number the Brief Answers (and call that section "Brief Answers," not "Brief Answer") to correspond to these Questions Presented.

If you write your Question Presented before writing your Discussion section, remember to go back to review and revise it. There's no particular order in which you must write the components of your memo. You'll generally want to have a draft Question Presented to get you started and guide your analysis, but after you've completed your full analysis you'll better understand the key facts and issues. For this reason, it's a good idea to review and revise your Question Presented after you've finished writing the Discussion section.

HOW TO WRITE AN OFFICE MEMO'S QUESTION PRESENTED

Using a social host scenario and the cell phone manslaughter problem in Appendix A, we'll walk you through the process of writing an objective Question Presented. To use the "Under/Does/When" format, follow the steps below.

Problem

> Here is a quick overview of the cell phone manslaughter problem (for details see Appendix A). Allison King used her wireless phone, without a hands-free device, while driving in dense fog on a winding road on the edge of an ocean cliff. King placed the call to warn her friends about the dangerous conditions, as they would be meeting later. While she was making the call, she hit and killed a bicyclist. The prosecution will attempt to convict King of vehicular manslaughter by showing that she drove while committing an illegal act (driving while using a wireless phone without a hands-free device) and with gross negligence. King will argue that her actions fit within the emergency exception to the wireless phone prohibition. She will also argue that she did not act with gross negligence.

Step 1: Articulate the applicable law — the "under" component. In this part of the Question Presented, identify the relevant jurisdiction and the controlling legal authority in a broad sense. You generally won't identify the specific statutory citation or the controlling cases, unless the case is so central to the analysis that the case name serves as a shorthand to the reader for the governing principle (as might be the case with *Miranda* for confessions).

Some readers prefer — and some situations lend themselves to — using a relatively generic description of the applicable law. For instance, if you're asked to research whether there's any theory of liability under South Dakota law under which your client could make a claim, you would probably identify the applicable law very generally:

Under South Dakota law . . .

On the other hand, often you will have a more discrete problem to address. For instance, imagine your client has been sued for providing alcohol to a minor at a party, and one of his guests that evening caused a car crash that seriously injured the plaintiff. Assume that the party and accident occurred in New Jersey, and that social host liability in New Jersey, when the host provides alcohol to a minor guest, is governed by common law (and not a statute). That section might look something like this:

Under New Jersey common law . . .

Now we'll draft a Question Presented for the cell phone manslaughter problem in Appendix A. That case is governed by a California statute, which makes it illegal to drive "a vehicle in the commission of an unlawful act, not amounting to felony, and with gross negligence." Another California statute makes it illegal (not a felony) to "drive a motor vehicle while using a wireless telephone unless that telephone is specifically designed and configured to allow hands-free listening and talking, and is used in that manner while driving." That section creates an exception when the driver is using the cell phone for "emergency purposes." You need interpretive case law to finally resolve the issue, but in this step identify only the applicable law for the main issue. That law is California's vehicular manslaughter statute, so you could phrase the "under" portion of the Question Presented like this:

Under California's vehicular manslaughter statute . . .

This wording doesn't refer to the governing statute by its citation. Instead, it's referred to by name, which the reader will understand much more easily. (Few readers memorize statutory citations.)

If the issue were simply whether the cell phone use was for "emergency purposes," the first section might be phrased like this:

For purposes of California's vehicular manslaughter statute, under the prohibition on using a cell phone while driving . . .

Step 2: Determine the specific legal question—the "does" component—and state it as briefly as possible. Here, identify for the reader the underlying legal issue that's in dispute. Use the rule's actual language. If the rule comes from a statute, refer to the legal issue in statutory language, not in the generic wording that you might otherwise use (such as "homicide" for the cell phone manslaughter problem). If your rule comes from court opinions, use the terms of art the courts use. Using these "buzz words" helps the reader understand the key elements you're going to address.

This section of the "under/does/when" formula of the Question Presented might be written like this for the cell phone manslaughter problem:

. . . does a person commit vehicular manslaughter . . .

Similarly, for the social host issue, you might write:

> . . . is a person liable as a social host . . .

Generally, you'll refer to the main rule in this section, although some readers will expect more detail here, including the terms of art from the disputed element or elements. (In the latter situation, the main rule's terms of art would be included in the "under" section.) There, the "under" and "does" components might look like this:

> Under the fair use exception of the Copyright Act, does a new song target and transform the original without taking too much or becoming a substitute in its market . . .

Similarly, if you're focusing on the "emergency purposes" exception outlined in the cell phone manslaughter problem, this section might look like this:

> For purposes of California's vehicular manslaughter statute, under the prohibition on using a cell phone while driving does a person use a cell phone for "emergency purposes" . . .

Note how the statute's terms of art are included (both "vehicular manslaughter" and "emergency purposes"). If this were the only contested issue, a Question Presented framed this narrowly immediately lets the reader know the exact issue you're discussing.

Step 3: Identify the determinative facts—the "when" component—and state them as briefly as possible. Determinative facts are the key facts that most affect the outcome. You can't include every fact, and you don't need to. But you should remain objective and include the key favorable and unfavorable facts. In addition, the facts should be actual *facts*, not legal conclusions. Similarly, principles of law, like "damages have to be mitigated," aren't facts. Save them for the Discussion section of your memo instead. And what's a fact versus what's a conclusion depends, in part, on your legal issue. For instance, whether a person was "negligent" is generally a legal conclusion, not a fact (the underlying fact creating negligence may be that the defendant ran a red light, for instance). But imagine that the negligence of the plaintiff is uncontested and the issue is whether the negligent plaintiff is barred from suing the defendant, who also caused the plaintiff's injuries. In that case, the plaintiff's own negligence is a fact. Including the determinative facts in the Question Presented allows the reader who doesn't know your facts to still understand the issue.

Let's consider the relevant facts in the cell phone manslaughter problem in Appendix A. If the issue was whether King acted with "gross negligence," this section of the "under/does/when" formula might be written like this:

> . . . when she dialed her cell phone while driving on a winding two-lane road on the edge of a cliff in dense fog?

If, on the other hand, the issue you're concerned with is whether King was entitled to the "emergency purpose" defense, this section might look like this:

> . . . when she placed the call in order to warn her friends not to drive because road conditions were so dangerous?

For the social host hypothetical mentioned earlier in this chapter, the determinative facts component might look like this:

> . . . when he provided alcohol to the minor guest after the minor displayed signs of intoxication, including slurred speech, and the minor later killed another motorist?

Notice how the relevant facts change depending on the issue. The facts necessary to resolve the "gross negligence" element are different from the facts necessary to resolve the "emergency purposes" defense.

Step 4: Put them all together. Simply add the three sections to make one complete sentence phrased as a question. You may need to rearrange the order or edit for conciseness, but generally, you can just plug the steps in using the same order you drafted them. Hence, the Question Presented for the California cell phone manslaughter problem might look something like this:

> Under California's vehicular manslaughter statute, does a person commit vehicular manslaughter when she hit and killed a bicyclist as she dialed her cell phone while driving on a winding two-lane road on the edge of a cliff in dense fog?

Assume you are focusing on the narrow "emergency exception" issue, the final Question Presented might look something like this:

> For purposes of California's vehicular manslaughter statute, under the prohibition on using a cell phone while driving, does a person use a cell phone for "emergency purposes" when she placed the call in order to warn her friends not to drive because road conditions were so dangerous?

And for the New Jersey social host hypothetical, the complete Question Presented might look like this:

> Under New Jersey common law, is a person liable as a social host when he provided alcohol to the minor guest after the minor displayed signs of intoxication, including slurred speech, and the minor later killed another motorist?

You can also switch the order of the sections. For instance, in the context of a contract dispute, you could draft the Question Presented like this:

> Is there consideration for a contract under New York common law when an uncle promises to give his nephew money in exchange for the nephew refraining from drinking, smoking, and swearing?

Each of these Questions Presented works, because the reader understands all of the components (the "under," the "does," and the "when").

EXAMPLES

Here are some examples of objective Questions Presented. For each example, choose the best answer. Explain to yourself why you've chosen that answer. Then read the explanations in the last section of this chapter to check your work.

Example 13-1

> Is King likely guilty when she made a cell phone call while driving on a narrow winding road in dense fog, but did so to warn her friends of the dangerous driving conditions?

This is an . . .

A. effective Question Presented because it includes the determinative facts.
B. effective Question Presented because it poses the key legal question—whether King is guilty.
C. ineffective Question Presented because it omits the applicable law.
D. ineffective Question Presented because it provides too much detail in terms of the determinative facts.

Example 13-2

> The issue is whether Jones is liable for negligent infliction of emotional distress under Indiana common law, considering the fact that the plaintiff was not married to the deceased when he died, and whether Sanchez is barred from suing because the statute of limitations has expired.

This is an . . .

    A. effective Question Presented because it includes the applicable law, the legal questions, and the determinative facts.

    B. ineffective Question Presented because it omits determinative facts.

    C. ineffective Question Presented because it isn't phrased as a question.

    D. ineffective Question Presented for the reasons stated in both B and C.

Example 13-3

Under California's vehicular manslaughter statute, does a person commit vehicular manslaughter when she violates a traffic law and drives with gross negligence, killing someone?

This is an . . .

    A. ineffective Question Presented because it fails to identify the specific legal question.

    B. ineffective Question Presented because it fails to include the determinative facts.

    C. effective Question Presented because it includes all three components of a good question presented: under, does, and when.

    D. effective Question Presented because it's short and easily readable.

Example 13-4

Under California's vehicular manslaughter statute, does a person commit vehicular manslaughter when she makes a cell phone call while driving on a narrow, foggy road, or does she have to do more than drive unsafely even though she thought she was driving safely?

This is an . . .

    A. effective Question Presented because it includes the applicable law, the specific legal question, and the determinative facts.

    B. effective Question Presented because it identifies both the main legal question and the potential defense.

    C. ineffective Question Presented because it isn't capable of being answered with a yes/no answer.

    D. ineffective Question Presented because it omits the applicable law and specific legal question.

Example 13-5

Under Indiana common law, can a bystander recover for negligent infliction of emotional distress when the person the defendant negligently killed was the bystander's fiancée rather than legal spouse?

This is an . . .

A. effective Question Presented because it includes the applicable law, the specific legal question, and the determinative facts.

B. effective Question Presented because it's short and easy to read, even though it omits some determinative facts.

C. ineffective Question Presented because it omits the determinative facts.

D. ineffective Question Presented because it's too long.

EXPLANATIONS

Explanation 13-1

A is incomplete, and therefore wrong. This Question Presented does describe the determinative facts, and it does so objectively by including facts that suggest King might have acted with gross negligence as well as facts that suggest she may be eligible for the "emergency purposes" exception. But this Question Presented does not identify the applicable law, so it is not effective. **B** is also wrong. As with answer A, this answer is incomplete. The Question Presented is ineffective for other reasons. And the ultimate legal question can be phrased more clearly than "is King guilty." The reader doesn't know what King might be guilty of. In the broadest sense, the legal question is more clearly phrased as "does a person commit vehicular manslaughter." In a more narrow sense, the underlying legal question may be whether King acted with gross negligence or whether King made the call for an emergency purpose. Any of these three options would provide the reader with more guidance than the generic "is she guilty" phrase. **C** is correct. This Question Presented doesn't identify the applicable law, which is the California vehicular manslaughter statute. The Question Presented could also be improved by phrasing the ultimate legal question more clearly, as explained in B. **D** is wrong. As noted in the explanation for answer A, the determinative facts are well described.

Explanation 13-2

A is wrong. Although the Question Presented includes the applicable law for the first issue, it doesn't for the second. It's also phrased as a statement rather than a question, and it doesn't include sufficient determinative facts to understand the issues. It's therefore ineffective. In addition, some professors might expect this Question Presented to be divided into two separately numbered questions (one for each issue), although this varies. **B** is true, but it isn't the correct answer because **C** is also true; hence, **D** is the correct answer. This Question Presented includes two separate legal questions—negligent infliction of emotional distress and the statute of limitations. But as noted in B, the example omits determinative facts. How long after the incident occurred was the suit filed? And what was the relationship between the plaintiff and the deceased? The Question Presented tells us they weren't married, but it doesn't tell us what their relationship was. In addition, as noted in C, a Question Presented isn't usually phrased as a statement. Readers will generally expect a question that is answered by the Brief Answer (see Chapter 14).

Explanation 13-3

A is wrong. This Question Presented does identify the specific legal question —vehicular manslaughter. **B** is correct. The phrases "violates a traffic law" and "drives with gross negligence" are legal conclusions, not facts. The reader needs to know the underlying determinative facts, such as "when she uses a cell phone while driving" (the act that violates the traffic law) or "when she places a call while driving on a narrow two-lane road over a cliff in a dense fog" (the acts that constitute gross negligence). In addition, this Question Presented merely states the elements of the statute, making the answer an indisputable "yes": if a person violates a traffic law and drives with gross negligence and kills someone, she has committed vehicular manslaughter. But the reader needs to know whether, in this case, the defendant has in fact violated the traffic law and driven with gross negligence. More facts are necessary to answer that question. **C** is wrong. Although the Question Presented uses "under," "does," and "when," for the reasons stated in B the determinative facts are absent. **D** is also wrong. This Question Presented is short, which is good, but it omits determinative facts, which outweighs the benefit of having a shorter and easily read Question Presented.

Explanation 13-4

A is wrong. Although this Question Presented includes all the necessary components, it's ineffective for the reason C is correct. **B** is also wrong. Having to "do more than drive unsafely" isn't a defense. To the extent it infers a lack of gross negligence it's simply the absence of an element. **C** is correct. This Question Presented isn't capable of being answered with a simple yes/no answer. It is also phrased a bit casually for a Question Presented. **D** is wrong. The applicable law and specific legal question are included. But they are clouded by the complex question.

Explanation 13-5

A is correct. This Question Presented includes all the necessary components —the under/does/when sections—and they are properly developed. **B** is wrong. The Question Presented is relatively easy to read, but it doesn't omit any determinative facts. Although it describes the defendant's actions as "negligently" killing the deceased, for purposes of this issue—who can recover—his negligence is a fact, not a legal conclusion. **C** is wrong for the same reasons that the explanation for B stated. **D** is also wrong. Make your Questions Presented as short as possible, but they need to contain all three parts of the "under/does/when" formula, and this example does in one sentence.

Writing the Brief Answer

Unlike detective television shows, legal memos are best when they tell the reader the answer in the beginning. That's because lawyers tend to be most comfortable when they know exactly where they're going. When busy readers know the answer at the outset they can read the rest of the memo to discover the reasons for this and ask themselves whether it seems correct.

WHAT YOU NEED TO KNOW ABOUT A BRIEF ANSWER

The Brief Answer should answer the Question Presented and briefly summarize the key reasons for that answer. Assert your answer and then give your key reasons for it, which will typically include key "buzz words" from the legal rule that applies, combined with the determinative facts. Don't go into unnecessary detail. Most lawyers think it's sufficient to write the Brief Answer in a way that assumes the reader is familiar with the legal and factual analysis you provide in your Discussion. Brief Answers are typically two to three sentences. Some professors and attorneys may prefer a slightly longer version that includes a concise statement of the applicable rule and more summary of the reasons for the conclusions. Generally, even counting these "slightly longer" versions, Brief Answers come in two sizes: small and extra small!

The first sentence should be a one- or two-word answer to the Question Presented, such as "Yes.", "No.", "Probably Yes.", "Probably No." Aim to indicate an accurate degree of certainty about your answer. Avoid sending mixed signals about your level of certainty within your Brief Answer or between your Brief Answer and the rest of your memo. Also, don't waffle when you have confidence in an answer. But if you really can't accurately answer the Question Presented because of legal or factual uncertainty, use a term that suggests your uncertainty such as "Maybe yes . . ." and explain briefly why your conclusion is tentative or what additional facts you'd need to know.

Be conclusory: don't discuss or evaluate the strength of arguments. Writing is conclusory if it states a legal conclusion without supporting it with analysis. In your Brief Answer, that's the approach to take: state your answer and the key reasons for that conclusion, without explaining your underlying analysis. (Conclusory writing is usually a mistake in the Discussion, but in the Brief Answer, it's the right thing to do. The answer is supposed to be brief.)

For instance:

> Yes. The defendant committed burglary because he entered his neighbor's apartment without permission and with intent to steal her jewelry.

And if you wanted to include a concise statement of the rule in your Brief Answer, it might instead look like this:

> Yes. Under relevant state law, a person commits burglary when he enters a building without authority and with intent to commit a felony or theft inside. The defendant committed burglary here because he entered his neighbor's apartment without permission and with intent to steal her jewelry.

These examples provide the key conclusions that led to the answer ("because . . ."), melding law and fact without going into a detailed explanation of the analysis that supports the conclusions. Don't explain that the answer depends on whether the facts show the legal conclusion at issue, such as "Whether the defendant committed burglary depends on whether he had authority to enter. Several facts show that he had authority, such as his past history of helping his neighbor bring in the mail while she was on vacation and that they recently started dating. But some facts do not, such as that she was not on vacation when he entered and that she had not asked him for help for over a year or given him a key." The reader can turn to your Discussion section for your analysis and discussion of alternative arguments. Keep your Brief Answer concise and conclusory.

Generally, don't include citations or discussions of authority. Your conclusions will come from your analysis of authority, but your Brief Answer shouldn't cite or discuss any particular authorities. There are a couple of exceptions. First, when the Question Presented poses a statutory issue, you may refer to the statute and include any essential statutory requirements in your Brief Answer. Second, when you have a seminal case that controls all or nearly all of your analysis, it's okay to note and cite the case.

You should have a Brief Answer for each Question Presented. As explained in Chapter 13, when you have multiple Questions Presented, number them 1, 2, and 3, and number the Brief Answers to correspond to them. Remember to use the header "Brief Answers," not "Brief Answer."

HOW TO WRITE A BRIEF ANSWER

Using the copyright and fair use problem in Appendix B, we'll walk you through the process of writing a Brief Answer.

Problem

> Here is a quick overview of the copyright and fair use problem (for details see Appendix B). Young is suing Olds for violating the Copyright Act when Olds wrote a song based on Young's original, "Rockin' in the Free World." Olds' song uses the structure and many lyrics of the original but changes the original song's political message. The music of the two songs is not at issue, only the lyrics. Young expects that Olds will argue that his song is a parody that falls under the fair use exception to the Copyright Act. The court will consider the relevant factors set out in the fair use statute, 17 U.S.C. § 107 (2006): whether the copy was transformative and targeted the original; whether it took more than necessary of the original; and whether it will interfere with the original's market.

Step 1: Carefully read your Question Presented and decide on the answer. You'll want to do this after you've written the Discussion section of your memo because often writing that section will crystallize the answer in your mind. Look at the phrasing of the Question Presented. Does the factual and legal analysis warrant a certain "Yes." or "No." answer? Would a "Probably yes." or "Probably no." better capture your degree of certainty?

An office memo on the copyright and fair use problem might include the following Question Presented:

Does Phil Olds' rock song fall under the Copyright Act's fair use exception when it purposely used lyrics from Neil Young's anti-war rock anthem to imitate its pattern but critiqued its message of pacifism?

Step 2: Write the first sentence of your Brief Answer, starting with a one- or two-word answer to the Question Presented. Imagine that after a thorough legal and factual analysis in the Discussion section you decide that Olds' song is probably fair use. Responding to the Question Presented, the first sentence of your Brief Answer might be:

Probably yes.

Step 3: Write another sentence or two summarizing the reasons for the answer. Be conclusory. If your professor or supervising attorney expects a slightly longer version that includes more detail, then your Brief Answer might be a bit longer and include more specificity.

Here, you might add the following:

Probably yes. Olds used Young's song as a means to criticize the original and create an identifiable parody. The copy thus transforms the original work's anti-war message to an opposing political viewpoint and creates a different market for the critique.

This Brief Answer works. It starts with a one- or two-word answer to the Question Presented. It briefly summarizes the key reasons for that answer in a conclusory manner, melding law and fact, without evaluating the strength of various arguments. It doesn't cite or discuss specific authority. It's brief.

EXAMPLES

Here are some examples of Brief Answers. They respond to this Question Presented:

Does Phil Olds' rock song fall under the Copyright Act's fair use exception when it purposely used lyrics from Neil Young's anti-war rock anthem to imitate its pattern but critique its message of pacifism?

For each example, choose the best answer. Explain to yourself why you've chosen that answer. Then read the explanations in this chapter's last section to check your work.

Example 14-1

Brief Answer

Likely yes. The fair use statute provides various factors to weigh when determining whether an allegedly infringing work is fair use. Whether the parody is transformative enough or borrows too heavily from the original are questions that a jury will end up deciding, as there is no bright line rule to determine these factors. It is undisputed that Olds' song is for commercial purposes and, while not a pivotal issue, this nonetheless weighs in Young's favor. Also, Olds' song uses the same musical genre and might compete in the same market. On the other hand, Olds could argue that his work criticizes the political message of Young's song and as such is parody that falls within the fair use exception.

A. This is typical of good Brief Answers because it tells the reader about the various important arguments.

B. This Brief Answer should be more concise and conclusory instead of weighing alternative arguments.

C. This Brief Answer should include specific references to cases and provide citations.

Example 14-2

Brief Answer

Olds' song is parody, which constitutes a fair use of copyrighted material for commercial use. Although the large amount of original lyrics he used may weigh against fair use, his critical transformation of the lyrics changed the song in such a way that it would no longer appeal to the same market as the original.

The writer could improve this Brief Answer by . . .

A. starting with a "yes" or "no" type of answer.

B. cutting out the factual detail.

C. softening the first sentence's tone.

Example 14-3

Brief Answer

Probably not. Olds' lyrics are not entitled to fair use protection because his song would likely serve as a substitute for Young's original. Unlike the allegedly infringing work in *Mattel v. Walking Mountain Productions*, 353 F.3d 792 (9th Cir. 2003), which served a different market than the original, Olds' work is similar to Young's in that both provide political commentary set to rock music, potentially confusing listeners and causing market harm to the copyright holder.

A. This Brief Answer should state what action the client wants the court to take.
B. This Brief Answer should state and explain the rule of law first.
C. This Brief Answer should not include the case reference and citation.

Example 14-4

Brief Answer

Probably yes. The owner of a copyrighted work usually has exclusive rights over the work. There is, however, a fair use exception. To qualify as fair use, a work must transform the original work without copying more than necessary or harming its market value. These are statutory factors. Olds borrowed significantly from twenty-three of the original thirty-six lines of Young's song. Some words and phrases are exactly the same such as "Red, white and blue." By changing some of the lyrics, however, Olds significantly changed the meaning of Young's song. Specifically, the political message of Olds' song is different than that of Young's song. A court will therefore probably rule in favor of Olds because he borrowed the amount of lyrics necessary to invoke the tension of a parody between his work and Young's. A court will probably also rule that Olds' parody will do minimal damage to Young's market value because Young has an established fan base of listeners who oppose war and conservative politics and who will not support Olds' lyrics. Thus, Olds' song probably falls within the fair use exception to the Copyright Act.

The writer could improve this Brief Answer by . . .

A. editing for conciseness.
B. adding analogical reasoning.
C. concluding more broadly at the end.

EXPLANATIONS

Explanation 14-1

A is wrong. Save your evaluation of reasons and alternative arguments for your Discussion. The Brief Answer should simply state your conclusions and very briefly summarize the essential reasons in a way that assumes the reader is familiar with your legal and factual analysis. You can tell that this example weighs alternative arguments because it uses language like "on the other hand." Likewise, you can tell that this example doesn't assume the reader is familiar with the law because it starts out by explaining that the statute provides factors and that there's no bright line rule. Further, you may have spotted the language "while not a pivotal issue" and noted that this example fails to focus on only essential reasons. **B** is correct. This Brief Answer should be more conclusory instead of weighing alternative arguments. **C** is wrong. Brief Answers typically do not provide specific references to cases or citations.

Explanation 14-2

A is correct. A Brief Answer should start with a one- or two-word answer to the Question Presented. **B** is wrong. Unless the Question Presented is a pure legal question, good Brief Answers meld legal conclusions with the facts. **C** is wrong. The conclusory tone is characteristic of good Brief Answers.

Explanation 14-3

A is wrong. Brief Answers do not state what action the client wants the court to take. They provide answers to Questions Presented, giving legal conclusions based on the essential facts. **B** is wrong, though perhaps partly correct. Some readers indeed prefer a concise statement of the applicable rule in the Brief Answer. But Brief Answers typically do not include an explanation of the rule. The Discussion section is where the memo provides more detailed rule development, as addressed in Chapter 8. **C** is correct. Brief Answers usually don't refer to specific cases or provide case citations. In this example, the reference to *Mattel* is unnecessary because, although useful, it's not a blockbuster case that controls all of the analysis. The Brief Answer would be improved by editing this case reference and citation out.

Explanation 14-4

A is correct. This Brief Answer could be improved by editing for conciseness. Readers' tastes will vary, but most would probably agree that you could improve it by distilling down its critical conclusions and reasoning and stating those in a concise, conclusory manner. Here's one way you could revise it:

> Probably yes. Olds borrowed the amount of lyrics necessary to invoke Young's original, but changed some of the lyrics to transform it into a critical parody of Young's anti-war stance. The parody will do minimal damage to Young's market value because Young has an established fan base of listeners who oppose war and conservative politics and who will not support Olds' lyrics.

B is wrong. Brief Answers should not include analogical reasoning. Save that for the analysis in your Discussion. *C* is wrong. A Brief Answer should summarize conclusions precisely and doesn't need to broaden its conclusions at the end as essays in the liberal arts sometimes do.

Writing the Facts

CHAPTER 15

In the Facts section of the memo, you tell the story. It's probably the easiest section to write—because the facts are often (but not always) the easiest part of the problem to understand. But don't let this lull you into believing you can write the Facts section without much thought or effort. And don't just copy and paste into your memo the facts provided by your professor in the assignment (which may be considered plagiarism). This is a genuine writing task requiring effort and skill.

WHAT YOU NEED TO KNOW ABOUT AN OFFICE MEMO'S FACTS SECTION

Include every fact you mention in the Discussion section as well as any other fact that's necessary for the story to make sense. Describe the client and what she wants first, and then develop the facts more fully. Some writers like to think of this as the "who, what, where" part of the memo. Include as much detail as necessary either for the analysis or to understand the story. Because including lots of specific dates can clog up your writing and make it harder for the reader to follow, leave out specific dates unless they're relevant to the legal issue (for instance, when the legal issue depends on the timing of particular events, such as in statute of limitation issues, claims regarding default for failure to file an answer, etc.).

Include procedural facts. The Facts section should note what has happened in terms of legal action to date. And as with substantive facts, specific dates aren't necessary unless they're legally significant.

State the facts and just the facts. This section is called the "Facts" for a reason. Don't include the law. That will go in the Discussion section. Similarly, the Facts section is not the place for analysis, characterizations of the facts, or inferences. You'll have plenty of space to do that in the Discussion section. Keep the Facts section clearly factual.

Frame the facts objectively. The facts should not be told just from your client's perspective (assuming you have been put in the role of an attorney drafting a memo on behalf of your client). The reader needs to understand all sides of the issue. Include facts that hurt your client's case, not just those that help.

Because objective memos are usually used for predictive purposes and strategy, you're not doing the client any favors by making the facts sound more compelling than they actually are. Be accurate, objective, and neutral. This contrasts with a persuasive brief, where you still have to avoid making overt arguments and leaving out relevant facts, but your goal there is for the facts to have a subtly persuasive effect.

Generally write the facts in chronological order. Stories usually make the most sense when they start at the beginning, then explain what happened in the middle, and then tell what happened at the end. Sometimes, though, another organization makes more logical sense. For instance, if two parallel situations were brewing, explaining the facts in true chronological order would jumble the two scenarios together and likely confuse the reader. As with all writing tasks, use your best judgment, but absent a reason to do otherwise, ordering the facts in chronological order is wise. And because the facts already happened, you'll generally use past tense in the Facts section.

Facts sections are usually written in regular paragraph format. Unlike complaints and some Statements of Material Facts for motions, which are often drafted using numbered sentences or very short numbered paragraphs, Facts sections in office memos are most often written in regular narrative format. If you have a long Facts section, consider using subheaders to break the facts into logical chunks. This will make the Facts section easier to read and understand.

Be sure to revise the Facts section after you've completed the Discussion section. Some writers like to begin with the Facts because it's the part of the memo they understand the best. If you do that, be sure to go back and review the Facts section after you've completed the Discussion section, because only then can you appreciate which facts are truly relevant and which aren't.

Every fact that's necessary for the analysis needs to be in the Facts section, so double-check to make sure you've included them all (and correspondingly omit facts irrelevant to the legal analysis unless they're necessary to understand the story). Even though it may seem repetitive to include everything in the Facts section (because all the necessary facts are also in the Discussion section), readers won't always read the memo in order. They may jump around. And Facts sections have a separate purpose. Clients are often told to review the Facts section carefully and make sure that all the facts are correct and none are omitted. In that sense, the Facts section ensures the factual basis for your analysis is accurate and it protects you in the event your analysis is based on a fact that turns out to be inaccurate.

HOW TO WRITE AN OFFICE MEMO'S FACTS SECTION

Using the cell phone manslaughter problem in Appendix A, we'll walk you through the process of writing the Facts section of an office memo.

Problem

> Here is a quick overview of the cell phone manslaughter problem (for details see Appendix A). Allison King used her wireless phone, without a hands-free device, while driving in dense fog on a winding road on the edge of an ocean cliff. King placed the call to warn her friends about the dangerous conditions, as they would be meeting later. While she was making the call, she hit and killed a bicyclist. The prosecution will attempt to convict King of vehicular manslaughter by showing that she drove while committing an illegal act (driving while using a wireless phone without a hands-free device) and with gross negligence. King will argue that her actions fit within the emergency exception to the wireless phone prohibition. She will also argue that she did not act with gross negligence.

Step 1: Gather and read all the facts, whether in a case file, a memo from the assigning attorney, or some other source (provided by your professor). In the cell phone manslaughter problem, the facts are provided in a short summary form. Often, the relevant facts have to be gleaned from other documents. For instance, for a breach of contract claim, you might review the contract and possibly a complaint and answer. Discovery may also be relevant; you may need to review deposition testimony, affidavits, responses to interrogatories, and other evidence. In whatever form you find the facts, your task is to locate and closely review every source that may contain factual information.

Step 2: Determine which facts are relevant. To determine whether a particular fact is relevant, you need to have some knowledge of the legal issue and the applicable rules. Whether a particular fact is relevant also depends on the surrounding circumstances. For instance, in a negligence suit, the fact that a car involved in an auto accident was white is generally irrelevant. If, however, the accident occurred during a blizzard and the defendant claims he couldn't see the plaintiff's vehicle, the fact that the car was white may very well be relevant.

The following hypothetical, which is based on a new scenario, illustrates how to determine which facts are relevant:

You represent Mark Yokus, who owns R & J Construction Company. Yokus was recently served with a complaint by the Equal Employment Opportunity Commission (EEOC). One of his employees filed a complaint with the EEOC alleging R & J Construction engaged in unlawful employment discrimination in violation of Title VII.

The claimant, Sarah Clark, worked for R & J for five years as a supervising electrician. In that capacity, she regularly earned overtime (working approximately 57 hours per week).

On Friday, May 28, 2010, Yokus learned that Clark was four months pregnant. Yokus became concerned about health and safety risks for Clark and her fetus if she were to continue working as a supervising electrician. The same day, Yokus shared his concerns with Clark and offered to transfer her to an office job for seven months while continuing to pay her at her current hourly rate. But that position is a 40-hour-a-week job that rarely involves overtime, and thus Clark would suffer a reduction in total pay. Clark declined this offer on the spot, but Yokus refused to allow her to continue performing electrician duties.

Clark's next day at work was Tuesday, June 1. (Monday, May 31, was a holiday.) Yokus again refused to allow Clark to perform electrician duties. At noon that day, Clark went home. On the following day, June 2, Yokus told Clark her employment was formally terminated. Clark filed a complaint with the EEOC on November 29, 2010.

If the only issue you're asked to address is whether Title VII's definition of "sex" (in its prohibition of sex discrimination) includes pregnancy, the Facts section might be very short:

Our client, Mark Yokus, owns R & J Construction Company. One of R & J's employees, Sarah Clark, became pregnant, and Yokus attempted to transfer her position. Clark refused, and Yokus terminated her employment. Clark then filed a complaint with the EEOC alleging sex discrimination in violation of Title VII.

However, if the issue is whether R & J Construction unlawfully engaged in sex discrimination in violation of Title VII, the Facts section would be longer and might look like this:

Our client, Mark Yokus, owns R & J Construction Company. R & J employed Sarah Clark for five years as a supervising electrician. Yokus learned that Clark was four months pregnant. Concerned for her health and safety as well as the fetus's, Yokus offered to transfer Clark, at her usual hourly rate, to an office position until after the baby was born. Clark refused that offer because the office position did not include regular overtime and as a supervising electrician Clark had averaged seventeen hours of overtime per week.

Clark then filed a complaint alleging sex discrimination in violation of Title VII with the EEOC. The EEOC recently filed a complaint against Yokus on behalf of R & J Construction.

This Facts section doesn't include specific dates. Imagine, though, that Clark has now sued, and the issue is whether Clark has exhausted her administrative remedies in a timely fashion. Some legal research reveals that Title VII requires the employee to file a complaint with the EEOC within 180 days of the adverse employment action. Imagine a case where the definition of "adverse employment action" is an issue. Several events happened and the question is which one of them triggered the start of the 180-day time limit. In that case, additional facts—including dates—would be relevant. That Facts section might look like this:

Our client, Mark Yokus, owns R & J Construction Company. On May 28, 2010, Yokus learned that one of R & J's employees, Sarah Clark, was pregnant. On that day, Yokus told Clark that she could not continue to work as a supervising electrician and could be transferred to an office position at the same rate, although she would lose her customary overtime pay. Clark refused that offer on the spot, and Yokus refused to allow her to perform electrician duties. Her next work day was June 1, 2010, and Yokus again refused to allow her to perform electrician duties. Clark went home at noon. The next day, June 2, Yokus formally terminated Clark's employment.

Clark filed her complaint with the EEOC on November 29, 2010, 185 days after May 28, when Clark was told that she could not continue to work as a supervising electrician and when she refused Yokus' offer to transfer to an office position. November 29, 2010, was 181 days after June 1, when Clark was again prohibited from performing supervising electrician duties and went home at noon. It was 180 days after June 2, when Yokus told Clark that her employment was terminated.

Note how the relevant facts change, depending on the specific legal issue being addressed. The facts themselves don't change, but because the issue changes, their relevancy changes. Some facts are relevant to one issue, and some are relevant to another issue. Some are relevant to all issues. Your Facts section would include the facts relevant to the issue or issues you're addressing. For this reason, don't just copy and paste the facts you were given into your memo.

Step 3: Be especially careful to include the relevant facts that allow you to analogize or distinguish the facts in the precedent cases from the client's facts. For example, in the copyright and fair use problem in Appendix B, the following facts might be helpful in the Facts section—first because they are relevant, and second because they allow you to compare and contrast those facts with the facts in the controlling cases:

> Young's song is critical of American politics, and Olds' song reflects pride in American politics.

These facts are relevant and helpful under the Copyright Act's first statutory factor, the "purpose and character of the use." But these facts also create a point of comparison with the *Mattel* case: In *Mattel*, the defendant's works criticized women's traditional role in society, emphasizing that role can put women in ridiculous and even dangerous positions. On the other hand, Mattel's works represented women's traditional role positively, associated with beauty, wealth, and glamour. You'll be able to create stronger analogies and distinctions in the Discussion section if you've included enough facts in the Facts section to draw those explicit comparisons later.

Step 4: Draft a preliminary Facts section. Start at the beginning and work your way through the facts chronologically (unless some other structure works better in your particular case). At this stage, err on the side of over-inclusiveness. You can always delete facts later, but if you've left them out here, you might forget about them when drafting the Discussion section, and that can cause greater problems. Don't worry too much yet about whether each fact will ultimately be relevant. You'll be better able to answer that question after you've completed the legal research and considered how all of the pieces fit together.

Step 5: After you've completed the Discussion section, revise the Facts section. Now you're ready to decide whether each fact in your Facts section is relevant or needed for context. You can tell how much detail the reader needs to understand the analysis in the Discussion section. And now you're ready to revise—not just edit—your Facts section. Recall the first thing you need to know about Facts sections: "Describe the client and what she wants first, and then develop the facts more fully." So start there, explaining, briefly, the client's legal predicament. Then tell the story, making sure that every fact in the Discussion section is indeed in the Facts section. Also make sure the Facts section leaves out irrelevant facts, unless they are necessary for the story to make sense. And make sure it flows, so the reader can follow the story with one quick read.

EXAMPLES

Here are some examples of Facts sections and portions of Facts sections. Most, but not all, are based on the cell phone manslaughter problem in Appendix A. For each example, choose the best answer. Explain to yourself why you have chosen that answer. Then read the explanations in the last section of this chapter to check your work.

Example 15-1

Facts

Our client, Allison King, has been charged with vehicular manslaughter.

On October 22, 2010, Ms. King was driving from Jenner to Gualala on State Highway 1. This road is well known for being a winding two-lane highway on the edge of a cliff with the sea below. The highway offers very few places to pull over. Ms. King planned to meet several friends from San Francisco for a weekend vacation on the coast near Gualala.

The night Ms. King was driving, the fog was rolling in from the ocean and driving conditions were even more hazardous than usual. She was terrified and kept her bearings in near-whiteout conditions by hugging the road on the side of the cliff.

She also became concerned that the fog presented such dangerous driving conditions that she should warn her friends and suggest that they refrain from driving until road conditions improved.

Ms. King pulled out her cell phone and, while driving slowly along the cliff, she dialed one of her friends, June Coughlin, to give the warning. Suddenly a bicyclist appeared from out of the fog. Ms. King's car struck the cyclist, and he slipped across the road and over the cliff. The fall killed him. Ms. King has been charged with vehicular manslaughter.

Note: It would be helpful here to review the facts on the first page of Appendix A.

This is an . . .

A. effective Facts section because it includes all the facts provided by the supervising lawyer verbatim.

B. effective Facts section because it includes names and dates, and without those details, the reader would be confused by the story.

C. ineffective (but thorough) Facts section primarily because it repeats the exact fact summary provided to the writer without considering the relevance of each particular fact.

D. ineffective Facts section because it's too long and fact statements should never exceed two paragraphs.

Example 15-2

Consider the following opening paragraph to the Facts section for the cell phone manslaughter problem:

> Allison King, who turned forty-six years old on May 11, 2010, drove a silver 2006 Mercedes-Benz four-door sedan. On Friday, October 22, 2010, she was driving approximately 23 miles per hour heading northbound on California State Highway 1 near milepost 56. The time was 2:47 p.m.

This is an . . .

A. ineffective opening paragraph in the Facts section because it doesn't include the deceased bike rider's name, which is a relevant fact.

B. ineffective opening paragraph in the Facts section because it doesn't state the client's problem.

C. effective opening paragraph in the Facts section because it includes enough relevant facts to allow the reader to picture the story.

D. effective opening paragraph in the Facts section because Facts sections should read like novels: they should be interesting, include lots of detail, and save the legal issue for the Discussion section.

Example 15-3

Facts

Our client, Allison King, was charged in California with vehicular manslaughter. Ms. King was driving in dense fog when her car struck a cyclist, who died. Ms. King had been trying to call a friend on her cell phone when the accident happened.

This is an . . .

A. effective Facts section because it includes all the relevant facts.

B. effective Facts section because it's brief and avoids unnecessary detail.

C. ineffective Facts section because the reader isn't told the date of the accident, the name of the cyclist, or who King was calling when the accident happened.

D. ineffective Facts section because it omits relevant facts.

Example 15-4

Facts

Our client, Steve Morris, has been sued for breach of contract. He entered into a written contract last fall to supply B & G Foods with 3,000 pounds of pineapples. Because of an early winter frost, all of his crops were destroyed. Morris was therefore unable to deliver the pineapples to B & G.

The contract includes no provision for inability to perform or Acts of God. B & G claims Morris is liable for the difference in price between their contracted price and the price B & G had to pay for pineapples on the open market. Morris claims B & G should bear the risk of natural disaster, as Morris was unable to perform through no negligence or acts of his own and any potential breach was not voluntary.

This is an . . .

A. effective Facts section because it begins with the legal claim and includes the relevant facts.

B. ineffective Facts section because it includes argument.

C. ineffective Facts section because the reader isn't told the exact date of the contract, the date of the frost, and the date the crops were destroyed.

D. ineffective Facts section because it includes the parties' claims about the contract.

Example 15-5

Facts

Our client, Allison King, has been wrongfully charged with vehicular manslaughter. King acted reasonably and responsibly, and should not be found guilty.

The accident occurred on October 22, 2010, when Ms. King was driving on California State Highway 1. Highway 1 is a winding two-lane road that sits atop a high cliff with the sea below. It was exceptionally foggy on Oct. 22, with "near white-out" conditions. Despite these hazardous conditions, a bicyclist decided to ride on the narrow cliff-top road.

Ms. King was terrified of the road conditions and feared that her friends, whom she would be meeting, would be in danger by driving on Highway 1 in those conditions. There was no place to pull over, so Ms. King called her friends to warn them not to drive. This single act of using her cell phone is the sole reason she is charged with vehicular manslaughter.

This is an . . .

A. effective Facts section because it includes all the relevant facts.
B. effective Facts section because it's told from the client's perspective.
C. effective Facts section because it begins by introducing the client and the legal claim.
D. ineffective Facts section because it omits negative facts, does not frame the facts objectively, and includes legal argument.

Example 15-6

Facts

Bob Fulton and José Garcia got into a heated argument in March. They had previous negative encounters, all because Fulton believed Garcia was paid too much. In August the year before, Fulton, Garcia's immediate supervisor, told his department manager that Garcia was "underperforming" and began making a record in an effort to fire him. After the March argument, Garcia demanded to speak with the department manager because Fulton had made working conditions unbearable. Fulton was paid only $3,000 per year more than Garcia, and Fulton believed he should be paid substantially more.

Finally, in July, Fulton fired Garcia. Garcia's previous performance reviews, for two years before August, were all "satisfactory" or "excellent." Garcia wishes to sue B & G Banking for wrongfully terminating his employment contract.

This is an . . .

A. ineffective Facts section because the facts are not organized logically.
B. effective Facts section because the facts are framed objectively.
C. effective Facts section because it includes all the relevant facts.
D. ineffective Facts section because it omits the legal claim.

EXPLANATIONS

Explanation 15-1

A is wrong. Although this Facts section is thorough, it's not particularly effective because the writer has simply copied, verbatim, the facts provided. Part of your job as a writer is to discover which facts are (and which are not) relevant, and to leave the irrelevant facts out. **B** is also wrong. It's unlikely the reader would be confused if she weren't told the name of the friend Allison King was calling, for instance. **C** is correct for the same reasons that A is wrong. It's your job to distinguish between relevant and irrelevant facts, and to relate only the relevant facts to the reader. **D** is wrong. Although a Facts section should omit irrelevant facts or details, it should be as long as needed to convey all the relevant facts. A strict rule on length—such as that all Facts sections should be two paragraphs or less—won't work when you have a complex case that requires greater space to recount all the relevant facts.

Explanation 15-2

A is wrong. The bike rider's name isn't a relevant fact. (Is King guilty only if the bike rider's name is Smith and not if it is Jones?) What's relevant—and what the reader needs to know—is that he was riding a bike when King drove her car into him and killed him. **B** is correct. Telling the reader at the beginning that King has been charged with vehicular manslaughter helps frame the rest of the facts in context. Without knowing that, the reader wonders why it's worth caring about King, what she was driving, or where she was. **C** is wrong. Facts sections generally don't need to personalize the client to this degree. This level of detail is irrelevant both to the legal issue and to understanding much about the client. In persuasive briefs, personalizing the client may be more appropriate, but still this much detail is likely unnecessary. **D** is wrong for the reasons stated in C, and because the reader needs to know the legal issue at the beginning.

Explanation 15-3

A is wrong. This Facts section fails to include many relevant facts, including where she was driving, the characteristics of Highway 1, and why King made the call. **B**, too, is wrong. Although the Facts section should be as brief as possible, it needs to include all the relevant facts, and this one doesn't for the reasons stated in A. Furthermore, this Facts section doesn't avoid unnecessary detail. Instead, it *leaves out* necessary detail. **C** is wrong. The reader needs more facts, but not, for instance, the cyclist's name. Instead, the reader needs to know more about the driving conditions, the accident, and the reason for the call because these facts are relevant to the issues of whether the elements of vehicular manslaughter are met and whether the emergency exception would apply. **D** is correct for the reasons A, B, and C are wrong.

Explanation 15-4

A is correct. A good Facts section identifies the client and his legal problem, and then includes the relevant facts in chronological order. This Facts section does that. The reader is told that the client is being sued for breach of contract and why he didn't perform under the contract. The reader is also told that the contract's language does not address this situation together with what each party claims at this stage. **B** is wrong. An objective description of the claims being made isn't the same thing as argument. The Facts section doesn't suggest one version is correct, so that is not a problem. **C** is wrong. The exact date of the contract, the date of the frost, and the date the crops were destroyed do not appear, from the claims made, to be relevant to the issue. If the issue had been one of timing—such as a statute of limitations issue—some of those dates might be relevant. But as the problem is posed, the dates do not appear to be relevant, and the Facts section wisely omits them. **D** is wrong. As noted in the explanation for answers A and B, the parties' claims are facts. Including them here helps the reader understand the significance of the legal arguments.

Explanation 15-5

A is wrong. This Facts section omits a number of key facts, including that King's car hit a bicyclist, who then slid across the highway and off the cliff, resulting in death. **B** is wrong. A memo's Facts section should identify the client and include facts relevant to the client, but it needs to be told from an objective point of view, not the client's point of view. The reader can't decide whether to agree or disagree with your analysis if the facts aren't stated here objectively. (In persuasive writing, on the other hand, facts are most often told from the client's point of view—although negative facts still need to be included and addressed. See Chapter 23.) **C** is wrong. Although this Facts section introduces the client and legal claim, it's not effective, for the reasons stated in A, B, and D. **D** is correct. This Facts section omits negative facts. Here, King's hitting and killing a bicyclist is essential to the analysis. Furthermore, these facts are not framed objectively. Criticizing the bicyclist's decision to ride on Highway 1 and at the same time portraying King's decision to drive on that road—and place a cell phone call—highlights the lack of objectivity in the writer's description of the facts. In addition, the last sentence in the Facts section misstates the facts. King's "single act of using her cell phone" is not the "sole reason she is charged with vehicular manslaughter." Rather, she has been charged because she hit and killed a bicyclist when she placed that call during dangerous driving conditions. Finally, this Facts section includes legal argument. The Facts section isn't the place to state that King has been "wrongfully charged with vehicular manslaughter." That is argument. If it's true, it belongs in the Discussion section. And whether she acted "reasonably and responsibly" and therefore "should not be found guilty" are not facts, but instead are legal conclusions that belong in the Discussion section.

Explanation 15-6

A is correct. The organization of this Facts section detracts from its effectiveness. The facts are not relayed chronologically, making it hard for the reader to follow the sequence of events. **B** is wrong. The facts seem at least somewhat slanted in Garcia's favor. But even if they are framed objectively, that is not enough—alone—to make a Facts section effective. **C** is wrong. Some key facts are missing, including how the working conditions were unbearable and what information was used to "make a record" against Garcia. In addition, as with B, even if all of the facts are included, that does not guarantee an effective Facts section. The information must be organized logically, as noted in A. **D** is wrong. This Facts section does include the legal claim—wrongful termination of an employment contract.

Persuasive Writing

PART

III

Overview: Motions and Briefs

16

Picture a lawyer at work. You're probably picturing someone arguing. After all, that's what lawyers get paid to do, right? Argue other people's cases for them—orally, in court. We picture the brilliant lawyer bantering with the Supreme Court or eliciting that confession as the witness breaks down on the stand. There's some truth in that picture, but it's not the whole picture.

Even when lawyers advocate, a good chunk of it occurs in writing. Only in a very small percentage of appellate cases, for example, does the outcome turn on the oral argument. Instead, the written briefs are most influential.

The good news is that in persuasive writing, you'll use many of the same analytical and organizational tools that you'll use in objective writing—so the principles discussed in Parts I and II of this book apply here as well. But persuasive writing has some unique features. To excel at persuasive writing, you need to know certain techniques of persuasion and understand some unique document sections that appear primarily in appellate briefs. You also need to think about a theory of your case and themes that can tell a persuasive story.

This chapter provides some tips and discusses pitfalls to avoid. It also includes an overview of the audience and purpose of motions and briefs as well as their general format.

Terminology Notes: Textbooks use a variety of terms to describe the document of legal analysis that lawyers file with a *trial* court when seeking a specific ruling. Some call it a "trial brief." Some call it a "motion brief." Others call it a "motion memo." Those terms are also used for the document the opposing lawyer submits asking the trial judge to deny the motion. For conciseness, this book uses the more simplified term "motion" to describe the persuasive document that accompanies the request to the court as well as the document the opposing lawyer submits. When discussing these documents in class or with your professor, we suggest you use whatever term your textbook or your professor uses.

SOME TIPS FOR PLANNING YOUR TIME

Just like when you're writing memos, writing motions and briefs takes a lot more time than you probably expect. Start researching and writing as early as possible. Revising and polishing will also take more time than you expect, so plan for that on the front end. Judges are not likely to trust your arguments if you don't cite cases correctly or follow other basic rules. Finally, because you're trying to do more than convey objective legal analysis, you'll want to spend extra time working on persuasion after you have the analysis and arguments down. So build in that time as well.

Just as with office memos, you'll rarely write a motion or brief from the first section to the last. You'll usually write some form of introduction or summary last, even though those sections appear near the beginning of the final document.

One key difference between memo writing and motion or brief writing, though, is that court rules apply to motions and briefs. These court rules may cover items such as font size, page limits, citation style, and required document sections. They vary by jurisdiction, so be sure to find and read the court rules that apply to the document you're drafting.

SOME COMMON PITFALLS

Beware of these common pitfalls:

- leaving out unfavorable facts or authorities;
- framing your argument as a response to your opponent's argument;
- not supporting your factual assertions;
- not including all the required sections for your document (or not including them in the required order); and
- going overboard/hitting the judge over the head with attempts at persuasion.

The first problem on this list sometimes happens in office memos as well, but it happens more often in persuasive writing. Just remember that you can't refute that negative information, whether it's factual or legal, unless you address it. Don't leave the only discussion on the point to the other side. See Chapters 20, 21, and 23.

The second problem is the flip of the first problem. Rather than wishing away the other side and their arguments, you mistakenly start with their arguments and react. A defensive position isn't persuasive. Instead, show why you should win. Again, see Chapters 20, 21, and 23. Chapters 18, 19, 22, and 24 might also help. Most significantly, generating and using a persuasive theory of the case and themes that help advance your position will help ensure you aren't just reacting defensively to your opponent's arguments. Chapters 18 and 23 will be helpful with these skills.

Third, courts expect proof for each assertion you make, including factual claims. Citations to the underlying facts are less common in office memos. But when drafting persuasive documents, you need to cite documents that you put in the factual record as sources of support for your factual assertions.

The fourth problem is usually the result of not budgeting enough time for the project. Legal analysis and drafting takes time, and when you're reading authorities for the first time at 4:30 in the morning and the brief is due at 9, chances are you're going to miss something. So look at the authorities early and create a template with all the document sections. Figure out from the court rules which sections count toward the page limit and which don't. Format your template so that once you add the content, you're ready to submit.

Finally, the fifth problem usually happens because students haven't had enough exposure to good persuasive writing this early in their careers. Chapters 20 and 21 will help, as will time and experience. To get some of that experience more quickly, take the time and review some good persuasive writing. Read briefs submitted to the U.S. Supreme Court, for example, especially those by the Solicitor General, which are often excellent. Check for samples in your legal writing textbook. No matter where you find them, reading good briefs will help.

AUDIENCE AND PURPOSE OF MOTIONS AND BRIEFS

Even though the analytical process is the same, the audience and purpose for objective and persuasive writing are very different. In terms of audience, you're now writing for a judge (and perhaps for the judge's clerks as well as secondary audiences like your opponent who might be persuaded to settle in the shadow of the litigation). Judges are busy and usually won't spend extra time trying to understand poorly made arguments.

In terms of purpose, in contrast to office memos, your goal when drafting a motion or a brief isn't to "inform" the reader or provide an objective analysis of the case. As a writer, your goal with persuasive writing is to make the reader agree with you. Whether that reader is a judge reading your motion, an appellate judge reading a brief, or someone else, you're trying to get the reader to act in a way that favors your client. Even if you objectively think your client should lose, you must argue as though you believe in your client's position.

MOTION AND APPELLATE BRIEF FORMAT

There's no universal format for motions and briefs. That's because, as noted previously, documents filed with courts are subject to various court rules. Be sure to check the rules in your jurisdiction. But here are a few general guidelines.

Motions usually have fewer restrictions in terms of required sections, but they typically have formatting requirements (margins, etc.). Motions usually have two parts: (1) the motion page itself, stating very briefly what you want, and (2) the memorandum or brief, arguing that the trial court should grant your motion. The lawyer on the other side of the case will submit a memo or brief arguing that the court should deny the motion. As we said at the beginning of this chapter, textbooks use different terms to describe these memos or briefs, and for conciseness we simply use the term "motion" to refer to them. In many jurisdictions, certain motions, most notably motions for summary judgment, also include a separate statement of facts.

The supporting memorandum or brief often has three parts: (1) an Introduction or Factual Statement to give the reader an overview or factual background (see Ch. 23 on writing a persuasive Fact Statement, sometimes also called a Statement of the Case); (2) an Argument, which is organized like an objective memo's Discussion section (see Ch. 6 and Ch. 12) but framed persuasively (see Chs. 18, 19, 20, and 21); and (3) a short Conclusion, which typically states the action you want the court to take.

Appellate briefs also follow court rules, so their format also varies by jurisdiction. The rules even govern details like the color of the brief cover, how it is to be bound, and other matters. But the typical sections that are required in appellate briefs and not in trial-level motions or memos include:

- the Question Presented (see Chapter 24);
- a Table of Contents, where you identify each section in the brief and reproduce the text of your point headings and subheadings, with page references;

- a Table of Authorities, where you list all the statutes and cases and other authorities cited, with page references;
- a Statement of Jurisdiction;
- a Summary of the Argument (see Chapter 22);
- a Standard of Review section or statement (see Chapter 17); and
- a Conclusion.

You'll often include the verbatim language of any relevant statutory provision, sometimes near the beginning of the brief and sometimes as an appendix at the end.

In summary, persuasive writing builds on objective writing, but there are special considerations with motions and briefs. Be sure you know the rules, and then be sure you actually follow them!

Handling Standards of Review

(Standards of review are part of appellate practice. You don't need this chapter if you're writing for a trial court. Come back to it later if you're assigned an appellate brief.)

"Counsel, what's the standard?" If you're appearing before an appellate court, the court is likely asking you about the standard of review, meaning the level of deference it should apply to the finding or ruling of the lower court. This can be quite important, and in many appeals, outcome determinative. Because courts and lawyers use the term *standard of review* in various ways, however, it's natural to feel confused. In fact, standard of review is a complex topic and the subject of several legal treatises. This chapter describes on a basic level the various usages and meanings of the term *standard of review* and explains how to write the standard of review section for an appellate brief.

WHAT YOU NEED TO KNOW ABOUT STANDARDS OF REVIEW

When an appellate court hears an appeal it *reviews* the decision below. It does not retry the case. Instead of holding a new trial with witnesses, cross-examinations, and the like, the appeals court reviews the written record of the claims made on appeal and considers the evidence already in the record for those claims. This system promotes judicial economy and respects factual findings made at trial where the fact-finder observed the witnesses firsthand and was not relying on a "cold" appellate record.

The appellate court's power to decide is limited by the standard of review applicable to the lower court's decision. The standard of review determines the level of *deference* the appellate court must give to the decisions of the court below. This level can range from no deference to a lot of it.

In this sense, to defer is to accept, at least to some extent, someone else's decision, largely because of who, or what institution, made it. If you give someone no deference at all, you judge her decisions on their own merits, without assuming that she's probably right because of her knowledge or skill. If you give a lot of deference, you start off assuming that she's probably right and disagree only if you have some special reason for doubting her in this instance. How much doubt do you need before you'll disagree? That depends on how much deference you're giving.

For some types of issues, appellate courts give trial courts no deference and will reverse if they simply disagree with the trial court. For others, appellate courts defer to some extent, but not a lot. They'll reverse only if they disagree strongly. For still other types of decisions, appellate courts defer a great deal to trial courts, and they'll reverse only if they disagree emphatically with what the trial court did.

The standard of review the court applies depends on what it's reviewing: a factual finding, a legal ruling, an evidentiary ruling, or some other type of decision. The standard for factual findings is usually very deferential, while the standard for legal conclusions is usually low or no deference. This reflects the relationship among different levels of courts and the view that the fact-finder — either trial judge or jury — is in the best position to evaluate the evidence, particularly witness testimony, while the appellate court is in the best position to rule on the law and promote a uniform body of law.

The standard of review is itself a matter of law that you must research to determine and cite authority to support. Appellate courts apply standards of review on an issue-by-issue basis, so there may be more than one that applies in any given case. Research the applicable standard of review in your jurisdiction for each issue. In many instances, you'll be able to find a recent case from the appellate court your case is before, or the highest one in the jurisdiction, that provides the applicable standard of review for your issue.

Usually the applicable standard of review is not a controversial issue and the research required is not terribly time-consuming. Sometimes, however, it's not clear what standard applies and the standard will determine the outcome. In those instances, the standard of review may be at the core of the parties' dispute. For instance, one party might argue that the lower court applied the wrong standard of review and if it had applied the correct one, the other side would have prevailed.

The three most common appellate standards of review in civil proceedings are de novo, clearly erroneous, and abuse of discretion. These phrases don't have definitions agreed upon by all courts, and courts haven't uniformly applied them, but the basic concepts can be generally summarized as follows:

- **De novo review** applies to questions of law (about what the law means) and often to mixed questions of law and fact (usually a question about how the law applies to certain agreed-upon facts, such as whether the facts meet a legal standard). De novo review means reviewing the issue anew, without any deference to the lower court.
- **Clearly erroneous review** applies to factual findings. It requires a high level of deference to the lower court. The appellate court will not reverse unless the lower court made a decision based on a clearly erroneous understanding of the facts.
- **Abuse of discretion review** applies to procedural rulings and other discretionary decisions such as admissibility of evidence, objections, and non-dispositive motions. Like the clearly erroneous standard, abuse of discretion requires the appellate court to give a high level of deference to the lower court's decision. Depending on the circumstances, this may amount to a determination that the decision was one no reasonable person would have made or that it was arbitrary and capricious.

Follow court rules, if any, about where to address the standard of review in your brief. If court rules don't specify where to put it, use good writing judgment. You could put it in a separate section with its own header or in the beginning of your Argument section. If you have multiple issues with different standards of review, you could put the applicable portion in the introductory part before each issue. If the standard is controversial, then treat it like any other major issue and develop the section further with argument.

If a deferential standard of review applies, that standard will frame the brief's argument. If a deferential standard of review applies, do more than just state it: incorporate it into your argument as well. It's like a filter or lens through which the court will be viewing your arguments, so when the standard of review favors your side, emphasize it, and when it's not favorable, show how you should win even with the bar set that high. For instance, if you're appealing an evidentiary admissibility ruling, you must assert that the trial court abused its discretion by admitting certain evidence, identify that evidence and the ruling with a citation to the record, and argue why the decision changed the outcome of the case. It wouldn't be enough for the appellate court to be persuaded that it would've ruled differently. It must be persuaded that the trial court abused its discretion in admitting certain evidence and that this changed the outcome of the case.

The phrase "standard of review" can be confusing because courts also use the phrase to describe the legal tests or constitutional standards for trial-court motions and government actions. Specifically, courts use the term to refer to the legal test the trial court applies to decide whether to grant a motion and the standard that courts use to review the constitutionality of a statute or government action (i.e., strict scrutiny, intermediate scrutiny, and rational basis). Sometimes the necessary certainty and evidence for trials, known as the burden of persuasion and burden of proof, is also confused with standard of review. Don't let this confuse you into thinking that appellate courts are applying trial burdens. If you're writing an appellate brief that doesn't concern the constitutionality of a statute or government action, then "standard of review" simply refers to the appellate standard of review as discussed in this chapter.

HOW TO WRITE THE STANDARD OF REVIEW SECTION OF AN APPELLATE BRIEF

Using the copyright and fair use problem in Appendix B, we'll walk you through the process of writing a standard of review section.

Problem

> Here is a quick overview of the copyright and fair use problem. Young is suing Olds for violating the Copyright Act when Olds wrote a song based on Young's original, "Rockin' in the Free World." Olds' song uses the structure and many lyrics of the original but changes the original song's political message. The music of the two songs is not at issue, only the lyrics. Young expects that Olds will argue that his song is a parody that falls under the fair use exception to the Copyright Act. The court will consider the relevant factors set out in the fair use statute, 17 U.S.C. § 107 (2006): whether the copy was transformative and targeted the original; whether it took more than necessary of the original; and whether it will interfere with the original's market.

Step 1: Identify the issue or issues on appeal and figure out the standard or standards of review that apply in your case. To do this, you'll need to do legal research. Look for binding case law that states the standard of review that a court applied to the same kind of decision that is at issue in your appeal.

Here are some considerations that can help you think about what you're looking for. Who made the ruling on the record below? Was it a judge, jury, or administrative body? Also consider the kind of decision. Was it an evidentiary ruling (e.g., that certain evidence was admissible)? A procedural ruling (e.g., that a motion should be granted)? A factual finding (e.g., whether the defendant pulled the gun trigger)? A decision of law (e.g., whether a collateral debt obligation is a "security" within the meaning of the statute)? A mixed question of law and fact (e.g., a district court's finding of fair use under the Copyright Act)?

Imagine that the copyright and fair use problem resulted in litigation between the parties in a district court within the Ninth Circuit. Young claimed that Olds infringed his copyright. Olds argued that his song was a parody and within the fair use exception to the Copyright Act. Imagine further the district court granted summary judgment to Olds, holding that Olds' parody was indeed fair use. If you were working on Young's appeal of the district court's grant of summary judgment, you'd need to find the standard of review that the Ninth Circuit would apply when reviewing such a ruling. Preferably, you'd find this information in a recent case on a similar posture and area of law.

Here, your research finds the *Mattel* case in Appendix B, which provides that an appellate court reviews de novo a district court's grant of summary judgment. Likewise, an appellate court reviews de novo a district court's finding of fair use under the Copyright Act, which is a mixed question of law and fact. It's always a good idea to check that your research results are still "good law" and up to date.

Step 2: Once you've found the standard or standards of review that apply, make a note of the authority that stands for that proposition. Cite authority for the standard of review: it's a legal proposition.

Here, make a note of the proper citation for *Mattel* and include a pinpoint citation to the part of the opinion that discusses the applicable standard of review.

Step 3: Check whether the court where you're submitting your brief has rules regarding where the standard of review should be included and whether it should be in a separate section with its own header. If the court rules don't require a separate statement, then, as noted previously, use your good writing judgment about where to fit it into your organization.

Here, you'd check what the Ninth Circuit requires. Ninth Circuit Rule 28-1 provides that appellate briefs should conform with the Federal Rules of Appellate Procedure (FRAP) Rule 28, which in turn provides that the appellate brief must contain "for each issue, a concise statement of the applicable standard of review (which may appear in the discussion of the issue or under a separate heading placed before the discussion of the issues)." Ninth Circuit Rule 28-2.5 similarly provides: "As to each issue, appellant shall state where in the record on appeal the issue was raised and ruled on and identify the applicable standard of review." Thus, when filing a brief in the Ninth Circuit we could either state the applicable standard of review for each issue under a separate heading or within the discussion of the issue in the Argument.

Step 4: State the applicable standard of review for each issue on appeal and cite authority. Either paraphrase or use a direct quote. Use simple language.

Here, you might write:

Standard of Review

This Court reviews de novo a district court's grant of summary judgment. *Mattel, Inc. v. Walking Mountain Prods.*, 353 F.3d 792, 799 (9th Cir. 2003). A "district court's finding of fair use under Copyright Act," a "mixed question of law and fact," is also reviewed de novo. *Id.*

This statement of the standard of review works. You did research to find the applicable standard or standards, you checked local court rules for formatting, and you stated simply the standard of review and cited authority. Remember that if a deferential standard of review applies and favors your client, you should also incorporate that into your argument. In the instance of the copyright and fair use problem, the standard of review is de novo, so the appellate court would give no deference to the lower court's decision. However, if the problem involved an issue on appeal that required applying the clearly erroneous, abuse of discretion, or some other deferential standard, then you'd want to frame your argument in terms of that standard of review.

EXAMPLES

Here are some examples of statements of the standard of review. You should be able to tell enough from these examples to follow along, although they don't come from the cell phone manslaughter problem or the copyright and fair use problem. For each example, choose the best answer. Explain to yourself why you have chosen that answer. Then read the explanations in the last section of this chapter to check your work.

Example 17-1

This example comes from a brief in which the appellant appeals the district court's award of costs to the prevailing party under a federal statute.

Standard of Review

This Court reviews de novo a district court's interpretation of a federal statute. In addition, this Court reviews de novo whether the district court has the authority to award costs to a prevailing party.

This standard of review statement . . .

 A. works well.
 B. needs citations to authority.
 C. needs to tell the appellate court how much deference to give the lower court's decision.
 D. is too repetitive.

Example 17-2

This example comes from a brief in which the appellant appeals the district court's order compelling arbitration and dismissal of the action for failure to prosecute pursuant to Federal Rule of Civil Procedure 41(b).

Standard of Review

The Plaintiffs-appellants brought a proposed class action in federal court against the Defendant company, alleging that it had sold defective products to them in violation of California state law. Based on the terms and conditions of the product purchase agreement, the Defendant moved to stay proceedings and compel arbitration. The district court granted the motion, and the Plaintiffs refused to comply with it. Subsequently, the Defendant moved under Federal Rule of Civil Procedure 41(b) for the district court to dismiss the action for failure to prosecute or comply with a court order. The district court granted the Defendant's motion to dismiss. The Plaintiffs-appellants now appeal the district court's dismissal, which this Court should review for abuse of discretion. *Omstead v. Dell, Inc.*, 594 F.3d 1081, 1084 (9th Cir. 2010). Further, this Court should review the district court's order compelling arbitration de novo. *Davis v. O'Melveny & Myers*, 485 F.3d 1066, 1072 (9th Cir. 2007).

This standard of review statement . . .

A. works well.
B. needs more citations to authority.
C. includes unnecessary information for the section.
D. confuses the standard the trial court applied to the motions it granted with the appellate standard of review.

Example 17-3

This example comes from a brief in which the appellant appeals the district court's award of attorneys' fees to the defendant under the Copyright Act and the Lanham Act.

Argument

The district court's award of attorneys' fees should be reversed. First, the district court abused its discretion in awarding attorneys' fees under the Copyright Act. Based on the factors to be considered in copyright infringement cases in this Circuit, the defendant was not entitled to attorneys' fees here. The defendant had not advanced the purpose of the Copyright Act and the award was not an appropriate deterrent to further the purposes of the Copyright Act. Second, the district court abused its discretion in awarding attorneys' fees under the Lanham Act because it failed to apportion the attorneys' fees for work only related to the Lanham Act claim, as required.

This Court reviews decisions by the district court awarding attorneys' fees under the Copyright Act and under the Lanham Act for abuse of discretion. *Stephen W. Boney, Inc. v. Boney Servs., Inc.*, 127 F.3d 821, 825 (9th Cir. 1997).

I.   The District Court Abused Its Discretion in Awarding Attorneys' Fees Under the Copyright Act Because Defendant Had Not Advanced the Purpose of the Copyright Act and the Award Was Not an Appropriate Deterrent to Further the Purposes of the Copyright Act.

. . . .

The writer . . .

A. should revise this because the standard of review should always be in its own separate section of the brief.

B. has made an acceptable choice to include the standard of review in the beginning of the Argument.

C. should add more citations to authority.

D. should specify how much deference to give the lower court's decision.

EXPLANATIONS

Explanation 17-1

A is incorrect. Although this is a good start, the statement lacks the necessary citations to authority. **B** is correct. The applicable standard of review is a legal proposition that should be supported by authority. Each sentence in this example should have a citation to authority after it. **C** is incorrect. This statement does tell the court how much deference to give because it states the review is "de novo," which means that the appellate court will review the matter anew with no deference to the lower court's decision. **D** is incorrect. Although it repeats the phrase "de novo," this statement is not too repetitive because there's a question of statutory construction and a question of authority to award costs, and the standard of review for each issue should be explicit.

Explanation 17-2

A is incorrect. In this example, the author chose to put the standard of review in a separate section of the brief with its own header. After so choosing, the author should have put only the standard of review in this section and shouldn't have included the procedural history as well. **B** is incorrect. The portions of this example that relate to standard of review have appropriate cites to authority. The author should, however, edit the section by moving the beginning portion devoted to procedural history to a different section of the brief. **C** is correct. As noted in A, this separate standard of review statement shouldn't include tangential information such as the procedural history. Note that the problem with this example isn't length. Sometimes the applicable standards of review can be complicated and require a detailed explanation or argument. The problem here is simply a lack of focus on the standard of review in a section devoted to it. A better standard of review statement would be as follows:

Standard of Review

This Court reviews for abuse of discretion a district court's dismissal pursuant to Federal Rule of Civil Procedure 41(b) for failure to prosecute or comply with a court order. *Omstead v. Dell, Inc.*, 594 F.3d 1081, 1084 (9th Cir. 2010). This Court reviews de novo a district court's order compelling arbitration. *Davis v. O'Melveny & Myers*, 485 F.3d 1066, 1072 (9th Cir. 2007).

D is incorrect. Although the section unnecessarily includes procedural history, it doesn't discuss the legal test that the trial court applied in granting the motions. If you're feeling confused about the term *standard of review*, you might review the beginning of this chapter again.

Explanation 17-3

A is incorrect. The standard of review doesn't always have to be included in its own separate section of the brief. If court rules don't specify where to put it, use good writing judgment. You could put it in a separate section with its own header or in the beginning of your Argument section, as the writer did in this example. **B** is correct for the reasons explained in A. **C** is incorrect. The writer has appropriately included a citation to authority for the standard of review—the *Stephen W. Boney, Inc.* case, which states that the standard of review is abuse of discretion for awards of attorneys' fees under the Copyright Act and under the Lanham Act. **D** is incorrect. This statement does tell the court how much deference to give because it states the review is "abuse of discretion," which means that the appellate court must give a high level of deference to the lower court's decision.

18

Developing a Theory of the Case and Themes

A good brief is not a patchwork of required sections. A good brief tells a coherent story. It makes the reader understand the issue from your client's point of view and why your client should prevail. An excellent brief can in fact make the reader believe that your client prevailing isn't only the legally correct result, but also the just result.

"Theory of the case" is a term that lawyers use to describe the overarching narrative or idea about a case that a lawyer uses as a guide when making decisions about the trial plan and brief writing process. A good theory of the case is the glue that holds your brief together, forming a cohesive storyline between facts and argument that illuminates what the case is about and the key reasons your client should win.

WHAT YOU NEED TO KNOW ABOUT A THEORY OF THE CASE AND THEMES

A theory of the case is an overarching narrative or idea that concisely explains the key issues and why your client should prevail. It's a view of the law and facts that puts your client in a favorable light and makes the result you advocate seem both legally correct and just. You might not state your theory of the case expressly in your brief, but after reading your brief, the reader should have a clear idea of what you think the case is about and why your client should prevail. Thus, a good theory of the case:

- accounts for, or is at least consistent with, the key facts;
- plausibly explains the controversy, consistent with common sense;
- has a solid legal basis;
- is concise;
- is easily understandable;
- is persuasive; and
- leads to a conclusion that your client should win.

A good brief will weave the theory of the case and core themes throughout, while not overpowering the reader. Every part of your brief is a potential persuasive moment that should advance or at least comport with (and not conflict with) your theory of the case.

The introduction is an entryway for the reader to understand your overarching narrative and what you're asking the court to do. If your brief includes a Question Presented or a Summary of the Argument, craft these so that they're consistent with your theory of the case.

Carry the theory of the case through your Facts section, which should tell a compelling story, with persuasive techniques that are not obvious. Avoid an argumentative tone. Include contextual facts that help to subtly build your narrative. Of course, you must present the key facts accurately, even unfavorable ones. Ask yourself whether you can also present them in a light favorable to your client while maintaining accuracy and integrity. Consider the perspective, order, and amount of detail in your Facts section. Make the reader start from and follow the story through your client's eyes or a favorable vantage point. A chronological order is usually easiest for the reader to understand. You might consider starting at a point in the chronology that is favorable to your side, or using a nonchronological order if you carefully ensure it is still easy for the reader to digest. Use vivid, specific detail to describe favorable facts. Do not omit important facts even if they're unfavorable, but you can describe unfavorable facts more briefly and with less vivid detail.

Your arguments should also fit your theory of the case. Choose words that evoke the core themes of your narrative. Emphasize the strong aspects of your theory of the case, whether that is the law itself, the facts, or policy. Choose arguments that are coherent with each other, or easily understandable alternatives that still fit with your theory of the case.

Themes support the theory of the case. Themes can be captured in words, phrases, or even a sentence that evokes or symbolizes the theory of the case or related key points. Themes should be easy to understand, concrete, and emotionally compelling. For instance, in a breach of contract case where your client is seeking to enforce the contract, a word that evokes the theory of the case might be "promise."

Carefully choose the labels you use to describe the parties as well as those facts that can subtly reinforce your themes. For instance, if you're writing a brief in support of prosecuting a minor as an adult, you might call the minor a "juvenile" instead of a "minor" or "child" because the word "juvenile" evokes a juvenile delinquent who seems more like an adult than the word "child" would suggest. In a case about an automobile collision, the defendant might describe it as an "accident" while the plaintiff might call it a "car crash."

Don't worry about trying to vary elegantly your word choice so as to avoid repetition. Using the same words that evoke your core themes throughout your brief will enhance its cohesion and clarity.

A theory of the case can be formed at various stages of litigation and it might change over time as the key facts develop and litigation continues. For instance, in civil litigation a lawyer might form a theory of the case based on a client interview or informal investigation even before formal discovery starts. In a criminal case a lawyer might develop a theory of the case after reading the initial facts such as in a police report. The theory of the case could start as a broad idea and get refined as more evidence is gathered, as you better understand the strengths and weaknesses of your case, or as the litigation continues and the court rules on motions and issues. Remember, though, that the theory of the case must be driven by the facts; don't try to force or manipulate facts to fit into a theory that doesn't account for the key facts and the particular situation at hand.

HOW TO DEVELOP AND USE A THEORY OF THE CASE AND THEMES

Step 1: Gather and review foundational information to determine what will likely matter to the outcome of the case. Research and review the legal requirements, such as elements for the claims or defenses, and the relevant facts, whether favorable, unfavorable, or neutral. A good theory of the case has to have a solid basis in the applicable law and it must take into account the facts that will matter to the outcome.

Using the copyright and fair use problem, this would mean reviewing the materials in Appendix B, which includes the applicable law and the document in the case file that provides the known background facts.

Problem

> Here is a quick overview of the copyright and fair use problem. Young is suing Olds for violating the Copyright Act when Olds wrote a song based on Young's original, "Rockin' in the Free World." Olds' song uses the structure and many lyrics of the original but changes the original song's political message. The music of the two songs is not at issue, only the lyrics. Young expects that Olds will argue that his song is a parody that falls under the fair use exception to the Copyright Act. The court will consider the relevant factors set out in the fair use statute, 17 U.S.C. § 107 (2006): whether the copy was transformative and targeted the original; whether it took more than necessary of the original; and whether it will interfere with the original's market.

Step 2: Identify each side's strengths and weaknesses, considering the evidence for each side and the weight of authority supporting each side's arguments. At this point you're evaluating the foundational information with an analytical purpose.

With the copyright and fair use problem, you might jot down a list of strengths and weaknesses for Young's side. For instance, you might note that a strong point for Young's case is that Olds used a lot of Young's song lyrics. The third statutory factor for determining fair use considers whether "'the amount and substantiality of the portion used in relation to the copyrighted work as a whole' . . . [is] reasonable in relation to the purpose of the copying." *Campbell v. Acuff-Rose Music, Inc.*, 510 U.S. 569, 586 (1994) (internal citations omitted). A weakness for Young's case might be that Olds' song is a parody of his, and while it uses some of the lyrics and evokes Young's song, Olds' song critically changes the message. The first statutory factor for determining fair use considers this "purpose and character of the use." Under that factor, "transformative" work, like Olds' parody, weighs in favor of finding fair use. You'd continue in this way making a list of strengths and weaknesses in light of the applicable law and facts.

Step 3: Brainstorm ways of looking at the case that would make your client a winner. Reviewing and analyzing the applicable law and facts probably got your brain buzzing with ideas. Now it's time to think of a logical and persuasive narrative about what happened. It should emphasize your side's strengths, while neutralizing or at least being consistent with your side's weaknesses. This stage can be quite creative and it's often best to focus on simply generating ideas. You might try jotting down ideas without stopping to evaluate them—phrases or sentences for a theory of the case and words to use for your themes. If you get stuck, imagine you're telling a colleague about the case by completing the sentence "My client should win because . . ." or "This case is about . . ." Don't worry too much about the phrasing at this stage because you won't necessarily use the same language in your brief.

With the copyright and fair use problem, you might start by jotting down words for Young's side:

- unreasonable
- unfairly
- inequitable

Phrases and full sentences would be good too, so you might jot down:

- Olds takes too much
- Olds' song does not creatively transform
- Olds attempts to capitalize on Young's work
- Olds' song supplants the original

And then you might start thinking about completing a sentence, with results like these:

- My client Young should win because Olds unfairly took too much from Young's song in an attempt to financially capitalize on the market for Young's song.
- My client Young should win because instead of creating a new or transformative work, Olds stole an unreasonable amount from Young to try to take advantage of the market for Young's song. It's not fair because Olds took too much.
- This case is about a guy who lacked creativity and tried to take advantage of a successful musician by copying his song and targeting the original song's market.

It's okay if you start to feel your mind wander and you start jotting down ideas that go a little beyond the construct of "My client should win because . . ." or "This case is about . . ." At this stage, you're just brainstorming. For instance, you might start to feel your emotions rise and write down:

- People like Olds shouldn't be able to hide behind the fair use defense when they unfairly steal from someone else's successful work.
- It's okay to make a parody, but it's not okay to copy huge amounts from someone else and try to get people to buy your song instead of theirs.

Step 4: Evaluate possible strategies and choose what you think will be the most effective theory of the case and themes. This may be a matter of simply choosing the best idea from your brainstorming session if you have something good or it may require you to synthesize and distill multiple ideas into one concise theory.

Remember the theory of the case needs to be a credible and specific explanation of what happened, consistent with the evidence and not in legalese. Choose a theory of the case that fits with the case you have—the applicable law and actual facts. It should persuade your audience that your client should win. For instance, "the defendant infringed the copyright" or "the fair use exception does not apply" is too generic and conclusory, and won't likely speak to a juror or judge.

With the copyright and fair use problem, the court will weigh the statutory fair use factors. Which would be strong factors for you to emphasize in your theory?

Reviewing the case law, you'd find that the second factor, "the nature of the copyrighted work," is usually not significant in cases involving parodies. Although you've brainstormed the idea that Olds didn't creatively transform Young's work, the facts suggest that Olds' song is arguably a parody and that many of the lyrics actually were different and critical of Young's message. Therefore, the first factor probably doesn't weigh very strongly in Young's favor. You might avoid emphasizing it in your theory of the case for that reason. The theory of the case must fit well with the facts you have, not the facts you wish you had. It would be better for Young to emphasize the third and fourth factors regarding "the amount and substantiality of the portion used" and "the effect of the use upon the potential market for or value of the copyrighted work." The ideas from your brainstorming highlight these with the core themes of Olds taking too much of Young's song and Olds trying to take advantage of the market for Young's song. Synthesizing these, you might come up with something like:

- Olds took an unreasonable amount from Young and unfairly tried to take advantage of the market for Young's song.

Step 5: Use the theory of the case and themes throughout your brief. Unify your key points and assertions with your theory of the case and themes.

For instance, when writing an introduction to your brief consider the purpose of the section and what you need to include, such as some contextual facts and stating what action you'd like the court to take. Also consider how you might get in your theory of the case or core themes. Start with a line that will spark the reader's interest and that suggests a narrative explanation for the case. For the copyright and fair use problem, you might start with this:

- Although the fair use exception protects certain parodies from violating the Copyright Act, in this case Phil Olds has taken too much of Neil Young's original popular song lyrics to qualify for such protection.

This orients the reader to your situation, where Olds claims his song is a parody that falls under the fair use exception but Young claims that Olds took too much of the original and infringed his copyright. This sentence subtly gets in the core theme of "taking too much" and you can build on this in the rest of the introduction.

Remember that you'll want to use the theory of the case and themes at multiple places throughout your brief. You won't necessarily use the exact words that you jotted down. This is just to get the idea clear in your mind as you're writing your brief. Keep your notes close by, however, so that they can guide your choices and provide a memorable focal point for the reader to grasp.

EXAMPLES

Here are some examples of theories of the case, based on the cell phone manslaughter problem and the copyright and fair use problem in the Appendices. For each example, choose the best answer. Explain to yourself why you've chosen that answer. Then read the explanations in the last section of this chapter to check your work.

Example 18-1

Which of the following is the most comprehensive and persuasive theory of the case, on behalf of Allison King, for the cell phone manslaughter problem? (Answering this example gives you a chance to test your ability to strategically evaluate whether, given the relevant law and facts, a theory of the case would persuasively explain why your client should prevail. Remember that you can find the facts and law for the cell phone manslaughter problem in Appendix A.)

A. The near-whiteout conditions were dangerous and Allison King's decision to use her cell phone to prevent others from entering is what most anyone would have done in that situation.

B. Allison King's decision to give June Coughlin a call was the right thing to do because she was a friend and they were planning to get together. King was terrified and was doing her best. She had to dial the friend to be able to warn her. The law allows for this kind of cell phone use when there's an emergency.

C. Allison King did not drive with gross negligence, so she is not guilty of vehicular manslaughter.

D. The bicyclist appeared from out of the fog, so it wasn't Allison King's fault that she couldn't see him.

Example 18-2

Can you identify a theory of the case in this introduction? In which portions of the text? Circle or underline the portions you identify and then read the explanation.

> Although the fair use exception protects certain parodies from violating the Copyright Act, in this case Phil Olds has taken too much of Neil Young's original popular song lyrics to qualify for such protection. Olds produced and marketed a song entitled "Stop Knockin' the Free World," targeting Young's copyrighted original "Rockin' in the Free World." Olds patterned song lyrics after Young's in an attempt to capitalize on Young's significant financial and musical success. The Copyright Act protects rightful copyright holders like Young from this kind of unfair use. Under the statutory four factor test, Olds' use, which closely copies a famous original work, taking more than necessary from the original and targeting its market, does not constitute a fair use and therefore infringes Young's copyright. Accordingly, the Court should deny Olds' motion for summary judgment.

Example 18-3

Assume your theory of the case for the copyright and fair use problem is that instead of creating a sufficiently transformative work, Olds copied an unreasonable amount from Young to take financial advantage of the successful musician's original work. Which of the following point headings would best weave in this theory of the case?

    A. Olds' Song Is Not Fair Use Because It Conjures Up the Original Song by Targeting a Recognizable Refrain and Unfairly Transforms Its Political Message.

    B. The Fair Use Exception Does Not Protect Parodies That Copy Too Much of the Original Copyrighted Work.

    C. This Court Should Deny the Motion to Dismiss Because Under the Relevant Statutory Factors, Olds' Song Infringes Young's Work.

    D. Olds' Song Is Not Fair Use Because It Unreasonably Copies Too Much from Young's Copyrighted Song Without Sufficiently Transforming It and While Aiming to Usurp the Original Market.

EXPLANATIONS

Explanation 18-1

A is correct. This theory of the case would plausibly work. It melds relevant facts and law: that the near-whiteout conditions Allison King was in were dangerous, which goes toward showing that it was an emergency situation under California Vehicle Code § 23123 and therefore that King was not driving "in the commission of an unlawful act" or "in an unlawful manner" for purposes of California Penal Code § 192, vehicular manslaughter. It also concisely melds relevant facts and law as to section 192's gross negligence requirement, suggesting that it was not vehicular manslaughter because King acted how others would have acted in that situation, not with gross negligence. **B** is not the best choice. Although it has the makings of a plausible theory of the case, this version is not concise and lacks the coherence necessary for an overarching narrative or idea that concisely explains why King should prevail. **C** is not the best choice. When choosing a theory of the case, avoid lawyerly language and simply stating the legal conclusion that you hope your audience will reach. Gross negligence is a legal term and simply asserting that King did not act grossly negligent does not provide reasoning or a concise narrative to understand her actions. **D** is not the best choice. Although D melds law (the concept of fault) and fact (that the bicyclist appeared from out of the fog), it doesn't provide a precise explanation or narrative explaining why King isn't guilty of vehicular manslaughter. In addition, it doesn't involve the idea of King making a cell phone call and this omission might leave the reader wondering a number of things, such as: (1) whether the cell phone call is relevant to the writer's theory of the case; (2) whether the writer's theory is that fault is related to visibility or that fog is an emergency; (3) whether the legal question presented is whether King could see the bicyclist; or (4) whether she was grossly negligent for not seeing him. In short, while D might be a decent start in a brainstorming session, it isn't yet a clearly crafted, precise theory of the case for the cell phone manslaughter problem.

Explanation 18-2

This introduction uses the theory of the case discussed in "How to Develop and Use a Theory of the Case and Themes" above, that instead of creating a sufficiently transformative work, Olds copied an unreasonable amount from Young to take financial advantage of the successful musician's original work. It uses the related themes of Olds' use as unfair and unreasonable. The bolded portions weave in this theory of the case and themes:

> Although the fair use exception protects certain parodies from violating the Copyright Act, in this case Phil Olds has **taken too much**

of Neil Young's original popular song lyrics to qualify for such protection. Olds produced and marketed a song entitled "Stop Knockin' the Free World," targeting Young's copyrighted original "Rockin' in the Free World." **Olds patterned song lyrics after Young's in an attempt to unfairly capitalize on Young's significant financial and musical success.** The Copyright Act protects rightful copyright holders like Young from this kind of **unfair** infringement. Under the statutory four factor test, Olds' use, which closely copies Young's **famous** original work, **taking more than necessary** from the original and **targeting its market**, does not constitute a fair use and therefore infringes Young's copyright. Accordingly, the Court should deny Olds' motion for summary judgment.

Explanation 18-3

A is wrong. It uses reasoning that doesn't reflect the theory of the case and in fact would likely weigh against the conclusion you're advocating. A parody may copy to a limited extent so that it "conjure[s] up" the original work, particularly memorable parts of an original, and a work's transformative nature weighs in favor of finding fair use. *See* Appendix B; *Campbell v. Acuff-Rose Music, Inc.*, 510 U.S. 569, 588, 579 (1994). **B** is not the best choice. Although this point heading weaves in the part of the theory regarding Olds using "too much," D is a better choice because it also weaves in the part of the theory regarding Olds trying to capitalize on Young's financial success by targeting the original work's market. Also note while B uses generic language about the fair use exception, D uses facts that are more specific to the copyright and fair use problem at hand and so is overall a stronger point heading. **C** is wrong. This point heading is conclusory and doesn't weave in a theory of the case. A reader might wonder what key facts specifically show that Olds' song infringes Young's work. Key facts are important to a strong theory of the case because they help to create an understandable narrative with persuasive effect. **D** is correct. This point heading gets in the theory of the case that Olds unfairly took "too much" from Young's original and is trying to capitalize on the original's financial success by taking over its market.

Writing Point Headings and Subheadings

Point headings and subheadings are often an afterthought for student writers, but they are usually the first thing judges read. The point headings and subheadings do a lot of structural and persuasive heavy lifting because they briefly summarize your entire argument. The reader will either page through the body of the Argument itself to find them or will find them neatly presented in outline form in a Table of Contents.

Two important aspects contribute to effective point headings and subheadings: organization and persuasive writing. Making good choices about how many point headings and subheadings to use and where to put them requires you to make smart choices about the organization of your Argument section. You'll want to think about how many separate legal issues you have, what you have to show to win, how your applicable legal rule is divided, and where logical spots for point headings and subheadings would be. A natural place to get more help on this is Chapter 6 on Organizing the Discussion. Once you've got a logical organization in place, use this chapter to help you write persuasive point headings and subheadings.

Terminology Notes: This chapter addresses the argumentative headings in the Argument section of your brief. Your professor may call all of them "point headings," or may identify the headings at the highest level as "point headings" or simply "headings" and the various divisions as "subheadings." In this book, the ones at the highest level are called your "point headings" and any that come at a level nested below those are called "subheadings."

WHAT YOU NEED TO KNOW ABOUT WRITING POINT HEADINGS AND SUBHEADINGS

Point headings and subheadings persuasively assert your main arguments, arranged in a logical order. Picture a formal outline in which your big points—the point headings—are each a sentence at the Roman numeral level of the outline (I., II., . . .). Nested at the level inside of those bigger point headings you have your subheadings (A., B., . . .), each being a sentence that provides a logical chunk of reasoning that proves your point headings.

A point heading is generally used for a dispositive argument. This means an argument that, if accepted, would independently win what you're seeking in the brief. Some professors expect that you'll use a point heading only for making such a dispositive argument. Other professors recognize that while this is the general custom, it's not a strict rule and there may be reasons to use a point heading for a non-dispositive argument. For instance, you may have a threshold issue that, although not dispositive, should be addressed before your first main point heading. Some writers would use a point heading for that threshold issue.

Use subheadings to set forth the steps of logic or conclusions that prove your point heading. Subheadings can neatly separate a long and complex argument into logical chunks that go toward demonstrating the assertion in your point heading.

Each point heading and subheading should generally (a) include one or more key facts; (b) relate to the legal issue; and (c) identify what you want the court to do or what conclusion you want it to reach. If your issue is a purely legal one, such as an argument before an appeals court about what the law is, then you won't include facts because they won't be necessary to your argument. But in most cases, your issue will not be purely legal, and you'll want to include facts because point headings that meld legal issues and key facts are more persuasive. Be specific, not generic. And phrase the point heading in terms of what you want the court to do ("This Court Should Dismiss . . .") or as the conclusion you want it to reach ("The Defendant Breached the Contract by . . .").

There's no official rule on numbering and typesetting, but there are typical conventions that most lawyers and professors follow. Use Roman numerals (I., II., III.), letters (A., B., C.), and numbers (1., 2., 3.) as in a formal outline. Professors tend to have varying views about whether you should give a point heading a Roman numeral if you have only one point. Some consider it permissible, while others believe that if you have only one point heading, there's no point in giving it a number. What about subheadings? Most professors agree that you should not use subheadings unless you have at least two subheadings for that level. For instance, you would not use a subheading "A." unless you also had a subheading "B."

Your best bet is to ask which typesetting convention your professor considers most effective and to follow your professor's recommendation. Traditionally, lawyers have used all capital letters for point headings at the Roman numeral level (I.). All-caps can be difficult to read, however. Some use bold print instead of all-caps. Subheadings may be in italics, in bold, or underlined, except when they appear in a Table of Contents. The first letter of each significant word is capitalized. All headings should be single-spaced.

Here are three versions of what these various typesetting choices might look like (not in the Table of Contents):

I.   OLDS' PARODY IS FAIR USE BECAUSE IT TARGETS A RECOGNIZABLE REFRAIN OF THE ORIGINAL SONG AND CRITICALLY TRANSFORMS ITS POLITICAL MESSAGE FOR A DIFFERENT ECONOMIC MARKET.

   A. Olds Fairly Created a Parody of Young's Song That Transformed Its Political Anti-War Message to Support for Traditional Values.
   B. Olds Fairly Used a Reasonable Amount of Young's Copyrighted Work as Necessary to Invoke the Original for Olds' Parody.
   C. Evidence Shows That Olds' Critical Parody Has a Different Market and Will Not Affect the Market for Young's Original Song.

I.   **Olds' Parody Is Fair Use Because It Targets a Recognizable Refrain of the Original Song and Critically Transforms Its Political Message for a Different Economic Market.**

   A. **Olds Fairly Created a Parody of Young's Song That Transformed Its Political Anti-War Message to Support for Traditional Values.**
   B. **Olds Fairly Used a Reasonable Amount of Young's Copyrighted Work as Necessary to Invoke the Original for Olds' Parody.**
   C. **Evidence Shows That Olds' Critical Parody Has a Different Market and Will Not Affect the Market for Young's Original Song.**

Style Format

I.   **Olds' Parody Is Fair Use Because It Targets a Recognizable Refrain of the Original Song and Critically Transforms Its Political Message for a Different Economic Market.**

   A. *Olds Fairly Created a Parody of Young's Song That Transformed Its Political Anti-War Message to Support for Traditional Values.*

B. *Olds Fairly Used a Reasonable Amount of Young's Copyrighted Work as Necessary to Invoke the Original for Olds' Parody.*

C. *Evidence Shows That Olds' Critical Parody Has a Different Market and Will Not Affect the Market for Young's Original Song.*

You can use your point headings and subheadings to ensure that you have an effective structure to your Argument. Read your point headings in order and perhaps copy and paste them out onto another page as you would when creating a Table of Contents for an appellate brief. Considered together, your point headings and subheadings should set out a complete and persuasive outline of your Argument. Ask yourself: Do they assert my Argument's main points? Are there gaps or inconsistencies? If you're not using enough point headings and subheadings, you'll see that you don't have an accurate and complete outline of your Argument. If you notice that two point headings or subheadings are similar, you might be making only one point and you should consider consolidating those sections of your Argument and adjusting your headings accordingly.

HOW TO WRITE POINT HEADINGS AND SUBHEADINGS

Using the copyright and fair use problem in Appendix B, we'll walk you through the process of writing point headings.

Problem

Here is a quick overview of the copyright and fair use problem. Young is suing Olds for violating the Copyright Act when Olds wrote a song based on Young's original, "Rockin' in the Free World." Olds' song uses the structure and many lyrics of the original but changes the original song's political message. The music of the two songs is not at issue, only the lyrics. Young expects that Olds will argue that his song is a parody that falls under the fair use exception to the Copyright Act. The court will consider the relevant factors set out in the fair use statute, 17 U.S.C. § 107 (2006): whether the copy was transformative and targeted the original; whether it took more than necessary of the original; and whether it will interfere with the original's market.

Step 1: Start with your draft outline. Here's one from the copyright and fair use problem:

I. Fair Use
    A. The purpose and the character of the use
    B. The amount and substantiality of the portion used in relation to the copyrighted work as a whole
    C. The effect of the use upon the potential market for or value of the copyrighted work[1]

This draft outline organizes the defendant's Argument section by three of the four statutory factors that courts consider in evaluating whether an appropriation of copyrighted material is fair use. The second factor, "the nature of the copyrighted work," is omitted because the case law shows that courts have consistently concluded it's of negligible significance in cases where, as in this copyright and fair use problem, the defendant claims the allegedly infringing work is "parody." This omission could be briefly explained in the introduction (also known as the umbrella section) of the Argument. That leaves the other three factors for the Argument section.

Step 2: Consider whether your headings are point headings or subheadings and whether you've appropriately numbered them. The draft outline envisions "Fair Use" as the big point of the brief. This makes sense because you're imagining writing a brief for the defendant who wants to assert fair use as a defense to copyright infringement. If the defendant prevails with the fair use defense, he wins the case and so it's a dispositive argument that warrants using a point heading.

What about the three statutory factors? None of them are dispositive. Each one, however, is a logical step toward showing that the use falls within the fair use exception to the Copyright Act. So these make sense as subheadings as in the draft outline.

Step 3: Craft a sentence for each point heading and subheading that melds the legal issue with key facts and is phrased as the conclusion you want the court to reach or the action you want it to take. Think about writing a point heading about fair use.

What's the legal issue here? The plaintiff has sued the defendant for copyright infringement of his original song's lyrics, "Rockin' in the Free World." The defendant wants to argue that the fair use defense applies to his song's lyrics, "Stop Knockin' the Free World." You could say the issue is whether the defendant's use of the original work in his parody song falls within the fair use exception. And you know that the defendant will argue

---

1. 17 U.S.C. § 107 (2006).

that the three relevant statutory factors weigh in favor of the court finding that his song's appropriation of the original falls within the fair use exception. You would then capture that idea in the point heading.

What are the key facts that you use to show this? Look at your arguments under each of the relevant statutory factors and consider what the most persuasive facts are for each factor. Is there a fact that goes to more than one factor and that you think will be especially important?

Finally, you want to phrase this as a conclusory sentence, either identifying what you want the court to do or the conclusion you want it to reach. Here, you want the court to conclude that the song is not an unlawful infringement because it falls within the fair use exception. Stated more briefly, Olds' song is fair use.

Capturing all three of these components, you might have:

I. OLDS' PARODY IS FAIR USE BECAUSE IT TARGETS A RECOGNIZABLE REFRAIN OF THE ORIGINAL SONG AND CRITICALLY TRANSFORMS ITS POLITICAL MESSAGE FOR A DIFFERENT ECONOMIC MARKET.

This one is a bit on the long side, but it's readable and gets in the important components. Next you'd craft the subheadings using the same method.

Step 4: Check that your point headings and subheadings set out a complete and persuasive outline of your Argument. Some people write point headings before they've written the Argument section and others keep a marker in the spot and write the point headings after they've finished writing the Argument section. Whichever way you do it, after you've finished writing the Argument section, go back and check your point headings and subheadings. Make any necessary adjustments to the number or phrasing of the headings.

EXAMPLES

Here are some examples of point headings and subheadings. For each example, choose the best answer. Explain to yourself why you have chosen that answer. Then read the explanations in the last section of this chapter to check your work. (We've all-capped these point headings only because that's commonly done in practice. In your own writing, as we said earlier in this chapter, you should use the typesetting your professor considers most effective.)

Example 19-1

I. OLDS' SONG COPIES SOME OF YOUNG'S SONG, TARGETING THE MOST MEMORABLE PARTS, AND CRITICIZES YOUNG'S NEGATIVE POLITICAL MESSAGE TO APPEAL TO A DIFFERENT AUDIENCE.

This point heading . . .

A. should state a legal conclusion or what the court should do.
B. is strong for a pure question of law and needs no improvement.
C. should include more key facts.

Example 19-2

I. OLDS' SONG IS FAIR USE BECAUSE, ALTHOUGH IT COPIES SOME OF YOUNG'S SONG, IT TARGETS THE MOST RE-COGNIZABLE REFRAINS AND TRANSFORMS THE SONG INTO A PARODY CRITICIZING YOUNG'S NEGATIVE MESSAGE ABOUT AMERICA AND WAR, WHILE NOT SUPERSEDING THE MARKET FOR YOUNG'S ORIGINAL WHICH CONSISTED OF MANY LOYAL AND LIBERAL FANS.
   A. The Relevant Statutory Factors Weigh in Favor of Olds' Song Being Fair Use.

A. The subheading is better than the point heading—it should be substituted for the point heading.
B. The point heading and subheading are strong and need no improvements.
C. The point heading is too long and the subheading should be cut.

Example 19-3

I. IN LIGHT OF THE APPLICABLE STATUTORY FACTORS AND LONGSTANDING DOCTRINE, THE COURT SHOULD FIND THAT OLDS' SONG IS FAIR USE.

This point heading . . .

A. would be more persuasive if it included facts supporting the legal conclusions.

    B. is strong and needs no improvement.

    C. should cite authority.

EXPLANATIONS

Explanation 19-1

A is correct. A point heading should include key facts, relate to the legal issue, and identify what the court should do or what conclusion it should reach. This example is heavy on the facts and fails to identify what the court should do or conclude. You could start to revise it by adding to the beginning "OLDS' SONG IS FAIR USE BECAUSE . . ." It would then be phrased as the conclusion that Olds wants the court to reach. With a few more small changes, you might then have: "OLDS' SONG IS FAIR USE BECAUSE IT IS A PARODY THAT TARGETS THE MOST MEMORABLE PARTS OF YOUNG'S SONG TO CRITICIZE THE NEGATIVE POLITICAL MESSAGE AND THUS APPEAL TO A DIFFERENT AUDIENCE." *B* is wrong. Our copyright and fair use problem is not a pure question of law. The issue requires the court to determine how the law applies to the facts. *C* is wrong. This point heading already includes lots of facts. What's missing is the conclusion or action the writer seeks from the court.

Explanation 19-2

A is wrong. The subheading does a good job clearly and concisely stating its point, but it does not incorporate key facts. So it wouldn't be a good idea to simply substitute the subheading for the point heading. In fact, as most professors agree that you shouldn't use a subheading if you have only one point to make under the point heading, it would make sense here to cut the subheading. Alternatively, if you liked the text of the subheading better than the text of the point heading in this example, you could revise the subheading to incorporate the key facts and use it instead of the point heading. For instance, you might revise the subheading to this point heading:

    I.   OLDS' SONG IS FAIR USE UNDER THE RELEVANT STATUTORY FACTORS BECAUSE IT IS A PARODY THAT TARGETS THE ORIGINAL'S MOST RECOGNIZABLE REFRAINS, CRITICALLY TRANSFORMING ITS POLITICAL MESSAGE, WHILE NOT SUPERSEDING ITS MARKET.

B is wrong. Although the point heading has some strong aspects, it's hard to read and could be improved by editing its length. Also, most professors agree that you shouldn't use a subheading if you have only one point to make under the point heading. Because there's only one subheading here, it should be cut. **C** is correct. This point heading is pretty good, but it's too long and needs some editing. Also, the subheading should be cut because you don't use a subheading if you have only one point to make under the point heading. The point heading should make that point.

Explanation 19-3

A is correct. Supplying reasons, particularly with key facts, is more persuasive than generic conclusions of law. **B** is wrong. This point heading could be improved by explaining its conclusion, particularly with key facts. **C** is wrong. Although point headings occasionally cite authority if there's a key statute or seminal case, they usually don't and there's no requirement that they should.

CHAPTER 20

Making Persuasive Arguments

If you came to law school because you love to argue, this part of writing ought to make you happy. Although the art of persuasion is just that—an art—certain principles will make your arguments more likely to succeed. After all, who likes to *lose* an argument?

WHAT YOU NEED TO KNOW ABOUT MAKING PERSUASIVE ARGUMENTS

Recall that your goal with persuasive writing is to get the reader to agree with you. As noted in Chapter 16, persuasive writing differs from objective writing. With objective writing, your purpose is to answer the Question Presented with objective/predictive analysis. With persuasive writing, on the other hand, you're trying to convince the judge that your client's position is the correct position. Sometimes this is your task even though you believe the opposing side has a stronger legal argument. But even in those situations, you need to write as though you are confident that your position is the winner.

The substance of your argument is the most important factor in overall persuasiveness. A losing argument, even when made artfully, is still almost always a losing argument. The good news is that (at least in law school) you rarely need to make arguments that are clear "losers." Usually, each side's position has merit—which is why your professor assigned the problem in the first place.

Your argument should include both (1) the reasons you are legally entitled to win (the "justifying" arguments), and (2) the reasons you *should* win (the "motivating" arguments).[1] The justifying arguments convince the judge she will not be overruled for deciding in your favor. But the motivating arguments are those that make the judge want to rule in your favor in the first place. Although rarely dispositive, in a close case making the judge think your side is right can matter. Your arguments need to incorporate all the relevant law and the record (if drafting an appellate brief) or the other factual basis for your argument.

Furthermore, limit your arguments to those with a reasonable chance of success. If you want a refresher on legal analysis and different types of arguments, you can review Chapters 9-11. And unless a weak argument is essential to your client's success (or unless you're trying to preserve the record in a criminal case by raising all possible arguments), generally you'll be more persuasive if you focus your attention, in detail, on the strongest reasons you should prevail. This allows greater focus on those winning arguments.

The second most important factor in a document's persuasiveness is the structure of your argument, and two organizational tools can help: (a) starting each section, argument, and paragraph with a thesis statement; and (b) putting important information at the beginning and end. The first tool, starting with thesis statements, helps with the second: putting important information at the beginning. But each technique involves different considerations.

Thesis statements: Your thesis is, at a very basic level, your main point. Some people think of the thesis statement as the conclusion that you state at the beginning of your argument. The same structure you use to organize an office memo's Discussion section—CRAC—is the foundation for persuasive organization. For a refresher on CRAC, see Chapter 6.

The beginning and end: Readers have certain expectations—mainly, that the most important information will be at the beginning and end—and these expectations should influence the organization of your argument. Knowing that the beginning and end are positions of strength—the beginning is the "topic" position[2] and the end is the "stress" position[3]—will help you write more persuasively. Furthermore, the concepts of primacy and recency suggest that readers remember most what is at the beginning and the end, and you want the reader to remember favorable information.

Although the end—the stress position—is the position of greatest emphasis and readers remember that information most clearly, this principle

---

1. *See* Richard K. Neumann, Jr., *Legal Reasoning and Legal Writing: Structure, Strategy, and Style* 309-13 (6th ed. 2009).
2. Joseph M. Williams & Gregory G. Colomb, *Style: Lessons in Clarity and Grace* 76 (10th ed. 2010).
3. *Id.* at 85.

is trumped by a special expectation in the law: Judges expect your strongest argument first. If you wait until the end, the judge may have stopped reading by then (or may only be skimming the document by that point). So if you have three main arguments, a good strategy is to start your Argument section with the strongest argument. Some readers expect the next strongest argument to follow, and so on; others expect a strong argument at the end, so they would suggest you save the second strongest argument for last and put the weakest argument in the middle. If you have more than three arguments, many writers put the weakest next to last.

Make your organization obvious with headings and transitions. This is true even for objective writing. Headings and transitions simply make your writing easier to read. But in motions and briefs, headings should be persuasive phrases or sentences that assert the conclusion you argue for, not just a word or phrase to introduce the issue. (Chapter 19 explains point headings.) Your thesis statement for a section ought to become that section's heading. And the thesis statement for a subsection ought to be that section's subheading.

Transitions are also key to your document making sense. Whether it's a simple "first, . . ." "second, . . ." "third, . . ."; "therefore"; or transition phrase or sentence, the reader will better understand your argument if you include explicit signals and transitions. (See Chapter 29 for more help with transitions.)

Your writing style can also add to the persuasiveness of your argument. Just as the way you write your facts can affect how the judge perceives your case, as noted in Chapter 23, the same holds true for your arguments. As with all legal documents, and especially all documents filed in a court, your writing style should be formal. Avoid contractions, using parentheses other than for citations, and writing in the first person. Similarly, as with other legal writing, avoid unnecessary legalese. The bottom line is this: If the judge has to stop and think about why you chose a particular word, you've lost the persuasion battle. Your word choice should help persuade the judge without him even thinking about it.

Techniques of persuasion work best when they are subtle, not obvious. Judges like to think of themselves as objective, neutral decision makers. If you make it obvious that you're attempting to sway a judge, she might put less trust in your brief or resist adopting your position. So follow all of the tips provided here, but don't go overboard in your attempts at persuasion. Similarly, you should avoid words like "clearly" and "obviously."

HOW TO MAKE PERSUASIVE ARGUMENTS

Using the cell phone manslaughter problem in Appendix A, we'll walk you through the process of writing persuasive arguments.

Problem

> Here is a quick overview of the cell phone manslaughter problem. Allison King used her wireless phone, without a hands-free device, while driving in dense fog on a winding road on the edge of an ocean cliff. King placed the call to warn her friends about the dangerous conditions, as they would be meeting later. While she was making the call, she hit and killed a bicyclist. The prosecution will attempt to convict King of vehicular manslaughter by showing that she drove while committing an illegal act (driving while using a wireless phone without a hands-free device) and with gross negligence. King will argue that her actions fit within the emergency exception to the wireless phone prohibition. She will also argue that she did not act with gross negligence.

Step 1: Draft a thesis statement for each argument. Because the most important piece of persuasion is the substance of your argument, thoroughly research your problem to ensure that you aren't missing helpful authorities or contentions. The same processes you used in objective writing apply to persuasive writing, even though the ultimate goal is different.

In persuasive writing, headings and subheadings that just name an issue, like "robbery," aren't very effective (although some readers prefer them in objective office memos). Hence, you should craft thesis statements—the main point of each argument. Those thesis statements will become your descriptive (and persuasive) section and subsection headings. You can write these thesis statements whether you're at the outlining stage or already have a draft.

For instance, your objective outline (in IRAC format) of the cell phone manslaughter problem might look like this:

Vehicular Manslaughter

  1. Unlawful Act
  2. Gross Negligence

Those same headings in a persuasive document might read as follows:

King did not commit vehicular manslaughter.

1. King's use of her cell phone did not constitute an "unlawful act" because she called for emergency purposes.
2. King did not act with "gross negligence."

Some readers expect each conclusion to be restated at the beginning of the textual paragraph that follows the heading. Others will treat the point headings and subheadings as the "conclusion" (using the CRAC structure described in Chapter 6). Those readers expect you to jump right into the rule as you begin the text below the heading.

Step 2: Organize your arguments by ranking their strength. Usually put the strongest argument first and order the rest by strength as well, but be sure to end on a strong note. Although your last argument may be the weakest you choose to include, don't end a section by trailing off with a weak argument. You should include a last sentence or two that reminds the reader of your strongest points. Using the previous outline, you might rank the sub-issues as follows:

Rank 2: King's use of her cell phone did not constitute an "unlawful act" because she called for emergency purposes.

Rank 1: King did not act with "gross negligence."

Even though the "gross negligence" element is last in the statute, if you determine that it's the strongest argument in your client's favor, you would probably lead with it. This general rule of leading with your strongest argument can be trumped, though. For example, readers generally expect threshold issues—those that would dispose of the case, like procedural questions—to be addressed first, even if not the strongest argument. Similarly, some readers expect the argument to parallel the test's elements (or factors) unless there's a good reason to vary from that structure. Here, if you assume point 1 is stronger than point 2 and the reader won't be confused by this order, putting it first makes sense. The same holds true of claims or contentions supporting each main argument. Rank them, and lead with the strongest unless that order is likely to confuse the reader.

When you have three or more arguments, you should find a way to end on a strong note. Typically legal writers put the strongest argument first. The convention to start strong is so widespread that readers will think whatever you put first is your strongest point. Many writers would then follow with the next strongest argument, afraid that if the first two arguments failed to convince the judge, she might stop reading. When dealing with the weakest argument, some might put it last while others might decide to minimize its impact by burying it in the middle or eliminating it entirely. But because readers tend to remember more about what they read last, you'll need to end the section with a reminder of the strong arguments that best support your position.

And just as you'll use the points of emphasis in your favor, use the points of de-emphasis—the middle—in your favor. As noted, weaker arguments might be put in the middle or cut altogether (unless they are essential for your success). Similarly, you might address unfavorable precedent or unfavorable facts in the middle of paragraphs or sections.

You might wonder why you should include negative information at all in a persuasive document. The answer is that your opponent will include it, and you don't want the judge left with only the other side's explanation of those arguments, authorities, or facts. You want to do the best you can to minimize their negative effect. Anticipate the other side's arguments. You don't make their arguments for them, but you can't just leave them out. For suggestions on this topic, review Chapter 21 on Making Persuasive Counterarguments. In addition, lawyers are ethically bound to disclose binding, adverse authority when the opposing party fails to disclose it to the court.

Step 3: Follow these first two principles when drafting subsections and even paragraphs. Just as these principles—starting with a thesis statement and putting your strongest argument first—provide an effective, persuasive organization for your main arguments, they are effective for subsections within each argument. Begin each section with the point of that section by using strong thesis statements. Similarly, start each paragraph with the point of that paragraph. If you need a refresher on doing this, review Chapter 27 on Starting Paragraphs Powerfully.

Organizationally, put your strongest contention or subsection within each argument first (as that is where the judge will expect it). As noted above, the next strongest argument can go next or at the end. Similarly, at the paragraph level, start strong and make sure the last sentence is important and favorable.

Look at the first main argument in our cell phone manslaughter problem: King did not act with "gross negligence." Imagine you had these three main points to demonstrate that King's actions did not rise to the level of gross negligence:

1. King exercised due care, so the presumption of "conscious indifference to the consequences" is not present.
2. A "reasonable person" in King's position would not have been aware that placing the call posed a serious risk.
3. King was attempting to minimize—not disregard—the risk to others, and these unique circumstances negate gross negligence.

You'd frame each as a thesis statement, as these samples do. Then, you'd rank them in terms of strength. If you concluded that the strongest contention was #3 and the weakest was #1 (hence, leaving #2 as a reasonably strong point, but not as strong as #3), you might reorder them as follows:

3. King was attempting to minimize—not disregard—the risk to others, and these unique circumstances negate gross negligence.
1. King exercised due care, so the presumption of "conscious indifference to the consequences" is not present.
2. A "reasonable person" in King's position would not have been aware that placing the call posed a serious risk.

The paragraphs within each of these contentions would all begin with thesis statements and be ordered in the same persuasive way: They'd have a strong beginning (the thesis statement), include less favorable information, including counterarguments, in the middle, and then end on a strong note.

Imagine you're drafting a paragraph within contention #3—that King was attempting to minimize risk, so she couldn't have disregarded risk. As with all persuasive writing, you'd need to address counterarguments. Here, you might expect the prosecutor to argue that the risk created by King's friends driving is different and a lesser risk than the risk King created when she made a phone call while driving on a dangerous, narrow, cliff-side road in fog. The paragraph where you address that might be structured like this:

> King was attempting to minimize—not disregard—the risk to others, and these unique circumstances negate gross negligence. The purpose of King's call was to warn others that the road conditions were dangerous. Although placing the call may have created a different risk, the overall purpose of the call demonstrates King's actions were not grossly negligent. Rather, the circumstances of this case suggest just the opposite; King acted reasonably.

This same persuasive structure that works for addressing counterarguments with entire issues works for paragraphs as well. For additional suggestions on dealing with counterarguments, review Chapter 21 on Making Persuasive Counterarguments.

Step 4: At the sentence level, be sure to end strong and think about your stylistic options. Readers tend to read a clause or sentence as the story of whoever shows up first—that is, in the "topic" position. So use the sentence's beginning to frame that story. And remember that the final portion of the sentence will garner the most attention, so place the most important information there.

Think about this sentence:

King acted as carefully as any conscientious driver would in an emergency situation and not with "gross negligence."

This sentence is a story about King. Note how the sentence ends on a strong note: King did not act "with 'gross negligence.'" Furthermore, consider these two sentences:

Mary is a good student, even though she sometimes fails to conduct the deeper analysis.

Although Mary sometimes fails to conduct the deeper analysis, she is a good student.

Audiences are more likely to think the first sentence's Mary isn't as good of a student as the second sentence's Mary.[4] You can use the end of the sentence to make your point. Which Mary do you want the reader to know?

Stylistically, six particular considerations are worth mentioning.

Stylistic Considerations:

- sentence/paragraph length
- passive voice
- repetition
- level of detail
- word choice
- transitions

Each is discussed here.

Length: First, short sentences and paragraphs are more persuasive than longer ones. They draw more attention. And attention may equal persuasion.

Chances are the previous paragraph, and especially the final sentence, captured your attention. As tempted as you may be to say everything you can in one sentence, avoid that temptation if you want to emphasize your point. Simply state the point:

King called to warn others.

Passive Voice: Second, although style manuals generally encourage writers to use active voice, there's a time and place for passive voice. Active voice is shorter and generally easier to follow because the actor in the sentence does

---

4. *See generally* Joseph M. Williams & Gregory G. Colomb, *Style: Lessons in Clarity and Grace* 82-98 (10th ed. 2010).

the acting. But when your client has done something wrong, you may not want to explicitly point that out to the reader.

For instance, if Mr. Smith is your client, the following statement isn't very persuasive:

> Mr. Smith punched Mr. Cole.

Instead, you can omit the actor and minimize the damage to your client:

> Cole was punched.

Passive voice also makes sense when you want the reader to focus on the object of the sentence rather than the actor. For instance, if your point is that the defendant was arrested, you probably don't want to say "the police arrested the defendant."

You can also use non-action verbs to deflect attention away from your client. For instance, if King was your client, it would be more persuasive to state that King "placed the call" rather than "called." "Call," an action verb, presents a particular mental image that "place" doesn't, even though the sentences mean the same thing.

Repetition: Third, repeat or otherwise connect topics (the beginning of your sentences) to create cohesion. You can fill the topic position with information that links it to previous sentences and topics to transition the reader from the old to the new. Or you can fill the topic position with contextual information that looks forward. Either way, the reader will more easily move through your writing and understand how your various ideas are connected. Using the paragraph from Step 3 about King and the cell phone manslaughter problem, we might connect topics as follows:

> King was attempting to minimize—not disregard—the risk to others. King attempted to minimize the risk to others by calling to warn them that road conditions were dangerous.

Level of Detail: Fourth, use more detail to emphasize favorable information. As you might have guessed, readers remember material better when told with more detail. Conversely, they are more apt to forget information that is told with less detail. Therefore, spend more time on favorable arguments, on favorable points within those arguments, and on favorable facts. This doesn't mean you should be redundant. It just means you should be more detailed in your discussion of positive, rather than negative, information.

If you were prosecuting King for vehicular manslaughter, you'd likely want to include a lot of details (without going obviously overboard) showing the dangerous road conditions when King decided to make a call on her cell phone. Although these facts may help King to some extent in showing an emergency, they also show that placing a call was risky. And you'd start by identifying the features that were known about the road to show they weren't that unusual, although dangerous. You'd begin with a thesis statement, and then proceed with the facts:

> King was driving on California's State Highway 1, a road well known for its dangerous conditions. Highway 1 is a winding, narrow, two-lane highway. It sits on the edge of a cliff. The Pacific Ocean lies below the cliff, and Highway 1 offers very few places to pull over.
>
> Conditions were even more precarious than usual when King pulled out her non-hands-free cell phone and called her friend. King was driving at night, and visibility was inherently lessened. Most significantly, a dense fog was rolling in from the ocean, creating near-whiteout conditions.

Word Choice: Fifth, think about each word you use and whether it helps or hurts your case. Words create particular connotations. Although you can't stretch the truth or appear to be "playing" the judge, some words are more likely to help than others. For instance, imagine you represent a plaintiff suing her former employer for wrongful termination. Think about the persuasiveness of these sentences:

> Crawford diligently completed every task her employer assigned to her.

> Crawford diligently completed every project her employer assigned to her.

The words "task" and "project" might be used interchangeably, but one suggests minimal effort and the other implies substantially more work. Similarly, whether you call a company a "corporation" or "conglomeration" or "family business" may impact the reader's perception of that entity.

Transitions: Finally, help the reader. Connect concepts (when appropriate) by using helpful transitions. "Therefore," "however," "furthermore," "similarly," and other common transitions make your writing easier to follow. After all, your goal is to make it as easy as possible for the reader to agree with you, and adding transitions is a relatively simple step toward that goal. If you need a refresher on transitions and making your document flow more smoothly, you can review Chapter 29.

EXAMPLES

Here are some examples of making persuasive arguments. Some of the examples come from the copyright and fair use problem in Appendix B. For others you should be able to tell enough from the example to make a good choice. For each example, choose the best answer. Explain to yourself why you've chosen that answer. Then read the explanations in the last section of this chapter to check your work.

Example 20-1

The following is a draft outline of arguments.

1. The trial court lacked jurisdiction over the Defendant and hence the ruling for the Plaintiff should be reversed.
2. Reversal is proper because the Defendant acted in self-defense.
3. The case should be reversed because the Defendant did not injure the Plaintiff.
4. Reversal is proper because the Plaintiff consented to any contact between the Plaintiff and the Defendant and hence the Defendant is not liable for assault.

This is . . .

A. a persuasive structure only if point #4 is the strongest argument.
B. a persuasive structure only if point #1 is the strongest argument.
C. a persuasive structure even if point #2 is the strongest argument.
D. an unpersuasive structure because you should never make more than three main arguments.

Example 20-2

The "fair use" exception is claimed to permit the use of a portion of Young's lyrics. Olds seeks to parody Young's lyrics and criticizes Young's message of pacifism. This statutory defense, however, is unavailable to Olds. Instead, using Young's lyrics constitutes copyright infringement because the songs appeal to the same market. It is true, though, that the messages are different and that the point of Olds' song is to reflect positively on pride in America without taking a critical look at our nation's failures.

This paragraph is . . .

A. unpersuasive in a brief for Young because it fails to state his underlying legal claim.

B. unpersuasive in a brief for Young because it puts the negative information at the beginning and end rather than in the middle and the writing style emphasizes the wrong facts.

C. persuasive in a brief for Young because it asserts his copyright infringement claim.

D. persuasive in a brief for Young because it responds to Olds' fair use claim.

Example 20-3

Neil Young does not want Olds to use his lyrics. Young holds the copyright to "Rockin' in the Free World," and the song has been quite successful. Olds, though, is marketing his song "Stop Knockin' the Free World," obviously a copyright violation of Young's original song under the Copyright Act, which prohibits reproducing copyrighted works, like Young's song.

This paragraph is . . .

A. persuasive because it clearly states the legal argument—copyright infringement.

B. unpersuasive because it does not begin with a thesis statement.

C. persuasive because it includes details about Young's song, which will reinforce those facts to the reader.

D. unpersuasive because it should include more words like "obviously" and "clearly."

Example 20-4

Olds is not entitled to the "fair use" exception to the general ban on reproducing copyrighted material. 17 U.S.C. § 107 (2006). Olds uses Young's music without any alteration. Furthermore, Olds uses over 80 percent of Young's lyrics. Although parody may constitute a fair use of copyrighted material, Olds' extensive use here goes beyond what is permitted to create a parody. Hence, Olds cannot rely on the exception for fair use.

This paragraph is . . .

A. unpersuasive because it addresses the counterargument that parody can constitute fair use.

B. unpersuasive because it does not begin with a thesis statement.

C. persuasive because it includes a percentage, and numbers are always persuasive.

D. persuasive because it focuses on Olds' wrongdoing and frames fair use as an exception to the general rule that prohibits reproducing copyrighted material, although it would be stronger if it used case law to support the argument.

Example 20-5

Williams did not see the victim until just before Williams smashed into him with his large SUV.

This sentence is . . .

A. unpersuasive in a brief for Williams because it uses active voice and poor word choice.

B. unpersuasive in a brief for Williams because it does not indicate the model of his SUV.

C. persuasive in a brief for Williams because it includes details of the incident.

D. persuasive in a brief for Williams because it's short and to the point.

EXPLANATIONS

Explanation 20-1

A is incorrect. Although the end is the place of highest emphasis, legal readers expect your strongest argument first, not last. Hence, saving your best argument for last is generally not an effective persuasive technique. **B** is also incorrect. It's true you should generally start with your strongest argument. But in this case, there's a threshold issue—jurisdiction—and courts often expect you to lead with that argument even if it isn't your strongest claim. **C** is correct. For the reasons stated in B, beginning with a procedural or other threshold issue is still a persuasive structure. You would then follow that argument with your strongest substantive claim. **D** is incorrect. The number of arguments will depend on the number of colorable claims. You shouldn't create a full argument for every minor point, but you shouldn't artificially limit the number of claims, either.

Explanation 20-2

A is incorrect. The paragraph does state Young's underlying copyright infringement claim, but it downplays that claim by burying it in the middle of the paragraph. **B** is correct. As noted in A, the favorable information to Young—his copyright claim—is buried in the middle. The paragraph starts and ends with information favorable to Olds, and those positions of emphasis should not be used for negative information. The paragraph also uses passive voice where active voice would highlight what Olds has done: "use" Young's lyrics (note "the use of Young's lyrics" in the first sentence contains no actor). Similarly, it uses active voice ("Olds seeks to parody Young's lyrics") where passive voice might be more effective. **C** is incorrect. Although it states the legal claim, burying it mid-paragraph is not very effective. **D** is incorrect for the reasons stated in B. Although you should respond to anticipated arguments, this paragraph emphasizes them rather than refuting them. See Chapter 21 for more help with Making Persuasive Counterarguments.

Explanation 20-3

A is incorrect. The paragraph does state that Olds' song is "obviously a copyright violation," but that statement does not make the paragraph persuasive. First, the reference to the copyright violation is buried in the middle of the paragraph. In addition, subtlety persuades more than bluntness. Terms like "obviously" and "clearly" actually detract from, rather than increase, persuasiveness. **B** is correct. The first sentence of the paragraph introduces the two parties, but it does not assert a thesis. It simply states what our client "wants," and that is rarely persuasive to a court (or to anyone else, for that matter). **C** is incorrect. This paragraph includes almost none of the actual facts. It includes broad characterizations, which are far less memorable. **D** is incorrect for the reasons stated in A.

Explanation 20-4

A is incorrect. To be persuasive, you need to address counterarguments. You should address them persuasively, but ignoring them will not strengthen your case. **B** is also incorrect. This paragraph begins with a thesis statement, and the paragraph develops that thesis. **C** is incorrect. Numbers or other facts can be helpful, but they aren't always necessary or even relevant. In addition, if the numbers aren't helpful, leave them out unless you need to refute them in some way. **D** is correct. This paragraph is generally persuasive, although as noted, comparisons to the case law would make it stronger.

Explanation 20-5

A is correct. Active voice is generally preferred, but when your client has behaved badly or you want to minimize her actions, use passive voice. In addition, the word choice is poor. Identifying the person Williams hit as the "victim" suggests Williams was an intentional perpetrator, and that is not an image Williams wants the court to have. Saying Williams "smashed" into the victim is also not helpful, and calling his vehicle a "large SUV" is probably also not the image of this incident that it makes sense for Williams to create. **B** is incorrect. Adding that information would only exacerbate the problems identified in A. **C** is also incorrect. Although related to the point in B, fewer details de-emphasize the material. **D** is incorrect. Short sentences can have more impact, but for the reasons in A, this sentence is unpersuasive in a brief for Williams.

21

Making Persuasive Counterarguments

Puzzled about how to make your paper stronger? One way is to think of arguments and counterarguments as two jigsaw puzzle pieces that fit together. That's because one side's strongest argument is often the other side's weakest argument. And if you ignore your weaknesses, you'll give the other side a clear shot at influencing how a decision maker will view that part of the argument. So although it may seem paradoxical, you can strengthen your argument by addressing its weak points.

Counterarguments are important because you want the court to know why those weaknesses shouldn't prevent it from ruling in your favor. Often you can strengthen your position by pointing out specific flaws in your opponent's arguments. In short, make counterarguments in two situations: (1) when you can anticipate and weaken strong arguments from the other side or address the court's likely concerns; and (2) when you're writing a brief responding to the other side and you have the opportunity to directly point out specific, significant flaws in the other side's arguments.

WHAT YOU NEED TO KNOW ABOUT MAKING PERSUASIVE COUNTERARGUMENTS

A counterargument is usually more persuasive when it's framed as part of the brief's affirmative argument, rather than as a digression that labels itself as a counterargument. This is called "anticipating" the counterargument. For instance, instead of saying "The defendant may argue that it gave the employee written warnings, but these were insufficient because . . . ," rephrase your point to sound like part of your own affirmative argument: "Although the employee received written warnings, they concerned only her attire and not the type of conduct which her employer ultimately cited as the cause for firing her." This phrasing emphasizes why a potential weakness is not convincing and the phrasing avoids emphasizing the opposing argument itself.

When brainstorming possible counterarguments, consider these commonly used techniques. Common ways to counter an opposing argument include showing that it's based on:

- an incorrect or incomplete view of the facts;
- an incorrect or incomplete view of the law;
- case law that is distinguishable from the case at hand;
- a misapplication of the law to the facts; and
- flawed reasoning or policy arguments.

Put your best arguments first, and then make your counterarguments. Most brief writers put their strongest arguments first because most readers expect them first. Your counterarguments, by their nature, usually aren't your strongest arguments even when you phrase them as an affirmative argument, so most writers wouldn't lead with them.

Be careful about using more space to address counterarguments than the arguments you planned for your side. You'll likely weaken the overall impression that the reader gets from your brief if you spend too much "air time" in your brief addressing defensive points.

Don't make arguments for the other side. Anticipating counterarguments in your brief should generally be limited to points that you think the other side will very likely raise, that the court will be concerned with, and that you can neutralize relatively well. For instance, whenever you see obvious weaknesses in your own arguments, you should preemptively address them. But be careful to only raise those points that will likely concern the court or arguments that the other side is likely to actually raise. Don't score points for the other side! If you're writing a reply brief in response to the other side's brief, then this is less of a concern because you have seen what the other side has actually argued.

Don't nitpick or create weak arguments just to shoot them down. You usually don't have enough space in the brief to devote time to anticipating weak or silly arguments the other side probably won't make. It makes you look petty or too willing to squabble over irrelevant issues.

HOW TO MAKE PERSUASIVE COUNTERARGUMENTS

Using the cell phone manslaughter problem in Appendix A, we'll walk through the process of making persuasive counterarguments. The first two steps explore identifying counterarguments the other side is likely to make. The final four steps address anticipating those arguments persuasively in your writing.

Problem

> Here is a quick overview of the cell phone manslaughter problem. Allison King used her wireless phone, without a hands-free device, while driving in dense fog on a winding road on the edge of an ocean cliff. King placed the call to warn her friends about the dangerous conditions, as they would be meeting later. While she was making the call, she hit and killed a bicyclist. The prosecution will attempt to convict King of vehicular manslaughter by showing that she drove while committing an illegal act (driving while using a wireless phone without a hands-free device) and with gross negligence. King will argue that her actions fit within the emergency exception to the wireless phone prohibition. She will also argue that she did not act with gross negligence.

Step 1: Put yourself in the other side's shoes. Some students become so engaged with the arguments for their side that they find it a struggle to see the other side at all. It's natural to identify with your client and to want her to win. But that tendency can blind you to your side's weaknesses.

If you're having difficulty putting yourself in the other side's shoes, make a list of your weaknesses because your weaknesses will usually be their strengths. Do you have any "bad" or undesirable facts? Is the lack of a fact making it hard for you to make an argument? Are there precedents you wish weren't out there? Answering these questions will uncover your weaknesses.

To apply some of these questions to King's problem, you might start with whether you wish any of the facts had been different:

> It would be better for King if it had been impossible for her to pull her car over before calling her friends.

Next, ask if any facts that are lacking make your argument tougher. Once again, you find a situation you wish were different:

> The facts are silent about exactly when King's friends would be on the road. It might even be possible that they were ahead of King, because the facts just say

that the group of friends planned to meet at a town on this road. Then her call would have been pointless for the purpose of warning them of the dangerous conditions.

The facts are also silent about whether her friends could have learned of the dangerous road conditions without the use of a cell phone. It would also be better for King if it was clear that her phone call was the only way her friends might learn of the potential problem.

Viewing these weaknesses as a strength for the State might look like this:

> King's situation was not a true emergency because it is possible that her friends had already driven on the foggy highway.
>
> King's situation was not a true emergency because a reasonable person would expect her friends to check road conditions before starting out.

Step 2: Identify the other side's arguments. Once you've put yourself in the other side's shoes and can see the weaknesses in your side, figure out what the corresponding arguments will be for the other side. One way to do that is to reread the facts and cases through your opponent's eyes. What are your opponent's strongest arguments? What will your opponent emphasize, whether facts or law? How will your opponent likely respond to your arguments?

To identify counterarguments in the cell phone problem, review the facts and law. First the facts: Allison King used her wireless phone, without a hands-free device, while driving on a winding road on the edge of a cliff over the ocean in dense fog. Her purpose was to warn her friends, who would soon be following her up the road, about the dangerous conditions. And now the law: One way of convicting King of vehicular manslaughter is to prove that she drove while committing an illegal act. Because it's illegal to use a wireless phone without a hands-free device unless the situation is an emergency, the State will try to prove that King's situation was not an emergency and King will try to prove that it is.

Suppose you're King's lawyer. You've made a strong argument that King's situation was an emergency because her concern about the physical safety of her friends was justifiable, since she knew her friends were likely to be driving over the same dangerous road very soon. You've compared your case to the *Newton* precedent in which the court found an emergency when a husband driving his wife to the hospital called his wife's specialist who had been caring for her throughout her high-risk pregnancy. And you've distinguished King's situation from the *Tompkins* case, in which the court found that a driver's concern about the safety of his family after danger had passed—an earthquake had already occurred—was not a genuine emergency. So, how can you lose?

Start by looking more closely at the cases. As you read *Newton* you see that although the appellate court found an emergency, the trial court had stated that the husband could have pulled over to make the call. The appellate court rejected that argument because a reasonable person would not want to pull over while his wife was in labor and they were on the way to a hospital. If you read *Newton* through the eyes of the prosecutor, you see that the prosecutor could argue that in *Newton* the time it would take to pull over might further endanger the pregnant woman. But King would not further endanger her friends by taking a minute or two to pull over. And that's one of the State's likely arguments:

> King's situation does not fall under the emergency exception because she could have waited to use one of the pull-offs provided.

Step 3: Evaluate whether your adversary is likely to raise the arguments you've identified, whether a court would be concerned with them, and whether your response lessens their sting. Decide what is worth including in your brief. Consider whether you're writing an opening brief or reply brief and whether you'll have a chance to later respond.

Here, representing King, you might decide that the strongest argument the State would probably make is that King could have pulled over, instead of continuing to drive, while calling. The State is likely to raise this argument, and a court will likely be concerned about this claim. The only remaining question is whether your brief will reduce that concern.

Step 4: Generate a response to the likely opposing argument. What are your best responses to arguments about your weaknesses? Why are they not fatal to your success? If you get stuck while brainstorming, consider the list of common ways to counter an opposing argument. Here, you can say that it's an incomplete view of the facts: The facts say that there were few places to pull off the road, that it was difficult to see, and they give no indication that King had an option to pull off.

Step 5: When writing a persuasive document, respond to the counterargument by anticipating it and not by making it for the other side. Phrase the counterarguments as part of your affirmative argument. Here, instead of saying "the State may argue" or "the State's argument X must fail because," just turn your response into an affirmative argument.

Here is a bad example. Instead of writing this:

> The State may contend that King could have pulled off the road to make a wireless call. King answers, however, that the road she was driving on had few places to pull off and furthermore it was foggy and she probably could not see them. She was not able to pull off.

You could avoid making the other side's argument and state your argument in the affirmative:

> Further, unlike cases in which a driver can pull off the road to make a wireless phone call, the road upon which King was driving had few places in which to pull over and the dense fog likely prevented her from seeing them. Pulling over to make the call was not an option for King.

Step 6: Check that you have not overemphasized or given too much "air time" to the opposing arguments. Note how the previous paragraph anticipates the other side's argument in just a short paragraph. Remember as well to lead with your own strongest arguments. That's the way to win.

EXAMPLES

Here are some examples concerning counterarguments. Most are based on the copyright and fair use problem in Appendix B. Some examples might have more than one correct answer. Explain to yourself why you've chosen your answers. Then read the explanations in the last section of this chapter to check your work.

Problem

> Here is a quick overview of the copyright and fair use problem. Young is suing Olds for violating the Copyright Act when Olds wrote a song based on Young's original, "Rockin' in the Free World." Olds' song uses the structure and many lyrics of the original but changes the original song's political message. The music of the two songs is not at issue, only the lyrics. Young expects that Olds will argue that his song is a parody that falls under the fair use exception to the Copyright Act. The court will consider the relevant factors set out in the fair use statute, 17 U.S.C. § 107 (2006): whether the copy was transformative and targeted the original; whether it took more than necessary of the original; and whether it will interfere with the original's market.

Example 21-1

Regarding the first factor, "the purpose and character of the use," Young expects that Olds will argue that his song is a parody that transforms the original song and that therefore that factor favors Olds. Young wants to anticipate this argument. Which of the following presents the most persuasive counterargument?

A. Olds argues that the factor weighs in his favor because his song is a parody that transforms the original's meaning from criticizing America to praising America. But the original song, although critical of America, has been used as a patriotic anthem supporting America at rallies after the September 11th tragedies.

B. Both songs are patriotic because both songs have been played at patriotic rallies.

C. Olds will likely assert that his song transforms the meaning of the original because it has a different viewpoint. However, both songs are political rock songs.

D. Young's song is a political statement that has several levels of meaning. This makes it nearly impossible to "transform" the song by choosing one meaning to parody.

Example 21-2

Regarding the second factor, "the nature of the copyrighted work," courts have often ignored it in cases involving parody, because parodies "almost invariably copy publicly known, expressive works." Consider the following statements about how Olds might make a counterargument about this factor.

A. Olds' counterargument should read: "Although courts usually do not apply this factor in parody cases, Young will argue that the court should apply it in this case. This argument will fail because precedent supports that the courts usually do not weigh this factor."

B. Olds should not waste space addressing this argument. He should deal with the factor in the introduction to the Argument section of the brief.

C. Olds should address this argument because there are four factors and there should be an argument and counterargument for each.

D. Olds' counterargument should read: "Young contends that this factor weighs in his favor. This factor, however, is not important in parody cases."

Example 21-3

Regarding the third factor, "the amount and substantiality of the portion used," Olds adopted the structure of the song and some of the lyrics. He will maintain, however, that the facts show it was a small amount of copying that was necessary for listeners to identify the song he was parodying. Consider how Young should respond:

A. Young should not respond because he should not bring the court's attention to his opponent's strong arguments.

B. "Any argument that Olds had to copy as much of 'Rockin' in the Free World' as he did must fail. Young's song is so well known that even the smallest reference to it would be recognized."

C. "Olds' argument that he needed to copy so much of the song is weak. Young's argument is much stronger and this Court should reject Olds' contention."

D. "The facts do not support the conclusion that Olds took only what was necessary to identify the target of the parody, because Olds took the entire structure of Young's song without changing enough lyrics."

Example 21-4

Regarding the fourth factor, "the effect of the use of the copy on potential markets," Olds is likely to rely on *Campbell* where the Court concluded that rappers and country western singers appeal to different markets. Consider which of these counterarguments for Young are most effective.

A. "In response to Olds' argument analogizing to the facts in *Campbell*, our case is different. In our case, Olds is likely to interfere with Young's market because Olds' song is the same type as Young's."

B. "Olds' reliance on *Campbell* is misplaced. This case is unlike *Campbell* because there the songs were performed in different genres and here both songs are rock songs with political messages."

C. "Further, in contrast to *Campbell* where the two songs were different genres, here both songs are in the rock music genre and the change in lyrics is so slight that music buyers may confuse the two songs."

D. "Under *Campbell*, Olds' copy will interfere with Young's market."

EXPLANATIONS

Explanation 21-1

A is less persuasive because its phrasing first makes Olds' argument. It also presents Young's argument defensively instead of affirmatively as part of Young's own argument. *B* is a pretty good start, but it's not yet a strong counterargument because it isn't clear how it's tied to the issue of whether Olds' song transformed Young's original. *C* has the same problem as A because it makes the other side's argument before answering it. *D* does the best job of anticipating the counterargument without making the other side's argument.

Explanation 21-2

A is not persuasive. It's a good example of wasting space to address a weak opposing argument. Most good writers would handle this factor by explaining that it's "not in dispute" in the introduction to the Argument section of the brief. *B* is therefore the most correct. If the other side has only a very weak argument on a factor, neither side will want to spend space or time addressing it. Both will most likely dispose of it in the introduction. *C* is wrong because often some part of a rule is not at issue. In those instances, you can usually use the introduction to tell the reader why it's not addressed. *D* is incorrect because it wastes space setting out a contention Young will probably not make.

Explanation 21-3

A is incorrect. When the other side has a strong argument, it's important to address it or else you will let the other side be the only voice the court hears on the issue. *B* has the common problem of making the argument before answering it. *C* is a weak counterargument because it doesn't tell why one argument is stronger than another. *D* is a better counterargument. It illustrates how you might make an affirmative counterargument by showing how the facts do not support the other side's position.

Explanation 21-4

A is incorrect because it announces itself as a counterargument by stating "in response to Young's argument." That wastes words and weakens the argument. **B** is a good counterargument that illustrates making a counterargument by showing how the other side has misread the law. This might work well in a reply brief. **C** is also a strong counterargument because it anticipates Olds' position and refutes it. **D** is weak as either an argument or counterargument because it doesn't say why the copy will interfere with the original's market.

CHAPTER 22

Writing the Summary of the Argument

"You never get a second chance to make a first impression." This old saying illustrates what we all know: First impressions count, whether formed when meeting a new person or reading a new brief. For many readers, first impressions of a brief are formed while reading the Summary of the Argument. You can make a good first impression if you rely on a few simple rules about writing this important section of your brief.

WHAT YOU NEED TO KNOW ABOUT WRITING THE SUMMARY OF THE ARGUMENT

Begin with an introductory paragraph that sets out a thesis statement and the rules that apply to the whole brief. If one of the parts of the rule will not be in dispute, let the reader know. Keep it as short as you can.

Write only one or two paragraphs for each main issue in the brief. The Summary of the Argument should be concise and not include the details of your Argument. Often one paragraph per main point is adequate.

Don't forget to write as an advocate: Using a thesis sentence to start each paragraph is especially important in the Summary of the Argument. Effective paragraphs in this section often start with an assertion about how the rule applies to your problem. These strong paragraph-thesis sentences combine to persuasively outline your argument. See Chapter 27 on

Starting Paragraphs Powerfully for hints on writing strong thesis sentences to start each paragraph.

After the paragraph-thesis sentence, most paragraphs in the Summary of the Argument simply state a rule and then use a few sentences to explain how the rule applies. No need for explaining the rule by describing precedent or making analogies. Omit citations unless a statute or key case is central to your position. Similarly, omit weaker arguments. Anticipate counterarguments rarely and only when they are unusually strong. Just state a rule, choose your strongest argument about this issue or sub-issue, and make the argument succinctly in a sentence or two.

Although the Summary of the Argument is one of the first sections of the brief, authors often draft it after they have finished the Argument section. You won't really know which arguments are your best until you've made them. After you've made your arguments and can evaluate them is often the best time to write the Summary of the Argument. If you instead draft your Summary of the Argument before you finish writing the Argument section, go back later and revise to be sure it is, in fact, a "summary" of the Argument you actually wrote.

HOW TO WRITE THE SUMMARY OF THE ARGUMENT

Using the cell phone manslaughter problem in Appendix A, we'll walk you through the process of writing a Summary of the Argument for the State.

Problem

> Here is a quick overview of the cell phone manslaughter problem. Allison King used her wireless phone, without a hands-free device, while driving in dense fog on a winding road on the edge of an ocean cliff. King placed the call to warn her friends about the dangerous conditions, as they would be meeting later. While she was making the call, she hit and killed a bicyclist. The prosecution will attempt to convict King of vehicular manslaughter by showing that she drove while committing an illegal act (driving while using a wireless phone without a hands-free device) and with gross negligence. King will argue that her actions fit within the emergency exception to the wireless phone prohibition. She will also argue that she did not act with gross negligence.

Step 1: Start by writing an introductory paragraph that sets out a thesis and the rules that apply to the whole brief. Begin with a thesis statement:

> King is guilty of vehicular manslaughter because she hit and killed a cyclist while using her cell phone without a hands-free device on a dangerous road during hazardous driving conditions.

Then set out the rules. The State is seeking to convict Allison King based on two statutes, so you'd set those out:

> California's vehicular manslaughter statute, Penal Code § 192(c)(1), holds accountable those drivers who drive "a vehicle in the commission of an unlawful act, not amounting to felony, and with gross negligence." Additionally, California Vehicle Code § 23123 declares it an unlawful act to "drive a motor vehicle while using a wireless telephone unless that telephone is specifically designed and configured to allow hands-free listening and talking, and is used in that manner while driving" unless an exception applies.

Setting out the two statutes is not complete, but the paragraph is growing lengthy. You might start a new paragraph to explain the exception. And then end the introductory section by stating the outcome you advocate.

> Further, King cannot escape culpability under the exception to the prohibition on using a cell phone without a hands-free device because she was not "a person using a wireless telephone for emergency purposes, including, but not limited to, an emergency call to a law enforcement agency, health care provider, fire department, or other emergency services agency or entity." § 23123. King is therefore guilty because (1) it was not an emergency and (2) she was driving with gross negligence in treacherous conditions. Her conviction for vehicular manslaughter should therefore be upheld.

Step 2: Once the general introduction is complete, summarize your argument on the first main issue in one or two short paragraphs. Usually, you'll follow the same organization of issues that you used in the Argument. Here that means you should address driving "a vehicle in the commission of an unlawful act" before gross negligence. You'll start the paragraph with a thesis statement on that issue—why King doesn't meet the exception—and then state the rule. So the beginning of the one or two paragraphs of the Summary of the Argument devoted to that section of your brief might look like this:

> First, King violated California law prohibiting the use of a wireless phone while driving, unless that phone is used with a hands-free device, and she does not meet the "emergency purposes" exception. California Vehicle Code § 23123 makes driving a car while using a wireless phone without a hands-free listening device an unlawful act, unless the person is using the wireless phone for "emergency purposes, including, but not limited to, an emergency call to a law enforcement agency, health care provider, fire department, or other emergency

services agency or entity." An emergency purpose exists only if there is a threat of imminent danger.

Then, you'll summarize your facts, bringing together the argument. Again you'll want to start the paragraph with a strong thesis statement:

> No emergency purpose existed here because King's friends were not threatened with imminent danger. King placed the call to advise her friends, whom she was to meet that day, that driving conditions were dangerous. King could have waited for an opportunity to pull over and make the call when it was safe, and legal, to do so. There is no indication that her call would have prevented any danger or that the friends were driving on or near the same stretch of road at the time King placed the call.

Step 3: Repeat the same process for each main argument, summarizing your points in one or two short paragraphs. After addressing the wireless phone statute and its exception, you'll turn to the second argument: that King acted with gross negligence. Remember to begin with a thesis statement, then the rule, and then apply that rule, very briefly, to your facts.

> Second, King acted with gross negligence. Courts use an objective test to determine gross negligence: whether a reasonable person in the defendant's position would be aware of the risk involved. King called her friend to advise her of the dangerous driving conditions. This demonstrates her appreciation of the risks involved in making the call. She knew driving in the dense fog on a winding road on the side of a cliff was dangerous. But King chose to place a call on her cell phone. King therefore acted with gross negligence.

Step 4: Finally, end on a strong note by stating your conclusion or your desired result. Should the court affirm the lower court? Reverse?

> Hence, King drove while committing an unlawful act, unexcused by emergency circumstance, and she was grossly negligent. King's conviction for vehicular manslaughter should be affirmed.

Putting it together, the Summary of the Argument might look like this:

> King is guilty of vehicular manslaughter because she hit and killed a cyclist while using her cell phone without a hands-free device on a dangerous road during hazardous driving conditions. California's vehicular manslaughter statute, Penal Code § 192(c)(1), holds accountable those drivers who drive "a vehicle in the commission of an unlawful act, not amounting to felony, and with gross negligence." Additionally, California Vehicle Code § 23123 declares it an unlawful act to "drive a motor vehicle while using a wireless telephone unless

that telephone is specifically designed and configured to allow hands-free listening and talking, and is used in that manner while driving," unless an exception applies.

Further, King cannot escape culpability under the exception to the prohibition on using a cell phone without a hands-free device because she was not "a person using a wireless telephone for emergency purposes, including, but not limited to, an emergency call to a law enforcement agency, health care provider, fire department, or other emergency services agency or entity." Cal. Vehicle Code § 23123 (West Supp. 2011). King is therefore guilty because (1) it was not an emergency and (2) she was driving with gross negligence in treacherous conditions. Her conviction for vehicular manslaughter should therefore be upheld.

First, King violated California law prohibiting the use of a wireless phone while driving, unless that phone is used with a hands-free device, and she does not meet the "emergency purposes" exception. California Vehicle Code § 23123 makes driving a car while using a wireless phone without a hands-free listening device an unlawful act, unless the person is using the wireless phone for "emergency purposes." An emergency purpose exists only if there is a threat of imminent danger.

No emergency purpose existed here because King's friends were not threatened with imminent danger. King placed the call to advise her friends, whom she was to meet that day, that driving conditions were dangerous. King could have waited for an opportunity to pull over and make the call when it was safe, and legal, to do so. There is no indication that her call would have prevented any danger or that the friends were driving on or near the same stretch of road at the time King placed the call.

Second, King acted with gross negligence. Courts use an objective test to determine gross negligence: whether a reasonable person in the defendant's position would be aware of the risk involved. King called her friend to advise her of the dangerous driving conditions. This demonstrates her appreciation of the risks involved in making the call. She knew driving in the dense fog on a winding road on the side of a cliff was dangerous. But King chose to place a call on her cell phone. King therefore acted with gross negligence.

Hence, King drove while committing an unlawful act, unexcused by emergency circumstance, and she was grossly negligent. King's conviction for vehicular manslaughter should be affirmed.

EXAMPLES

Here is an example of a Summary of the Argument for Olds using the copyright and fair use problem in Appendix B. For each question, more than one answer may be correct. Explain to yourself why you've chosen your answers. Then read the explanations in the last section of this chapter to check your work.

Problem

> Here is a quick overview of the copyright and fair use problem. Young is suing Olds for violating the Copyright Act when Olds wrote a song based on Young's original, "Rockin' in the Free World." Olds' song uses the structure and many lyrics of the original but changes the original song's political message. The music of the two songs is not at issue, only the lyrics. Young expects that Olds will argue that his song is a parody that falls under the fair use exception to the Copyright Act. The court will consider the relevant factors set out in the fair use statute, 17 U.S.C. § 107 (2006): whether the copy was transformative and targeted the original; whether it took more than necessary of the original; and whether it will interfere with the original's market.

Summary of the Argument

Olds' use of Young's original work was fair use. The fair use statute sets out a four-factor test to determine whether the use of copyrighted material is allowed. It requires the court to weigh: (1) the purpose and character of use, including whether use is of a commercial nature or for profit; (2) the nature of the copyrighted work; (3) the amount and substantiality of the portion used in relation to the copyrighted work as whole; and (4) the effect of the use upon potential market for value of copyrighted work. 17 U.S.C. § 107 (2006). The second factor is not in dispute, as both sides agree that the work in question is a copyrighted creative work.

Under the first factor, Olds' work criticized and transformed Young's song from an anti-war anthem that criticized Western society into a pro-Western song that directly counters Young's original message. The Court has found that such transformation satisfies the elements of a parody, a use allowed under the first factor.

Olds copied only the amount and substance he needed to successfully parody the original. The statute requires the court to consider the "amount and substantiality" the copyist took. Olds did take a substantial portion of the structure of Young's song to create his parody. However, he took less than a third of the words and only the material he needed to provide a direct point-by-point attack on the original. This factor favors Olds because the strong element of parody in Olds' work justifies the amount of material he took under the third factor of the statute.

Finally, it is unlikely that a Neil Young fan, some of whom have listened to his records for decades, will find Olds' song a satisfactory substitute for the original. Just as the rappers' market was different from the country western market in *Campbell*, the market for Olds' song is also a different genre of music. Olds' song may decrease the demand for the original, but only because of its critical nature, an effect the fourth factor allows. Because the new work satisfies the criteria included in the four-factor test, the Court should find it was fair use and Olds is not liable for copyright infringement.

Example 22-1

This example involves the first paragraph of the Summary, the introductory paragraph:

> Olds' use of Young's original work was fair use. The fair use statute sets out a four-factor test to determine whether the use of copyrighted material is allowed. It requires the court to weigh (1) the purpose and character of use, including whether use is of a commercial nature or for profit, (2) the nature of the copyrighted work, (3) the amount and substantiality of the portion used in relation to the copyrighted work as whole, and (4) the effect of the use upon potential market for value of copyrighted work. 17 U.S.C. § 107 (2006). The second factor is not in dispute, as both sides agree that the work in question is a copyrighted creative work.

This Summary's introductory paragraph is . . .

A. strong because it begins with a thesis statement.
B. weak because it analyzes factor two before factor one.
C. strong because it sets out the rule.
D. not very persuasive even though it starts with a thesis statement.

Example 22-2

This example involves the second paragraph of the Summary, the paragraph about the first factor, whether the copy transforms and targets the original:

> Under the first factor, Olds' work criticized and transformed Young's song from an anti-war anthem that criticized Western society into a pro-Western song that directly counters Young's original message. The Court has found that such transformation satisfies the elements of a parody, a use allowed under the first factor.

This paragraph . . .

A. is concise and complete.

B. starts with a thesis statement.

C. is not as strong as it could be because it doesn't state the rule that governs this factor.

D. applies the law to the facts of the problem (although the paragraph might have faults).

Example 22-3

This example involves the third paragraph of the Summary, the paragraph about the third factor—the amount and substantiality the copyist takes from the original:

> Olds copied only the amount and substance he needed to successfully parody the original. The statute requires the court to consider the "amount and substantiality" the copyist took. Olds did take a substantial portion of the structure of Young's song to create his parody. However, he took less than a third of the words and only the material he needed to provide a direct point-by-point attack on the original. This factor favors Olds because the strong element of parody in Olds' work justifies the amount of material he took under the third factor of the statute.

This paragraph . . .

A. starts with a strong thesis statement.

B. states the rule that governs the factor.

C. applies the law to the facts of the problem.

D. ends strongly by telling the court how to weigh the factor.

Example 22-4

This example involves the fourth paragraph of the Summary, the paragraph about the fourth factor, whether the copy will interfere with the original's market:

> Finally, it is unlikely that a Neil Young fan, some of whom have listened to his records for decades, will find Olds' song a satisfactory substitute for the original. Just as the rappers' market was different from the country western market in *Campbell*, the market for Olds' song is also a different genre of music. Olds' song may decrease the

demand for the original, but only because of its critical nature, an effect the fourth factor allows. Because the new work satisfies the criteria included in the four-factor test, the Court should find it was fair use and Olds is not liable for copyright infringement.

A. This paragraph begins with a strong thesis statement.
B. Although this paragraph doesn't state the rule from the statute, it states the rule by comparing the case at hand to an important precedent case.
C. This paragraph applies the law to the facts of the problem.
D. As the last paragraph in the Summary, this paragraph appropriately identifies the decision it wants the court to reach.

EXPLANATIONS

Explanation 22-1

A is correct in that it's good to start with a thesis statement. This thesis statement might be stronger if it included facts or more of the main reason supporting Olds' claim of fair use. **B** is incorrect. It's just fine to explain why one of the factors will not be in play. Although you ordinarily don't cite to cases in the Summary of the Argument, you might provide a citation for this assertion. **C** is correct. When a rule governs the entire issue, it's helpful to include it in the introductory paragraph of the Summary of the Argument. This example does so with the four-factor fair use test. **D** is correct. This example could be more persuasive by briefly stating that the relevant factors all favor Olds.

Explanation 22-2

A is incorrect. Although the paragraph is concise and has good points, it's not complete. It needs a thesis statement and a rule. **B** is incorrect. The first sentence tells how the rule applies to the facts, but it's not a thesis statement for this factor. A good thesis statement for this factor would be: "The first factor weighs in Olds' favor because he targeted Young's work and transformed it." **C** is correct. The paragraph should contain the rule governing the first factor. **D** is correct. The first sentence uses the problem's facts persuasively.

Explanation 22-3

A is correct. *B* is correct. *C* is correct. *D* is correct. This is an example of a good paragraph addressing one of the issues in a Summary of the Argument.

Explanation 22-4

A is incorrect. The paragraph starts by applying the law to the facts, without telling the reader about the law. *B* is incorrect. The sentence making an analogy to *Campbell* is not appropriate in a Summary of the Argument because the reader may know nothing about the precedent case. Further, you would not want to take the space in the Summary of the Argument to set out what the reader would need to know about that precedent to understand the comparison. *C* is correct. The author does apply the law to the facts of our problem. *D* is correct. As the last sentence of the entire section, this final sentence tells the court the precise outcome the author desires.

Writing a Persuasive
Fact Statement

A judge learns the facts from the Fact Statement of a trial court memo or appellate brief. In the movie *Amistad*—about a civil rights case involving Africans kidnapped into slavery—a group supporting them sends an emissary to ask the advice of John Quincy Adams, an eminent lawyer and former president. Adams responds that "*in a courtroom whoever tells the best story wins.*" Telling the client's story well is an important part of persuasive writing.

Terminology Notes: In some jurisdictions, this section is called the "Statement of Facts." In others, it's the "Statement of the Case." You should use the term in your textbook or in the applicable court rules. In this chapter, however, we'll refer to it simply as the Fact Statement. Most legal writers begin the Fact Statement by setting the context with the facts most favorable to their clients. We will call the paragraph that does this the "introductory statement."

WHAT YOU NEED TO KNOW ABOUT PERSUASIVE FACT STATEMENTS

Sound arguments alone are often not enough to persuade. You also need a good story. In persuasive writing, arguments and the story work together. Neither would persuade without the other.

Use the Fact Statement to tell a compelling story that motivates the court to rule for your client. If a judge is left with no desire, on a human level, to decide in your client's favor, it's hard to win. You need both: a compelling story and convincing arguments.

In the Fact Statement, tell the story. Don't analyze it or argue it. In the Argument, you persuade by telling the reader what you want her to believe, and then by explaining logically why she should believe it. But in a Fact Statement, only *state* the facts. Analyze them in the Argument.

How can you persuade in the Fact Statement if you're not allowed to argue there? *Tell the story in a compelling way.* Emphasize aspects of the story that would motivate a court to rule in your favor. Juxtapose favorable and unfavorable aspects of the story so the favorable outweigh the unfavorable. In this chapter, we'll show you how.

To write a good Fact Statement, you need to overcome the misconception that arguing is everything. Many law students are under the impression that the only way lawyers persuade is to make arguments. It's possible to influence the reader without making an argument. In the Fact Statement, that's your job.

Many students write a Fact Statement that's unpersuasive because it doesn't have a point of view. A teacher instantly recognizes this deficiency and might tell the student, "I can't tell from this Fact Statement whom you represent. It's a neutral telling of the story." If your teacher says something like this, you might be tempted, in a later draft, to start slipping argument into the Fact Statement. If you do that, your teacher will object—properly—to argument in a Fact Statement.

You might think that you have only two possibilities—either argue or tell a neutral story—with no ground between these two. But there is a middle ground, where you tell the story persuasively without arguing. And you might already have experience doing this.

Think back on some situation in which you were in some sort of difficulty and, to exonerate yourself, had to explain what you had done or somebody else had done. You probably did tell the story. And you probably told it from your point of view. If you were in conflict with somebody else, they probably told a similar story but from their point of view. Each of you tried to tell the story in a way that would persuade a third party, maybe someone in authority. If you've done this, you might have used a few of the techniques that lawyers use to tell compelling stories. As a lawyer, you will perfect those techniques and learn others as well.

Some writers prefer to tell the story twice. Any time you write to persuade, the way you begin is important. How you start writing the Fact Statement is especially important. Some writers prefer to tell the story in a short introductory summary that provides an overview of the factual picture. The writer can then tell the story again as the full story, with details.

If you decide to use this two-step approach, think of the introductory summary as the big picture. It comes at the beginning so the court can see an overview of the whole story. Unlike the remainder of the Fact Statement, it generally omits citations to the record because the same facts will appear again when you tell the story in detail, and you can provide record cites there. This introductory summary can be powerful because the beginning of any passage or section in the brief is a position of emphasis. It should focus on the facts that make your story compelling, but be careful to be selective. Ideally, it should fit into one paragraph. If it exceeds two paragraphs, it's not a summary.

After providing this introductory summary, you can tell the full story in detail. This gives a court the chance to see the details. Judges appreciate this twice-told presentation of the story because it tells them concisely what your factual theory is.

The Fact Statement must include every fact you mention in the Argument. Your Fact Statement will certainly include facts that do not reappear in your Argument. Some facts help tell the story in the Fact Statement but do not help in the Argument. But any fact that you use in the Argument must also appear in the Fact Statement. A judge needs to able to see all the relevant facts in one place, and that's the Fact Statement.

In the Fact Statement, don't say anything that your adversary could justifiably claim to be inaccurate. If you do, you're probably arguing and you might be losing credibility with your reader. Your story works only if your adversary has to admit that everything you say in the Fact Statement is true.

The Fact Statement must explain the procedural posture. The Fact Statement needs to describe what has already happened to the case in terms of court action. Judges make decisions only when the parties ask them to, through a motion or an appeal. A motion is a request that a court—usually a trial court—issue an order. An appeal is a request that an appellate court reverse a lower court's decision. Tell the court about the procedural events relevant to the decision the court is being asked to make.

In a trial court: If the court is being asked to decide a motion, explain who made the motion and what kind of motion it is:

> The defendant has moved for summary judgment on Counts I and III of the plaintiff's complaint. Count I alleges negligence, and Count III alleges fraud.

You can use the procedural posture as an opportunity to advance your theory. For instance, if you represent the plaintiff, you might add another sentence soon after the one above:

> . . . Count III alleges that the defendant defrauded the plaintiff of her life savings by selling to her stock in corporations that do not exist.

Be careful, though, to include only facts here. Be sure this complaint actually does allege that the defendant defrauded the plaintiff of her life savings by selling to her stock in corporations that do not exist.

In an appellate court: Explain what happened in the trial court and state which party has appealed and what that party claims the trial court did wrong. You don't need to do all this in the same place. You can wait until the end of the Fact Statement to say who has appealed and why. Or you can mention it earlier, even at the beginning of the Fact Statement, if that would help persuade.

Near the beginning of the Fact Statement, you'll need to explain what kind of case this is (a vehicular manslaughter prosecution, for example, or a copyright infringement action in which the defendant has pleaded the defense of fair use) and identify the trial court decision being appealed from (a jury instruction, for example, or the grant of a motion to dismiss the complaint). Without knowing the type of case and the decision being appealed from, the court won't know which facts are relevant and why.

If you're using an introductory summary, one challenge with this two-step approach is integrating the procedural posture while remaining persuasive. If your case is difficult to understand without knowing the procedural posture, you might try mentioning the key procedural components in the introductory summary and then explaining them in more detail later. If the procedural posture is less significant to understanding your case, you can describe it after the introductory summary and before the full story.

Every fact in the Fact Statement must be supported by a citation to the Record. The record includes whatever information could be the basis for a court's decision: pleadings, testimony, and affidavits, for instance. For every fact, cite to the place in the record where that fact can be found.

If you write an introductory summary, you don't need citations there. The judge knows that any fact in your introductory summary will be repeated with additional details in the full story, and those details will include citations to the record. But remember that the introductory summary is only a paragraph or two. After that, start citing to the record.

Citations to the record are also needed in the Argument wherever you refer to a fact in the story.

HOW TO WRITE A PERSUASIVE FACT STATEMENT

Using the cell phone manslaughter problem in Appendix A, we'll walk you through the process of writing a persuasive Fact Statement.

Problem

> Here is a quick overview of the cell phone manslaughter problem. Allison King used her wireless phone, without a hands-free device, while driving in dense fog on a winding road on the edge of an ocean cliff. King placed the call to warn her friends about the dangerous conditions, as they would be meeting later. While she was making the call, she hit and killed a bicyclist. The prosecution will attempt to convict King of vehicular manslaughter by showing that she drove while committing an illegal act (driving while using a wireless phone without a hands-free device) and with gross negligence. King will argue that her actions fit within the emergency exception to the wireless phone prohibition. She will also argue that she did not act with gross negligence.

Step 1: Sketch out the Argument first. Until you have a clear idea of your arguments, you won't know enough about your theory and theme to start working on the Fact Statement. Your argument and your story work together, but the story won't work if it isn't supported by the legal analysis. The legal analysis tells you what facts are legally relevant and why.

Some writers like to start their writing process with the Fact Statement because it's the part of the case they know best at the beginning — the story — and it sometimes helps break through writer's block to start there. If you've followed this method, be sure to go back and revise — not just edit — the Fact Statement once you've gained a better understanding, after writing the Argument, of which facts are truly relevant.

Step 2: Select the facts that *must* appear in the Fact Statement. Make sure it includes the following:

Facts relevant to legal rules. Make a list of facts that show whether elements of the governing legal rules have or have not been satisfied. If in the Argument you must show that your client has met the requirements of a six-element test, all the facts that satisfy those six elements must be in the Fact Statement.

Additional facts that help make your story more persuasive. Decide which facts show your client to be sympathetic and which facts show the other party to have behaved badly.

Any other facts that you mention in the Argument. If a fact is in the Argument, it must also be in the Fact Statement.

Facts that help your adversary. You have to tell the complete story, including the facts you don't like. An incomplete story lacks credibility. If a fact worries you, put it in the Fact Statement and try to neutralize it (see Step 4).

Step 3: Choose an organization that tells the story persuasively and can be easily understood by the reader. Generally the easiest sequence to understand is chronological—telling the story from beginning to end. You may decide to stray from chronological order for good reasons, but most readers follow facts quickly when the story is told in chronological order. Sometimes, however, a topical organization works better because you can use the way you organize the facts to imply the logical relationships between them. For instance, if your complaint alleges two separate causes of action based on mostly separate facts, you could first address the facts relevant to claim one and then address the facts relevant to claim two. If the facts overlap significantly, of course, this might not be the best structure.

Step 4: Write a draft of the full story. Your goals here are to emphasize favorable facts, neutralize unfavorable facts, point to gaps in the record, use strategic vividness, and eliminate distracting factual clutter.

Avoid using an argumentative tone. Some readers will react badly to any indication that you are manipulating the story as you present the facts. Typically your professor will expect you to tell a compelling story without crossing the line into manipulation or argument. It can be hard to find the line, but with time you'll develop a sense of how far you can go.

Emphasize favorable facts. Explain them in detail. Put them in prominent places, including the beginning of paragraphs. If your best fact is related to another fact, allude to that when you mention the other fact.

Suppose you represent the prosecution in the cell phone manslaughter problem. You decide that your best fact is that the road King was driving on (while using her cell phone) is on the edge of a cliff with a limited opportunity for survival in the event of an accident. Other favorable facts include the dense fog and the narrow, winding two-lane road. To be persuasive, paint a vivid picture of the cliff. Give enough detail so the reader can visualize the sheer drop to the ocean below. (Don't make up details, however. They all must be in the record.) Do this very early in the full story.

When you get to the dense fog, mention the cliff again so the reader can understand the cumulative effect of the dangers:

> Not only was the defendant driving along this cliff while using her cell phone, but she was doing so in dense fog with limited visibility.

Neutralize unfavorable facts. Hiding an unfavorable fact in an obscure part of the Fact Statement will not help you. Your adversary will explain it at length in her Fact Statement. To overcome that, you have to neutralize the fact, not hide it.

If a favorable fact lessens the impact of an unfavorable fact, mention them together. You might use "although" or "even though" clauses to show how the favorable fact helps to neutralize the unfavorable one, while being careful not to cross the line into an overall argumentative tone. If you represent the prosecution, your most unfavorable fact is the reason for the defendant's phone call. You can do something like this:

> Although the defendant telephoned her friends to warn them, no evidence in the record suggests that she was unable to stop her car for the few moments needed to make that call. Instead, she continued to drive while taking her eyes off the road to dial.

Point to gaps in the record. The absence of a fact is itself a fact. If that absence helps you, mention it. The example above does this: "no evidence in the record suggests that she was unable to stop her car for the few moments needed to make that call."

Use strategic vividness. Go back to the last example above. The words "while taking her eyes off the road to dial" help many readers see the scene: The defendant's eyes are on the road ahead and they move aside or down so that she can see the keys on the phone. If this were a movie, you'd be in suspense about what would happen next because as soon as her eyes leave the road, disaster can happen.

Eliminate distracting factual clutter. Too much information distracts from the most persuasive aspects of your story. Mention dates, times, and places only if they're essential to the story. You don't need to say that the accident happened at 4:17 in the afternoon. It's the same story if the accident happened at 11:31 in the morning. Discuss time only if it's relevant to a legal issue or if it helps you tell the story coherently.

Step 5: Check to make sure you've started the Fact Statement in an effective way. If you've decided to use the two-step approach, write the introductory summary. An introductory summary will be most persuasive if you write it after you write the full story because—as Chapter 12 explains—it's more efficient to write an introduction after you write the thing being introduced. If you represent the defendant in the cell phone manslaughter problem, you might write this introductory summary:

> Allison King, the appellant, was enveloped in a fogbank while driving on an isolated road along the top of a cliff. The fog was so thick that she worried about the safety of her friends, who had promised to meet her and were driving this same road. Her only way of warning them was with her cell phone. While making this call, she accidentally struck a bicyclist, who was enveloped in the same fogbank. The cell phone was not a hands-free device, and she was convicted of vehicular manslaughter. No other telephone was available to her.

If you were the judge, this introductory summary would give you the feeling that convicting King might have been an injustice. This summary leads the reader to think King had no alternatives and was doing the best she could in a dangerous situation.

Step 6: If you have a long Fact Statement, consider adding headings. Headings help the judge see your organization and find specific facts. If you use an introductory summary, the first heading should come afterward.

Step 7: Go back and forth between the Argument and the Fact Statement, revising, rewriting, and proofing in a coordinated way so these two parts of the brief support each other. As elsewhere in legal writing, you can't produce an effective document without rewriting it frequently. As you rewrite the Fact Statement, make sure you've included all the necessary facts, including those you use in the Argument. Review the Fact Statement to ensure that it tells a compelling story. And make sure that you've supplied a citation to the record for every fact.

EXAMPLES

Here are some examples of portions of Fact Statements without cites to the record. Each is based either on the cell phone manslaughter problem in Appendix A or the copyright and fair use problem in Appendix B. Some examples might have more than one right answer. Explain to yourself why you've chosen your answers. Then read the explanations in the last section of this chapter to check your work.

Example 23-1

These two paragraphs begin a Fact Statement:

> Neil Young, the plaintiff, has performed and recorded music for decades. His albums have sold millions of copies, both those he recorded as a solo performer and those he recorded as part of the band Crosby, Stills, Nash & Young. One of his songs, "Rockin' in the Free World," recorded in 1989, was often played in Europe as an anthem to freedom when Communism collapsed and the Berlin Wall fell. In 2004, *Rolling Stone* ranked it as number 214 in its list of "The 500 Greatest Songs of All Time."
>
> Phil Olds, the defendant, is a singer who is not well known. Last year, he recorded a song called "Stop Knockin' the Free World." In this lawsuit, Mr. Young alleges that this song infringes his copyright on the lyrics of "Rockin' in the Free World."

This is . . .

    A. an effective introductory summary for Olds. It portrays him as a struggling singer being taken advantage of by a much more successful performer.

    B. an effective way to start a Fact Statement for Young.

    C. an effective introductory summary for Young. It portrays Olds as an unsuccessful singer who is trying to profit from Young's work.

    D. not an introductory summary, although it begins the Fact Statement. It is more than one paragraph and it's the full story.

Example 23-2

The refrain in the plaintiff's song is "Keep on rockin' in the free world." In the defendant's song, the refrain is "Stop knockin' the free world." In the plaintiff's song, the first five lines are:

> There's colors on the street
> Red, white and blue
> People shufflin' their feet
> People sleepin' in their shoes
> But there's a warnin' sign on the road ahead

In the defendant's song, the first five lines are:

> There's flags on the street
> Red, white and blue
> People marchin' on their feet
> People shakin' in their shoes
> But there's a bright light on the road ahead

The defendant's lyrics infringe on the plaintiff's copyright.

    A. The entire passage is argument and inappropriate for a Fact Statement. The lyric comparison is intended to show that Olds' song infringes Young's copyright.

    B. None of the passage is argument. Everything is appropriate for a Fact Statement because only facts are stated in the passage.

    C. Everything except the last sentence states facts and is appropriate for a Fact Statement. The last sentence is argument.

    D. Everything except the last sentence is argument and is inappropriate for a Fact Statement. The last sentence states facts.

Example 23-3

A Fact Statement begins with this paragraph:

> Allison King, who turned 46 years old on May 11, 2010, owned a silver 2006 Mercedes Benz E350 four-door sedan. On Friday, October 22, 2010, she was driving approximately 23 miles per hour heading northbound on California State Highway 1 near milepost 56. The time was 2:47 p.m.

A. The level of detail in this Fact Statement is effective because it shows the brief's author knows all the details of the case.

B. The level of detail in this section of the Fact Statement is ineffective because it includes distracting factual clutter.

C. This section of the Fact Statement would be effective in King's brief because it personalizes her and allows the reader to picture her story.

D. This is an ineffective section of a Fact Statement because it doesn't support either the prosecution's theory or King's theory. It's neutral.

Example 23-4

King testified that she was surrounded by fog, could barely see over the hood of her car, and could not see whether there was any place to pull off the road. She knew that if she stopped on the road, another car could crash into hers. She also knew that parts of the road ran along the top of a cliff. She testified that she kept driving because she was afraid to do anything else.

A. This testimony should be cited to the record.

B. This passage does not favor either party. The reader can't tell whether the writer represents King or the prosecution.

C. The word "crash" does a better job here than "collide" or "hit" would have done.

D. This passage does nothing to neutralize any of the unfavorable facts.

EXPLANATIONS

Explanation 23-1

A is wrong. Nothing in the two paragraphs suggests that Young is doing anything other than defending his own legal rights. Olds' lack of success instead suggests that he has a motive to steal from Young's work, which supports Young's theory of the case. This introductory summary belongs in Young's brief, not Olds' brief. **B** is correct. Although these two paragraphs don't itemize the facts relevant to the fair use defense, they're an effective beginning to Young's Fact Statement because of the way they introduce the parties. **C** is also correct. The first paragraph vividly shows Young's lyrics to be known and appreciated all over the world. The second paragraph suggests that Olds can succeed only by appropriating Young's lyrics. **D** is wrong. The full story would include many facts that are missing here, such as the lyrics of both songs and, as noted in C, the facts relevant to Olds' fair use defense.

Explanation 23-2

A is wrong. It is not true that the entire Fact Statement is argument. Only the last sentence is. Everything else is facts. The lyric comparison creates a basis for concluding that the similarity is infringement, but that part of the passage makes no argument. It does not explicitly state any legal standard or compare the law to the facts. **B** is wrong. The last sentence mentions the legal claim—copyright infringement—and it explicitly states that the defendant has violated the plaintiff's copyright. This is the ultimate issue in the case, and although you should state this position in the Argument section, it should not appear in the Fact Statement. **C** is correct. The last sentence is indeed argument. Similarly, **D** is wrong. Everything but the last sentence is facts. The last sentence states an inference from facts and therefore is argument.

Explanation 23-3

A is incorrect. The purpose of a Fact Statement is to tell a compelling story and not to demonstrate the author's command of the case. Besides, most of the detail in the passage is irrelevant to the issues. **B** is correct. The time, the date, the car description, the age of the driver, and the exact location on the road are all interesting but not relevant to the issues. This is all factual clutter that distracts from the relevant facts. **C** is wrong. The reader may have learned more about King, but nothing in the paragraph portrays her sympathetically. **D** is also correct. This Fact Statement doesn't represent either side's viewpoint. It's neutral and thus it does not tell a compelling story for anybody.

Explanation 23-4

A is correct. This is not an introductory summary, where citations to the record can be omitted. It's a detailed description of testimony and would appear later in the Fact Statement, where citations to the record are mandatory. **B** is wrong. This testimony supports King by explaining the desperate situation in which she found herself and in which she had no good alternatives. **C** is correct. "Crash" helps you imagine the violent effect of one car running into another. "Collide" and "hit" don't provide the same vividness. **D** is wrong. A fact that hurts King is that she continued to drive in a blinding fog. The passage helps to neutralize that by showing that each of the alternatives was dangerous, too.

Writing the Question Presented (Persuasive)

The way a question is asked often influences the way it's answered. Suppose, for instance, that a cable news network has hired a pollster to find out whether the public feels Congress is doing a good job. A newspaper has hired a different pollster to do a poll on the same subject. One of the pollsters asks question A, and the other asks question B.

A. Do you think Congress is doing a good job of passing legislation that generally benefits the country?

B. Do you think Congress is failing in its responsibility to pass legislation that would resolve some of the basic problems facing the country?

Tomorrow the cable news network and the newspaper will separately announce their poll results. Based on the questions they asked, would you predict that these polls will agree or differ on the extent to which the public has confidence in Congress? What answer does each question encourage?

How you ask the question matters. In writing a Question Presented, you'll tell the court—as precisely as you can—the question it must answer about the law or about how the law treats your facts. You'll also use the Question Presented as an opportunity to persuade by framing the issue with the most essential facts of your theory and theme (see Chapter 18).

Don't confuse a persuasive Question Presented with an office memo's objective Question Presented, which is explained in Chapter 13. They look similar. Both are called the Question Presented. Both define an issue as precisely as possible. But a persuasive Question Presented has the added function of influencing the court to see the case from your point of view.

Typically, a Question Presented includes the most essential facts of your theory of the case. You can persuade by choosing your strongest facts and by expressing them in words that will motivate a judge to rule in your client's favor.

Terminology Notes: Sometimes professors will call the Question Presented the "QP." In some courts the Question Presented is called "Issue." If you have more than one Question or Issue, that part of the brief would be called Questions Presented (or Issues).

WHAT YOU NEED TO KNOW ABOUT WRITING A PERSUASIVE QUESTION PRESENTED

In an appellate brief, a persuasive Question Presented combines three ingredients:

- a reference to the applicable law
- the legal question the court must answer
- the facts you consider most significant to your theory

Typically, they are expressed in a single sentence.[1]

Assemble these ingredients in the most persuasive order as long as it can be understood quickly by the reader. General principles of persuasion should help you decide what order works best for your particular case. The beginning and end are positions of emphasis. Think about whether you want to emphasize the controlling law (which you may want to if, for example, it's unsettled and the court is being asked to clarify it), the legal question (which is often a good starting point), or the significant facts (which help if you have a particularly compelling factual scenario). Recall that the middle will be the position of least emphasis, so use that spot for any negative or less important part of the Question Presented.

Alluding to the applicable law: Although the following are phrased differently, they are essentially the same Question Presented. One uses *Under* to introduce the law. The other uses a verb (*Does*).

> Under the Antiquities Act, does the President have the authority to create a National Monument when . . . ?

---

1. An alternative and increasingly used format expresses the essential facts in one or more sentences and then, in a separate sentence, asks the question and alludes to the applicable law. Lawyers who use this format choose it when the facts are too complicated to fit into the traditional single sentence format or when there are several major issues that are all based on the same facts. But the alternative Question Presented format is not commonly used in legal writing courses.

> Does the Antiquities Act confer authority on the President to create a National Monument when . . . ?

Posing the question: The following use different interrogatory verbs: *Did, Do,* and *Is.*

> Did the police violate the defendant's Fifth Amendment rights when . . . ?

> Do school boards have the power to . . . ?

> Is a Congressional delegation of authority unconstitutional under the Separation of Powers Clause when . . . ?

Alluding to the facts: An easy way to start the list is with the word *when,* as you did in the objective question presented in an office memo (Chapter 13). Or you might incorporate them into the core of the sentence:

> Does Wyoming violate the Due Process Clause by exercising personal jurisdiction over a Nigerian citizen who has never been in the state, never caused harm there, and never derived any benefit from interests there?

Because of the nature of this particular issue, the facts flow without the introductory word *when.* In many situations, however, you will need to use *when* to introduce the facts.

The "Whether" dispute: In the past, the most popular format was to begin a Question Presented with the word *whether:*

> Whether this state should recognize the tort doctrine of social host liability in light of the increasing number of deaths and injuries caused by drunken driving.

> Whether Wyoming violates the Due Process Clause by exercising personal jurisdiction over a Nigerian citizen who has never been in the state, never caused harm there, and never derived any benefit from interests there.

Although some still favor this format, particularly in certain jurisdictions, a number of lawyers are beginning to avoid it. They believe that *whether* Questions Presented are harder to read and understand because they're not complete sentences and are not questions grammatically. They prefer to phrase a Question Presented as a grammatical question—so that it naturally ends in a question mark. Lawyers who continue to write *whether* Questions Presented might argue that a long tradition of doing so ought not to be abandoned. Unless your professor suggests otherwise, you might find it more effective to phrase the Question Presented as a question and not beginning with the word *whether.*

Put the wordiest ingredient at the end of the sentence unless other principles of persuasive organization outweigh this general advice. A sentence is most easily understood if the most complicated part comes at the end. Suppose it takes the following numbers of words to express each part:

applicable law	5 words
legal question	7 words
facts	16 words

Here, if you put the facts first, the reader might struggle to understand the sentence. The facts are more than half of the sentence, and the reader could get lost before realizing how the sentence is structured. Often—but not always—lawyers put the facts at the end of the Question Presented because the facts make sense only after the reader knows what the legal question is.

On the other hand, if the facts are unusually persuasive—even if the key facts can't be expressed very concisely—you might experiment to see if you can find a way to emphasize them by putting them first in the sentence without making the Question Presented hard to read.

A judge should be able to understand the Question Presented without having to read it twice. List only the most essential facts and eliminate unnecessary details. It takes a lot of writing and rewriting to make a Question Presented both concise and understandable. In many briefs, the Question Presented is the single hardest sentence to write.

State each fact in carefully chosen words so that your adversary cannot reasonably claim that you've stated the fact inaccurately. If a court doubts that you've accurately stated the facts, the Question Presented will not persuade. A good Question Presented persuades with facts that imply this message: "Judge, these undeniable facts are so strong that you should decide for my client." A judge who doubts that you've stated the facts accurately will ignore that message.

State only facts—and not disputable factual inferences or conclusions of law. "The defendant did not stop at the stop sign" is a fact. "The defendant carelessly ignored the stop sign" contains two factual inferences: that the defendant acted carelessly and that he ignored the stop sign (rather than didn't see it, for example). "The defendant negligently entered the intersection" is a conclusion of law. Unless your adversary concedes a factual inference or a conclusion of law, you cannot assume it in a Question Presented.

Phrase the Question Presented to invite a "yes" answer. One side will win the appeal, and the other side will lose. A positive tone ("yes") is associated with winning, and a negative tone with losing. Most lawyers draft Questions Presented to invite "yes" answers, and judges are used to reading them phrased that way. If you write one to invite a "no" answer, you'll confuse a judge, who will have to try to figure out whether you really want "no." And if you do, your Question Presented will suggest that your theory of the case is based on a negative reaction to the other side's argument rather than the positive merits of your own arguments.

Don't write too many Questions Presented. Write a Question Presented for each big, encompassing issue on which a large part or all of the appeal depends—but not more than that. Most cases include small issues in addition to one or more big issues. And a big issue will often include some sub-issues that help resolve the big issue. But don't write a separate Question Presented for each small issue or sub-issue. A typical law school appellate brief assignment will usually involve no more than one or two Questions Presented.

It's usually more efficient to write the Argument—or at least the first draft of the Argument—before writing Questions Presented. Sometimes it's efficient to write first drafts of both the Argument and the Statement of Facts first. Sketching out a Question Presented early doesn't hurt and might help, depending on your own writing process. Before writing the Argument, you might know what the legal question and the applicable law are. But usually writing the Argument helps you identify the facts—the very few facts that determine the answer.

HOW TO WRITE A PERSUASIVE QUESTION PRESENTED

Using the cell phone manslaughter problem in Appendix A, we'll walk you through the process of writing a persuasive Question Presented.

Problem

Here is a quick overview of the cell phone manslaughter problem. Allison King used her wireless phone, without a hands-free device, while driving in dense fog on a winding road on the edge of an ocean cliff. King placed the call to warn her friends about the dangerous conditions, as they would be meeting later. While she was making the call, she hit and killed a bicyclist. The prosecution will attempt to convict King of vehicular manslaughter by showing that she drove while committing an illegal act (driving while using a wireless phone without a hands-free device) and with gross negligence. King will argue that her actions fit within the emergency exception to the wireless phone prohibition. She will also argue that she did not act with gross negligence.

Step 1: Articulate the applicable law. Identify the controlling legal authority. Depending on the issue, you might do this broadly:

> Under California's vehicular manslaughter statute . . . ?

Or more specifically:

> For purposes of California's vehicular manslaughter statute, under the prohibition on using a cell phone while driving . . . ?

Step 2: Determine the specific legal question and state it as briefly as possible. Express the legal concepts precisely.

> For purposes of California's vehicular manslaughter statute, under the prohibition on using a cell phone while driving, does a motorist use a cell phone for "emergency purposes" when . . . ?

Where a statute is involved, the statutory wording is usually the most precise way to express the statutory concepts. In the vehicular manslaughter statute, for instance, the words "emergency purposes" have a precise meaning.

Step 3: Identify the key facts and state them briefly in words that best encapsulate your theory. For instance, if you represent the prosecution in the cell phone manslaughter case, you might use these facts to show that the defendant knew her conduct posed a risk to others:

> . . . she hits and kills a bicyclist while driving on a winding, two-lane road in dense fog on the side of a cliff while dialing her cell phone?

Step 4: Combine the components. Assemble the applicable law, the legal question, and the key facts into one sentence phrased as a question.

> Under California's vehicular manslaughter statute, does a motorist commit vehicular manslaughter when she hits and kills a bicyclist while driving on a winding, two-lane road in dense fog on the side of a cliff while dialing her cell phone?

If you represent the defendant and your theory is that she's exonerated by the "emergency purposes" exception, you might write this instead:

> Does a motorist use a cell phone for "emergency purposes," under the general prohibition on using a cell phone while driving and for purposes of California's vehicular manslaughter statute, when she places a call to warn her friends not to drive in dangerous conditions caused by fog?

EXAMPLES

Here are some examples of persuasive Questions Presented—written for the prosecution—based on the cell phone manslaughter problem in Appendix A. Some examples have more than one correct answer. Explain to yourself why you've chosen your answers. Then read the explanations in the last section of this chapter to check your work.

Example 24-1

Did King commit vehicular manslaughter when she made a cell phone call while driving on a narrow winding road in dense fog?

A. This is an effective Question Presented because it's concise and can be read and understood quickly.

B. This is an ineffective Question Presented because it omits the applicable law.

C. This is an ineffective Question Presented because it doesn't completely state the key facts.

D. This is an ineffective Question Presented because the writer has not used the facts to persuade the reader.

Example 24-2

Did King commit vehicular manslaughter under Cal. Penal Code § 192 (c)(1) when she violated Cal. Vehicle Code § 23123 by using a cell phone that was not configured for hands-free use, while operating a motor vehicle and, while using this cell phone, struck a bicyclist and forced him to fall to his death from a cliff?

A. This Question Presented is not concise. The same thoughts could be expressed in fewer words.

B. This Question Presented contains unnecessary detail.

C. The statutory section citations in this Question Presented are distracting. A description of the statutes (such as "the California vehicular manslaughter statute") would be sufficient without citations.

D. The statement that King violated § 23123 is a conclusion of law. It shouldn't be treated as a fact. Instead, it must be proved in the Argument.

Example 24-3

Under California law, does a motorist commit vehicular manslaughter when she makes a cell phone call, creating an unreasonable risk to others, and strikes and kills a bicyclist?

A. This Question Presented adequately identifies the applicable law.
B. This Question Presented is concise.
C. The facts listed in this Question Presented could be disputed by the opposing lawyer.
D. This Question Presented doesn't state all the essential facts.

Example 24-4

When King drove on a winding, two-lane road in dense fog near the side of a cliff while recklessly dialing her cell phone and hit a bicyclist, causing him to fall over the cliff to his death, did she commit vehicular manslaughter under California law?

A. The word "dense" expresses a factual inference that does not belong in a Question Presented. The prosecution and King agree that she drove in fog. The prosecution characterizes it as dense fog, but King could argue that it was not dense.
B. The word "recklessly" does not express a factual inference that King could challenge. Her conduct was undeniably reckless.
C. This Question Presented is hard to read because of the way it's structured.
D. Because the facts are compelling, placing them at the beginning of the sentence is effective.

EXPLANATIONS

Explanation 24-1

A is wrong. Although this Question Presented is concise and can be easily read and understood, it's nevertheless ineffective for the reasons stated in B, C, and D. *B* is correct. This Question Presented fails to articulate the applicable law. It could be improved by specifying the controlling state law, and specifically, the statutory provision at issue (though you could do this in descriptive terms rather than a citation). *C* is also correct. This Question Presented does not mention that someone died—an essential fact for the prosecution in a vehicular manslaughter case. *D* is also correct. The writer could do more to make this Question Presented persuasive. For example, it could refer to the death, as noted in C, and use details so the reader can visualize how the death occurred.

Explanation 24-2

A is correct. For example, instead of "operating a motor vehicle," it would be enough to write "driving." The reader knows from the context that there's a car. *B* is incorrect. The details used here—such as "forced him to fall to his death from a cliff"—help the reader visualize the actual incident and can help persuade the reader to favor the prosecution. The problem here is too many words (see A), not too many facts. *C* is correct. If a statutory section is ambiguous and the court must settle its meaning, it can be helpful to identify that section by its number. But typically, the description of the statute—such as California's vehicular manslaughter statute—is enough for the Question Presented. Of course, you'll refer to the specific statutory section, and cite it properly, within the Argument. But it doesn't help the reader much in this Question Presented. *D* is also correct. This Question Presented treats King's violation of § 23123 as a fact—which it isn't. In fact, it's part of the underlying question that helps resolve whether King is guilty of vehicular manslaughter. One clue that the writer treats this as a fact and not a question is its location in the under/does/when structure: It's in the list of facts that follows the word *when*.

Explanation 24-3

A is wrong. Most readers would think that the applicable statute should be specified. Some readers would prefer a descriptive approach to identifying the relevant statute—like "California's vehicular manslaughter statute"—and others would rather see a reference to the statute by section number, especially if the court is being asked to settle the meaning of that section. **B** is wrong. This Question Presented is short, but that's not the same as being concise. Conciseness is expressing ideas in few words. This Question Presented is short because it expresses too few ideas. The statute is not specified, and most of the key facts are missing. **C** is correct. The assertion that King "creat[ed] an unreasonable risk to others" is a conclusion of law. Because "gross negligence" is defined as creating an unreasonable risk, reasonableness is part of the governing legal rule. Thus, it's a conclusion of law to say that she acted unreasonably. **D** is correct. Many of the persuasive facts in this case, such as the dangerous driving conditions, are missing.

Explanation 24-4

A is wrong. "Dense" is an inference, but King will not challenge it. She will argue that in a dense fog, on a narrow road near a cliff, she had no choice but to keep driving, and she needed to call her friends and warn them of the fog, which would establish an emergency purpose under § 23123(c). If the fog isn't dense, her defense will fall apart. The prosecution needs a dense fog, too, to support its argument that she was ignoring risks. Both parties want this fog to have been dense. **B** is wrong for two reasons. First, one could reasonably argue that she was reckless, but one could just as reasonably argue that she was not. Whichever it was would be decided by argument, and it can't be inserted into a Question Presented as an undeniable fact. Second, whether or not she was reckless is irrelevant. None of the statutory tests in Appendix A measure recklessness. They do measure gross negligence, which is a different concept. **C** is correct. This Question Presented is made up of facts (the first 38 words of the sentence), a legal question (5 words, "did she commit vehicular manslaughter"), and a reference to applicable law (3 words, "under California law"). The reader gets lost in the first 38 words without being able to identify the sentence's structure. Generally, a sentence can be most easily understood if the wordiest or most complicated part comes at the end. This Question Presented should begin with the legal question and applicable law because they're expressed in few words and can be instantly understood. The facts should follow because they're wordier and more complicated. It's not always true that the facts should come last in a Question Presented. But it is true here. **D** is wrong. The facts are compelling, but placing them at the beginning of this Question Presented makes it hard for the reader to understand them.

Revising and Rewriting

PART IV

CHAPTER 25

Overview to Part IV: Revising and Rewriting

Revising and rewriting are essential to good legal writing. Everyone has to do it. Analysis, organization, and writing style in early drafts nearly always need polishing. Revise documents over and over again until they shine.

Knowing how to revise your written work is a valuable skill that you can learn. The next chapters aim to help you learn this skill and improve your writing.

- Chapter 26 helps you tighten up and add clarity to your sentences. This may be particularly useful when you receive comments like "awkward" next to sentences.
- Chapter 27 provides the essentials of crafting strong thesis sentences to start off your paragraphs and keep the reader moving effortlessly through your document.
- Chapter 28 focuses on conciseness and will help you write clearly and crisply, while staying within the word count or page limit of your assignment or court filing.
- Chapter 29 tackles the big-picture topic of coherence and gives you practice with transitions.

In Part IV, we've prioritized topics law students may find most useful as they revise. Even if you don't have a page limit problem or find yourself confused about sentence structure, this part of the book offers some of the key writing style principles that most lawyers value. If you find yourself struggling with writing mechanics or style, a number of good books can help you in more detail with writing basics. Don't be afraid to turn to other sources to get more practice. The payoff for being a good writer is immense.

SOME TIPS FOR PLANNING YOUR TIME

As mentioned before, keep in mind that you should leave plenty of time for your revision process. Have a smart plan of attack. Here are two big tips to keep in mind:

Plan to revise your document in multiple sessions. This way you'll have a fresh mind and eyes to tackle revising unclear analysis or to spot errors.

Revise in layers from big to small. Don't try to revise for everything all at once. It's nearly impossible to do a great job this way.

In your first session, you might check that your document has all the right components or sections, work on large-scale organization issues, and work on any sections where you need to do a lot of rewriting. Don't be afraid to scrap portions that aren't working well and start over! Be brutal with your written work. Don't keep something just because it's already written.

In your next session, work on the small-scale organization within your sections. Then, perhaps in another session or two, move on to the more detailed revising work of going line by line, editing out passive voice, revising for conciseness and sentence structure, fixing citation errors, etc.

The substance of your document is, of course, critical. Appearances count a lot, too. The polish of your document reflects on you not only as a writer but also on the care you take with your research and analysis. If you're sloppy with your writing, the reader might assume that you were also sloppy with your research and analysis. If your writing shines, the reader is more apt to assume that you were also careful and smart with your research and analysis. In short, your hard work revising your document is simply part of the process of excellent legal writing.

SOME COMMON PITFALLS

Be careful to avoid these common pitfalls when writing.

- not budgeting enough time for revising;
- revising only once;
- trying to revise and proofread for all issues, big and small, at the same time;

- being too hesitant to make changes; and
- not giving the revision process enough focus and energy.

The most common pitfalls occur when the tips provided in this chapter aren't followed. One of the easiest-to-avoid pitfalls occurs when the writer has to turn in an unpolished document because he or she didn't leave enough time to revise the document. Another pitfall is being too hesitant to make changes to a draft. It can feel difficult to cut or revise a sentence or paragraph you worked hard to write, or perhaps you've gotten some good comments on the draft. But in the revision process it's important to be tough with yourself. Ask yourself if that sentence or paragraph expresses something important and relevant to your analysis or argument. Ask yourself whether you've stated it as accurately and concisely as you can. Don't be afraid to rewrite something from scratch or delete a portion entirely if it'll make the document better. Few writers can write amazing first drafts. Amazing writing comes from lots of thoughtful revisions made over a period of time when the writer devoted focus and energy to the project.

26

Fixing Awkward Sentence Structure

Just what you need! A margin comment tells you that the reader finds your sentence "awkward," but gives you no clue how to fix it. Chances are that your problem involves sentence structure. The best way to solve this problem is to structure your sentences in the way that conveys information to the reader as quickly and painlessly as possible.

WHAT YOU NEED TO KNOW ABOUT FIXING AWKWARD SENTENCE STRUCTURE

Sentences are easiest to understand when they use a "subject-verb-object" structure. Compare these two sentences. One is easier to follow than the other:

> Due to the recognizable nature of the refrain in the original, which repeats the title four times, Olds' use, which repeats his similar title four times alone, will be recognized by anyone familiar with the song.

> Anyone familiar with the song will recognize the way Olds' song copies the original by repeating the title four times in the refrain.

Sentences are easiest to understand when the subject and verb are close together and near the beginning of the sentence. Compare these two sentences. One is easier to follow than the other:

Using the original children's book as a vehicle to comment on the O.J. Simpson trial, the defendant, without putting forth something new, copied a style to get his point across.

The defendant copied a style to get his point across when he used the original children's book to comment on the O.J. Simpson trial without putting forth something new.

Keep the length of sentences to four lines of type or less. This is one of those "rules" that isn't really a rule, but a handy guideline. In fact, the guideline may vary from professor to professor, with some suggesting three lines of type and others finding a sentence long if it is 25 words or more. (See Chapter 29 on Coherence.) It's possible to structure long sentences in ways that are easy to follow, but it's difficult. Save yourself the trouble by keeping sentences from growing beyond four lines of type. If it's four lines of text or more, break it up.

As you gain experience, you'll get better at drafting easy-to-follow sentences, but as a beginner, plan on time to review each sentence for structure and length. The most successful students plan time for a line-by-line edit before turning their papers in.

HOW TO STRUCTURE SENTENCES

Using the copyright and fair use problem in Appendix B, we'll walk you through the process of fixing awkward sentence structure.

Problem

Here is a quick overview of the copyright and fair use problem. Young is suing Olds for violating the Copyright Act when Olds wrote a song based on Young's original, "Rockin' in the Free World." Olds' song uses the structure and many lyrics of the original but changes the original song's political message. The music of the two songs is not at issue, only the lyrics. Young expects that Olds will argue that his song is a parody that falls under the fair use exception to the Copyright Act. The court will consider the relevant factors set out in the fair use statute, 17 U.S.C. § 107 (2006): whether the copy was transformative and targeted the original; whether it took more than necessary of the original; and whether it will interfere with the original's market.

Step 1: Read your draft sentence by sentence. Choose a sentence that is long or seems hard to follow, and use that to work on editing. Let's say you find this one:

> In examining how the infringing work further cuts against the fair use defense, the use of the title and the copying of the first stanza did not amount to an effort, decided the appellate court, to create a transformative work with new expression.

Step 2: Pull the sentence apart. Start with that long introductory clause. Do you need it? What does it add? Not much. It's not clear you need a signal or transition here, but if you do, it doesn't need to be this long introductory clause.

Try deleting it:

> The use of the title and the copying of the first stanza did not amount to an effort, decided the appellate court, to create a transformative work with new expression.

Step 3: Reorganize the sentence if necessary. In this step, decide what the actions in the sentence are and who is doing them. Here you have a court deciding, and the defendant copying and perhaps creating, and the defendant using the title. Recasting the sentence to order it into a subject-verb-object structure means you must choose one of these as the subject of the sentence. Try it both ways:

> The appellate court decided that copying the title and the first stanza did not create a transformative work with new expression.

> The defendant copied the title and the first stanza but did not create a transformative work with new expression.

Both of these sentences significantly improve the original. They are structured as subject-verb-object; they are shorter sentences; and the subject and verb are close together at the beginning of each sentence. Your choice may depend on what you want to emphasize—the court's decision or the defendant's actions. And, of course, you'll want to be careful to accurately characterize the law.

EXAMPLES

Here are some examples of awkward sentences. For each example, more than one answer may be correct. Explain to yourself why you've chosen your answers. Then read the explanations.

Example 26-1

When a court decides, depending on the situation and the ease in conjuring up the original in its medium, that the parody uses a greater amount of the original than necessary to assure identification, it finds against fair use.

    A. Even though the subject and a verb are close together here, the real action of the courts here is "finding," and because it's separated from the subject "courts" the sentence is difficult to understand.

    B. One way to fix this sentence is to break it into more than one sentence.

    C. This is a good solution for the sentence: "Depending on the situation and the ease in conjuring up the original in its medium, when a court decides that the parody uses a greater amount of the original than necessary to assure identification, it finds against fair use."

    D. This is a good solution for the sentence: "Courts find against fair use when the parody uses a greater amount of the original than necessary to assure identification."

Example 26-2

Mattel, noting that the defendant used the entire image of the Barbie doll, argued that it was copyright infringement by the defendant using more than needed to evoke the original, but the court stated that the purpose of the defendant's work was to critique the stereotyped female roles in American society, and as such it was acceptable for the defendant to use the entire image of the doll.

    A. This sentence is too long and one way to fix it is to break it into more than one sentence.

    B. The subject and the verb are close together because the subject is "Mattel" and the verb is "noting."

    C. This is a good solution for the sentence: "Mattel argued the defendant used more than needed to evoke the original. The court decided that fair use protected the defendant's use of the entire image of the doll to critique stereotyped female roles in American society."

    D. This is a good solution for the sentence: "The *Mattel* court found it acceptable to use the entire image of the Barbie doll in a critique of the stereotyped female roles in American society."

Example 26-3

The court has stated that no negative effect, regardless of the number of similar points in the product, is seen on the value or market for the original when the copy has been significantly transformed from the original, and confusion with the original is therefore not likely.

A. Although the subject "the court" and the verb "has stated" are close together at the start of the sentence, this sentence is too long and the intervening clause is confusing.

B. This is a good solution for the sentence: "When the copy has significantly transformed the original, and confusion with the original is not likely, there is no negative effect of the market."

C. This sentence is too long and one way to fix it is to break it into more than one sentence.

D. This is a good solution for the sentence: "The copy will not affect the original's market negatively if the copy is sufficiently transformative. If the copy is sufficiently transformative confusion with the original is not likely."

Example 26-4

Mr. Olds' song identifiably adapts Young's "Rockin' in the Free World" through its use of similar lyrics and the same music, just as 2 Live Crew identifiably adapted Orbison's "Oh, Pretty Woman" song through its use of the distinctive opening lyrics and music and thus, just as the U.S. Supreme Court found 2 Live Crew's use to be fair, a court is likely to find Mr. Olds' song is fair use.

A. This sentence is too long to understand easily and the author should break it into two sentences.

B. This sentence is long but it is fairly easy to follow because the subject and verb are close together and at the beginning of the sentence. You don't need to break up this sentence.

C. This sentence is long and you could best separate it into two sentences by breaking off the end of it, deleting the word "and" that comes before "thus," and starting the new sentences with "thus."

D. This sentence is long and you could best separate it into two sentences by making the break between the first part that describes Olds' song and the second part that describes 2 Live Crew's parody.

EXPLANATIONS

Explanation 26-1

A is correct. **B** may be correct. The phrase "Depending on the situation" doesn't add substance and you could delete it. If the part about the "ease of conjuring up the original" is important, you could make two sentences: "Courts consider the ease of conjuring up the original. If the parody uses more of the original than necessary to assure identification it is not fair use." **C** is incorrect. You still have a long introductory clause that makes the sentence hard to follow, or "awkward." **D** is correct. The revised sentence is easy to understand. It's okay that the phrase "Depending on the situation" was cut because it does not add substance to the sentence. If the part about the "ease of conjuring up the original" was important, however, you could put that concept in a separate sentence as noted in B.

Explanation 26-2

A is correct. The sentence runs "four lines or more" and would be easier to follow if it were shorter. **B** is incorrect. The subject here is "Mattel," but the verb is "argued." **C** is one possible solution that works well. **D** is another possible solution that works pretty well.

Explanation 26-3

A is correct. Although a subject/verb combination starts the sentence, the sentence does not follow the expected subject-verb-object structure that would make it easy to follow. **B** is incorrect. Although the proposed solution is slightly better, it lacks the subject-verb-object structure with the subject and verb close together at the start of the sentence. **C** is correct. The sentence has two ideas. It would work better as two sentences. **D** is correct. This solution is much easier to read.

Explanation 26-4

A is at least partially correct. It follows the guidance that if a sentence is more than four lines, you should break it up. But this sentence, although long, is fairly easy to follow. And thus, **B** is also partially correct. This is a pretty good example of a long sentence that works because the subject and verb of each of the major clauses come at the front of the clause and are close together. The parallel structure the author used to write an analogy between the current case and the precedent also makes this long sentence easier to follow. Despite good structure, however, it is a very long sentence. **C** is correct. This answer preserves the parallel construction and the analogy in the sentence, but makes it easier on the reader by breaking it up. **D** is incorrect. The purpose of the sentence is to make the analogy between the two cases, so breaking the sentence in the middle of the analogy is a poor choice. You can make analogies in more than one sentence, but you don't have to here. The other options are better choices. (For more on making analogies, see Chapter 10.)

CHAPTER 27

Starting Paragraphs Powerfully

Students often ask, "How do I change my B+ into an A?" Here is one practice that may not explicitly be listed on the grading matrix, but nevertheless contributes subtly and powerfully to making your paper one of the top papers in the class. *Use a well-crafted topic sentence that states a thesis for the paragraph.*

In grade school you learned to write paragraphs with a topic sentence — a sentence that tells the reader the topic discussed in the paragraph. In law school, that topic sentence should become a *thesis sentence* — a sentence that announces the topic of the paragraph *by making an assertion that the paragraph supports or proves.* The assertion should advance the argument made in the memo or brief. In this book we call them "paragraph-thesis sentences."

Terminology Notes: Talking about a "thesis" in legal documents can get confusing. It can mean the point or claim you want to make for the entire document; it can mean the point you want to make in a particular section of the document; or, as it's used here, it can mean the point of a paragraph. Some textbooks call these "persuasive topic sentences." Others will just say to put a thesis sentence at the beginning of your paragraph. To distinguish these thesis sentences at the beginning of a paragraph from other ways the term might be used, we call them "paragraph-thesis sentences."

WHAT YOU NEED TO KNOW ABOUT PARAGRAPH-THESIS SENTENCES

A thesis sentence at the beginning of a paragraph makes an assertion that tells the reader how the paragraph will advance your argument. The rest of the paragraph will either explain the legal sources that support the assertion or it will make the arguments about your case that support the assertion (or both). Some people would say that the paragraph "proves" the assertion you made in the topic or thesis sentence.

When you include a paragraph-thesis sentence that tells readers the point of a paragraph, you ensure that the paragraph actually has a point. You also ensure that it's not making so many points that it should be broken into separate paragraphs.

A paragraph-thesis sentence comes at the beginning of the paragraph. You may have learned that a "topic sentence" can appear anywhere in the paragraph. In contrast, a paragraph-thesis sentence works best at the start of each paragraph for a couple of reasons. First, it allows readers to see if the paragraph actually proves or supports the assertion you start with. Legal readers are critical thinkers and they expect this organization so that they can evaluate your argument. Second, putting it first makes it easy for readers to skim your argument and get the main points. If you write a list of your document's paragraph-thesis sentences in the order in which they appear in your paper, the list should form an outline of your argument.

To determine whether the paragraph-thesis sentence makes an assertion (a thesis) rather than an announcement (of a topic), ask yourself whether a reader would naturally ask "Why?" or a similar question.[1] A reader might want to see support for the sentence, but she should not be left asking, "and what did the court say about that?"

With practice you'll get better at writing strong paragraph-thesis sentences. But as a beginner, plan on going back over a draft to check paragraphs and add paragraph-thesis sentences as needed.

---

1. Thanks to Professor Michael Higdon for this tip. Michael Higdon, *The Legal Reader, the Legal Writer and the All-Important Thesis Sentence*, NEVADA LAWYER, September 2007. Professor Kirsten Davis also has useful suggestions for using strong thesis sentences to start paragraphs. *Persuasion Through Organization: Another in a Series*, ARIZONA ATTORNEY, September 2005.

HOW TO WRITE PARAGRAPH-THESIS SENTENCES

Using the copyright and fair use problem in Appendix B, we'll walk you through the process of writing a paragraph-thesis sentence.

Problem

> Here is a quick overview of the copyright and fair use problem. Young is suing Olds for violating the Copyright Act when Olds wrote a song based on Young's original, "Rockin' in the Free World." Olds' song uses the structure and many lyrics of the original but changes the original song's political message. The music of the two songs is not at issue, only the lyrics. Young expects that Olds will argue that his song is a parody that falls under the fair use exception to the Copyright Act. The court will consider the relevant factors set out in the fair use statute, 17 U.S.C. § 107 (2006): whether the copy was transformative and targeted the original; whether it took more than necessary of the original; and whether it will interfere with the original's market.

Step 1: Read the paragraph you've written and decide what point you're trying to make. Look at this paragraph from the section of the memo addressing the first factor of the fair use test, "the purpose and character of the work," where courts look at whether the copy "transforms" the original work.

> In *Mattel v. Walking Mountain Productions*, the court concluded that the first factor weighed in favor of fair use because the defendant's use of Mattel's Barbie doll in his artwork was transformative in nature. 353 F.3d 792, 802-03 (9th Cir. 2003). The court reasoned that Mattel established Barbie as "'the ideal American woman.'" *Id.* at 802. Mattel's advertisements showed the dolls "dressed in various outfits, leading glamorous lifestyles, and engaged in exciting activities." *Id.* To sell its product, Mattel used "associations of beauty, wealth, and glamour." *Id.* For purposes of social commentary, the defendant transformed these associations by using Barbie dolls in his photography. In some of his photos, kitchen appliances are about to destroy or harm Barbie dolls. Other photos portray a nude Barbie in sexual poses and contexts. The transformative nature of the work made clear that the defendant's commentary intended to show the harm that he perceived in Barbie's influence on gender roles in society. *Id.*

Here, the author is explaining what the court means by "transformative" by illustrating with facts from a previous case where the copy was transformative of the original.

Step 2: Put the main point in one declarative sentence. So far, the first sentence of the paragraph just tells you what the topic is—it's a topic sentence, but not a paragraph-thesis sentence. So, what is the point this paragraph makes? You want to illustrate what it means to be transformative, so start with that:

> A parody is "transformative" when . . .

Now go back to the paragraph. Which are the key facts used to point out what it means to be transformative? The second, third, and fourth sentences describe how Mattel has characterized the original. The fifth sentence tells the reader what the parody does to transform the original work's message. It is the last sentence, though, that makes the key point about the facts from *Mattel* when it says the parody "intends to show the harm that he perceived in Barbie's influence on gender roles and the position of women in society." Put that point in the paragraph-thesis sentence:

> A parody is "transformative" when it criticizes the original and what it signifies by showing its harmful social influence.

Notice that instead of naming Mattel or Walking Mountain Productions, this paragraph-thesis sentence uses the labels that make it easiest for readers to understand how a precedent will compare to the case—labels like "original," "copy," and "defendant."

What else does it need? A citation to authority:

> A parody is "transformative" when it criticizes the original and what it signifies by showing its harmful social influence. *Mattel, Inc. v. Walking Mountain Prods.*, 353 F.3d 792, 802-03 (9th Cir. 2003).

Notice that the citation tells the reader that your statement comes from the case even though the sentence doesn't start with: "In *Mattel*," or "In *Mattel, Inc. v. Walking Mountain Productions*, 353 F.3d 792, 802-03 (9th Cir. 2003), ..." Adding the citation not only made a stronger statement that advances your argument, but also saved words and eliminated the clutter at the beginning of the sentence. Effective paragraph-thesis sentences rarely start with a citation in text.

So putting the paragraph-thesis sentence in place, your paragraph might look something like this:

A parody is "transformative" when it criticizes the original and what it signifies by showing its harmful social influence. *Mattel v. Walking Mountain Prods.*, 353 F.3d 792, 802-03 (9th Cir. 2003). For example, the court in *Mattel* concluded that the first factor weighed in favor of fair use because the defendant's use of Mattel's Barbie doll in his artwork was transformative in nature. *Id.* The court reasoned that the plaintiff established Barbie as "the ideal American woman." *Id.* at 802. Mattel's advertisements showed the dolls dressed in various outfits, leading glamorous lifestyles, and engaged in exciting activities. *Id.* To sell its product, Mattel used associations of beauty, wealth, and glamour. *Id.* For purposes of social commentary, the defendant transformed these associations by using Barbie dolls in his photography. In some of his photos, kitchen appliances are about to destroy or harm Barbie dolls. Other photos portray a nude Barbie in sexual poses and contexts. The transformative nature of the work made clear that the defendant's commentary intended to show the harm that he perceived in Barbie's influence on gender roles in society. *Id.*

Your paragraph-thesis sentence works. It tells the reader the point of the paragraph. The rest of the paragraph "proves" or "supports" the assertion made in the first sentence, which allows readers to see if you correctly represented the case.

EXAMPLES

Here are some example paragraphs. Examine the first sentence of each paragraph and decide how well it works as a paragraph-thesis sentence. Most of the examples come from the copyright and fair use problem used throughout the book. Others are on another topic, but you should be able to tell enough from the example to choose good answers. More than one answer can be correct. Choose what you think are the correct answers and explain to yourself why you've chosen those answers. Then read the explanations.

Example 27-1

In *Mattel*, the court ruled that it is unlikely that the defendant's work could substitute for products that Mattel markets or licenses. *Mattel v. Walking Mountain Prods.*, 353 F.3d 792, 805 (9th Cir. 2003). The defendant's work portrayed Barbie in nude and sexualized positions, which serves a different market type than the one in which Mattel marketed the doll. *Id.* Furthermore, the court stated it was reasonable to assume that the defendant's work would not affect derivative works by Mattel because Mattel would not want to market products that are socially critical of themselves. *Id.*

The first sentence is . . .

A. a paragraph-thesis sentence because it tells readers what the paragraph is about.

B. a topic sentence, but not a paragraph-thesis sentence, because it doesn't make an assertion that tells the reader the main point this paragraph intends to make.

C. typical of good paragraph-thesis sentences because it starts by telling the reader what case it comes from.

Example 27-2

Here, Olds' lyrics are not entitled to fair use protection because it is likely that his song would serve as a substitute for Young's original. Unlike the defendant's work in *Mattel*, Olds' work shares many similarities with Young's work that result in confusion by listeners and market harm to the copyright holder. Both songs are social commentaries that deliver similar messages. The market that Olds is catering to is precisely the same as Young's market: rock music fans who want political commentary.

The first sentence is . . .

A. a good paragraph-thesis sentence.

B. a topic sentence, not a paragraph-thesis sentence.

C. not a good paragraph-thesis sentence because it's conclusory.

Example 27-3

Olds' song has many of the same lines and ideas as Young's song, but puts a slightly positive spin on it. Unlike the songs in *Campbell* and *Fisher*, which were of different genres, here the allegedly infringing song is in the same rock genre as the original and contains the same subject matter. Olds' song could easily replace the original as a sort of anthem because society tends to like happy endings and thoughts of hope, especially in times of trouble. Because of its happy nature it is likely to "substitute the original" at many concerts and events, "fulfilling the same demand."

This is . . .

A. a good paragraph-thesis sentence because it includes facts.
B. a good paragraph-thesis sentence because it tells the reader where the author is going.
C. not a paragraph-thesis sentence.

Example 27-4

In *Priebe v. Sinclair*, 90 Cal. App. 2d 79, 84 (1949), the court examined the question of implied conditions in giving gifts. Gifts given after the acceptance of a marriage proposal do not have the same implied conditions as an engagement ring given at the time of acceptance of a proposal. *Id.* at 86. In *Priebe*, the donor gave the donee gifts of money and a gold brooch after the proposal had already been accepted. *Id.* at 81. The donor did not state that these gifts were conditional upon the marriage taking place. Because of this the court rejected the claim for recovery under section 1590 and allowed the donee to retain them. *Id.* at 86.

A. The first sentence is a good paragraph-thesis sentence except it shouldn't start with a case's name.
B. The first sentence is a topic sentence, but not a paragraph-thesis sentence.
C. It would be a good idea to eliminate the first sentence and use the second sentence as a paragraph-thesis sentence.

EXPLANATIONS

Explanation 27-1

A is incorrect. The sentence might be acceptable as a topic sentence, but it fails our test for a paragraph-thesis sentence because it doesn't make an assertion that the rest of the paragraph proves. *B* is correct. It does not state a thesis. *C* is incorrect. Most of the time paragraph-thesis sentences will be stronger if they don't begin with the preposition "in" and a case name.

Explanation 27-2

A is correct. This is a paragraph-thesis sentence because it makes an assertion about the case that advances the argument. The rest of the paragraph supports the assertion with comparisons, or analogies, to precedent cases. **B** is incorrect. It's more than a topic sentence because it makes an assertion that advances the argument. **C** is incorrect. Remember that a paragraph-thesis sentence is often the conclusion you want the reader to draw after reading the paragraph. It's logical that a conclusion is "conclusory."

Explanation 27-3

A is incorrect. This is a statement of fact, not a paragraph-thesis sentence. The choice of facts announces the topic of the paragraph, but it's not an assertion that moves the argument forward. **B** is incorrect. This is not a paragraph-thesis sentence. It is not an assertion that the paragraph will explain and support. **C** is correct. It is not a topic sentence that acts as a thesis for the paragraph. It lacks a connection to a legal conclusion.

Explanation 27-4

A is incorrect. This is not a paragraph-thesis sentence that states a thesis for the paragraph. It is true, however, that it's rarely effective to start a paragraph-thesis sentence with a case's name. **B** is correct. It does announce the topic of paragraph, but only in the most general way. It does not make an assertion about the point of the paragraph. **C** is correct. The second sentence here would make a good paragraph-thesis sentence.

Writing Concisely to Stay Within the Word Count or Page Limit

28

Uh-oh! You've been working hard on an assignment and you've finally finished a full draft. But you suddenly realize that you're over the word count—substantially over the word count! What now?

Terminology Notes: If your professor calls your writing style "dense," "wordy," or "verbose," the tips in this chapter should help.

WHAT YOU NEED TO KNOW ABOUT WRITING CONCISELY

You can almost always cut down your document. Most law students feel they need every single word of their papers. But you can always find places to cut, and learning to cut with the least impact on the document's quality is an important skill. In fact, in practice you'll often need to make cuts. Sometimes you'll be part of a team of writers working on one document and the team will allot you only a little space because your issue is less important. Other times you'll be in charge of making decisions but your draft will exceed the court's page limit. You'll learn that you can almost always make your point more economically.

You can prune a lot with stylistic cuts before you turn to substance. It takes going through the document sentence by sentence, line by line, but most students can find the extra words they need for arguments or analysis by deleting useless words. Here are four ways to cut out unnecessary words at the sentence level.

1. Make verbs carry the action; use passive voice rarely and only when you have a good reason for using it; use few nominalizations.
2. Look for clusters of small words; look for unnecessary uses of the word *of*.
3. Avoid unnecessary "there is" and "it is" constructions.
4. Avoid throat-clearing; use concise introductory clauses; use signals; and use transitions.

Although you may repeat the same point in different sections of one document, avoid repetition within a single section of the document. Many times legal readers will have time to turn to only one section of the paper. Those hurried readers must be able to read a single section and understand what is going on. Therefore, you may need to repeat the same point in two different sections to make each section stand on its own for the reader. But within one section, ordinarily you should not repeat, unless you're repeating a thesis statement as a conclusion. Each sentence should move the reader forward.

Finally, when you must cut substance you can shorten an argument or eliminate a weak argument. Sometimes shortening a point can make it stronger and more forceful; including weak arguments can make you seem desperate. At first it's difficult to make good decisions about the relative strength of arguments and to know which arguments deserve the space needed to develop them. But cutting out the weak parts of your document is empowering! See Chapter 20 on Making Persuasive Arguments and Chapter 4 on Choosing Authorities for help on deciding what to cut.

HOW TO EDIT FOR A MORE CONCISE DOCUMENT

Using the copyright and fair use problem in Appendix B, we'll walk you through the process of writing more concisely. Although we suggest a step-by-step process, you can use the tips in these steps in any order that makes sense to you.

Problem

> Here is a quick overview of the copyright and fair use problem. Young is suing Olds for violating the Copyright Act when Olds wrote a song based on Young's original, "Rockin' in the Free World." Olds' song uses the structure and many lyrics of the original but changes the original song's political message. The music of the two songs is not at issue, only the lyrics. Young expects that Olds will argue that his song is a parody that falls under the fair use exception to the Copyright Act. The court will consider the relevant factors set out in the fair use statute, 17 U.S.C. § 107 (2006): whether the copy was transformative and targeted the original; whether it took more than necessary of the original; and whether it will interfere with the original's market.

Here's a passage of dense text from an office memo.

The first factor also includes an examination by the court of whether there is a commercial aspect in the new work. *Campbell v. Acuff-Rose Music, Inc.*, 510 U.S. 569, 584 (1994). In cases from some Circuits, it has been found that the derivative work's commercial purpose weighed against it. Plaintiffs in copyright infringement suits often present the commercial aspect of a derivative as a basis to rule against it. There are recent decisions, however, that have made clear the rule that the commercial character of a work does not automatically preclude a claim to fair use. The appeals court that ruled in the case of *Campbell v. Acuff-Rose* overruled an initial summary judgment that the new song was commercial, thus not able to claim fair use. Upon review the Supreme Court held that the decision was erroneous. The Supreme Court held that the song's commercial aspect is merely one point of consideration. *Campbell v. Acuff-Rose Music, Inc.*, 510 U.S. 569, 584 (1994). In the case of *Fisher v. Dees*, which was decided earlier, the court held likewise that the commercial purpose of the parody did not negate the claim of fair use. *Fisher v. Dees*, 794 F.2d 432, 437 (9th Cir. 1986). A parody may be commercial, but if it proves to be adequately transformative and if it comments on the original work then it will probably win more of the judges on the first factor.

Turning now to our case, it is possible that Phil Olds' song will be found to be a parody. The lyrics mirror the original topically, but ironically reflect the opposite images. It is noteworthy that many listeners regard the original song, "Keep on Rockin' in the Free World," as a cynical appraisal of the nation. Such listeners may therefore regard Olds' reworking as a mocking reflection, contrasting and correcting the original's pessimism with a message that the United States remains a healthy nation with a happy population. It may be argued that Olds' derivative is not a parody. There are other interpretations of the original that find the message strangely supportive of the United States. Despite the bleak images the song offers hope for the future and an assertion that America is still strong. The chorus of the song is a rallying cry and a celebration of freedom. In this sense the point of Olds' song is a mere appropriation of Young's vehicle, lacking the transformative quality necessary for parody.

These two paragraphs include 407 words. We'll explain how to reduce them. This isn't just an exercise in cutting words. When you tighten up the writing, you make it more powerful.

Step 1: Look for passive voice. Some students try to eliminate passive voice by looking for *is* or *was*, automatically getting rid of all forms of the verb *to be*, or by eliminating gerunds ("-ing" verbs). It is true that the verb *to be* often represents weak writing (see Step 4) and often you should replace it with an action verb. But looking for forms of *to be* and gerunds doesn't work to find passive voice in your writing because passive voice is not about verb tense or which verb one chooses. Instead, it occurs if the person or thing responsible for the action is either missing from the sentence or has become the object of the sentence.

The most effective method is to look at each sentence in isolation and ask yourself, "What is the action in this sentence and who is doing it?" Although the preceding sentence includes a form of *to be* three times, none of the three uses are in passive voice. Further, passive voice is not always bad. Sometimes you use passive voice because you want a different emphasis in the sentence. But eliminate passive voice wherever it obscures the action, weakens the writing, or adds too many words.

Remember, after you've identified the action, if you can't tell who's doing it, or the sentence uses the word "by" to identify the actor, then you have a passive voice problem. When you're trying to cut words, you'll usually save words if you use active voice.

Find the passive voice in the previous two-paragraph example. There's one in the second sentence:

> In cases from some Circuits, it has been found that the work's commercial purpose is weighed against it.
> [*16 words*]

This sentence includes two actions, "finding" and "weighing." In the phrase "it has been found," do we know who's finding? No. You know *where* it's found—in cases from the federal circuits—but the sentence doesn't tell you *who* found it. That's because the sentence is in passive voice. And who's weighing? Again, you don't know. If "finding" were the crucial action, you would need to supply a subject, such as "the courts within those circuits find." But here, weighing is the more important action, and the subject "circuits" works if we make "to weigh" the active verb. After recasting the sentence to save words, we get this:

> Some circuits weigh a work's commercial purpose against fair use.
> [*10 words*]

Step 2: Look for nominalizations. Nominalizations are words that could have been action verbs, but the writer instead has halted the action by turning the verb into a noun. For example, instead of saying "argue," you might be tempted to say "make an argument." There, "argument" would be a nominalization, the noun you've made out of the active verb "to argue." Or instead of saying "the court interpreted" (*three words*) you might be tempted to say "the interpretation of the court was" (*six words, three of which are unnecessary*). Many nominalizations are "-tion" words. To cure nominalizations, find the action in the sentence and incorporate it into the verbs.

For example, find the nominalizations in the two-paragraph example at the beginning of this section. There's one in the first sentence:

> The first factor also includes an examination by the court of whether there is a commercial aspect in the new work.
> [*21 words*]

Looking for the action here, you can see that the court is really *examining.* As the sentence is written, however, "examination" is a nominalization that stores the action in a noun instead of a verb. You also see "includes," which is a verb but not a terribly active or necessary one. Rewrite the sentence so it focuses on action:

> Under the first factor, courts examine whether the new work is commercial.
> [*12 words*]

Notice that you also got rid of the word "of" and other words cluttering the sentence. That's the focus of the next step.

Step 3: Look for small-word clusters that include the word "of." These small-word clusters can occur in phrases or clauses that have no function other than to take up space. Often you can cut a lot in these situations. Sometimes the whole phrase can disappear without changing the meaning of the sentence. Other times, you can at least trim a few words. Remember that you were able to cut words in Step 2 by changing "of whether there is a" — a classic small-word cluster — to "whether." Here's another opportunity:

> There are other interpretations of the original that find the message supportive of the United States.
> [*16 words*]

Cutting part of the "of" phrases and changing the nominalization "interpretations" to the verb "interpret," you get this:

> Others interpret the original's message to support the United States.
> [*10 words*]

We also eliminated the sentence's "there are" construction. (The tip in Step 4.)

Not every *of* is bad. Often you need to use it. But it's worth the time to check to see if you can save words by identifying small-word clusters.

Step 4: Avoid unnecessary "there is" and "it is" constructions.

These often present opportunities to cut—and to strengthen the writing at the same time. For instance, "there are many lawyers who believe that concise writing is important" (*11 words*) can become "many lawyers believe concise writing is important" (*seven words—and stronger writing as well*). This is from the two-paragraph example at the beginning of this section:

> There are recent decisions, however, that have made clear the rule that the commercial character of a work does not automatically preclude a claim to fair use. [*27 words*]

Changing the "there are" construction (and using some of the other Steps) produces this:

> Recent decisions have clarified that a work's commercial character does not preclude claiming fair use. [*15 words*]

Step 5: Avoid throat-clearing, and instead use concise introductory clauses, signals, and transitions.

Throat-clearing is an unnecessary introductory clause or phrase at or near the sentence's beginning. Often throat-clearing contains *metadiscourse*—writing that tells the reader how to think about the information in the sentence rather than simply providing that information. Examples of throat-clearing include "It is important to realize that," "Especially noteworthy is the fact that," or even something as simple as "it is clear."

Throat-clearing includes introducing a rule with something like "In the case of X, the court held . . . ." The citation tells the reader which court the rule comes from. Just state the rule, followed by a cite to the case.

Look for throat-clearing phrases or other long introductory clauses, signals, or transitions in the two-paragraph examples at the beginning of this section, where you'll find these sentences:

> It is noteworthy that many listeners regard the original song, "Rockin' in the Free World," as a cynical appraisal of the nation.

> In the case of *Fisher v. Dees*, which was decided earlier, the court held likewise that the commercial purpose of the parody did not negate the claim of fair use. *Fisher v. Dees*, 794 F.2d 432, 437 (9th Cir. 1986).

> Turning now to our case, it is possible that Phil Olds' song will be found to be a parody.

The first sentence here starts with a throat-clearing phrase. Just delete it and start the sentence "Many listeners regard . . ." *(saving four words)*.

The second sentence uses the long, unnecessary introduction to the rule. You can delete everything but "The commercial purpose of a parody does not negate a fair use claim" *(saving 16 words)*.

And the third sentence uses a lengthy transition. You can trim it to "Here the court may decide Olds' song is a parody" *(saving nine words)*.

Step 6: Check for repetition. The goal is for every sentence to move the reader forward. No marching in place! Look through the two-paragraph example at the beginning of this section. Do you see any repetition?

> The Supreme Court held that the song's commercial aspect is merely one point of consideration. *Campbell v. Acuff-Rose Music, Inc.*, 510 U.S. 569, 584 (1994). In the case of *Fisher v. Dees*, which was decided earlier, the court held likewise that the commercial purpose of the parody did not negate the claim of fair use. *Fisher v. Dees*, 794 F.2d 432, 437 (9th Cir. 1986).

The second sentence not only repeats the point, but repeats it with an older case from a lower court. Once you've cited the highest mandatory authority in your jurisdiction, there's no need to repeat the point with a lower court. You can cut the entire second sentence *(saving 30 words)*.

Step 7: When you've cut all you can with style, shorten some arguments or evaluate which of your points are weakest and cut them. Look at the first of the two paragraphs in the example:

> The first factor also includes an examination by the court of whether there is a commercial aspect in the new work. *Campbell v. Acuff-Rose Music, Inc.*, 510 U.S. 569, 584 (1994). In cases from some Circuits, it has been found that the derivative work's commercial purpose weighed against it. Plaintiffs in copyright infringement suits often present the commercial aspect of a derivative as a basis to rule against it. There are recent decisions, however, that have made clear the rule that the commercial character of a work does not automatically preclude a claim to fair use. The appeals court that ruled in the case of *Campbell v. Acuff-Rose* overruled an initial summary judgment that the new song was commercial, thus not able to claim fair use. Upon review the Supreme Court held that the decision was erroneous. The Supreme Court held that the song's commercial aspect is merely one point of consideration. *Campbell v. Acuff-Rose Music, Inc.*, 510 U.S. 569, 584 (1994). In the case of *Fisher v. Dees*, which was decided earlier, the court held likewise that the commercial purpose of the parody did not negate the claim of fair use. *Fisher v. Dees*, 794 F.2d 432, 437 (9th Cir. 1986). A parody may be commercial, but if it proves to be adequately transformative and if it

comments on the original work then it will probably win more of the judges on the first factor.

In addition to all the stylistic problems, this paragraph uses many words to make a simple point: that a parody's commercial nature may weigh against it but will not automatically preclude fair use. And you have the best authority for that statement—the U.S. Supreme Court. For most readers, you need say no more. Other historical cases leading up to that point don't make it more convincing. The reader cares about the state of the law *today*, and unless a historical trend is part of your analysis, the reader cares little how you got to today's rule. Ordinarily you should avoid a one-sentence paragraph. Thus, when you revise the paragraph, although you could cut most of it, you will keep two sentences:

> A parody's commercial nature may weight against it, but it will not automatically preclude fair use. *Campbell v. Acuff-Rose Music, Inc.*, 510 U.S. 569, 584 (1994). A song's commercial nature is merely one point of consideration. *Id.*

You've saved a whopping 200 words—which opens up a lot of space to develop your strongest arguments.

EXAMPLES

Here are some examples to provide practice cutting the word count. Make the paragraphs more concise and choose your answers. More than one answer may be correct. Explain to yourself why you've chosen your answers. Then read the explanations.

Example 28-1

On the other hand, one could make the argument that Olds' new work could be mistaken for Young's original, as was found in *Seuss*. Market confusion is not as likely as in *Seuss*, because in *Seuss* the amount of copying was extreme. In the case of *Seuss*, there were indications of seven recognizable features of the original. Further, the fact that the consumers of the work in *Seuss* are children who could easily mistake the gory parody for the original work of Dr. Seuss. This marketing to children foreseeably damages the market of the original. The facts support a conclusion that adult consumers would likely not mistake Olds' pro-government copy for Young's cynical original. Thus the court is not likely to find Olds' copy interferes with Young's market.

A. The argument comparing children purchasing books to adults purchasing rock music is weak because it assumes that only children purchase children's books. In fact, adults purchase most children's books to give as gifts to children. The comparison doesn't work.

B. This paragraph contains two instances of unnecessary passive voice.

C. The author used a grammatically incorrect "there were" construction in sentence three.

D. Passive voice is always in the present tense.

Example 28-2

Here, because of the case-by-case analysis of parody "fair use" cases, Mr. Young might be able to bring a suit for infringement, but it is not likely that he would win. Mr. Young's chances of winning are slight. There is no doubt that the law favors parody as fair use if it meets the four statutory factors, and it appears in this case that Mr. Olds' parody of Mr. Young's original work would likely be found by the court to win if he can prove those factors are in his favor. The four factors are set out below.

A. The author could cut this entire introductory paragraph.

B. The hedging in the first sentence wastes words.

C. "There is no doubt that the law favors" is not just a throat-clearing phrase because it tells the reader how strong the chances are that Olds will win.

D. The author could cut the second sentence because it's repetitious.

Example 28-3

A parody may be an infringement if it causes a severe economic hardship regarding the work of the original artist. One way to make the determination of whether economic harm exists is the examination of whether the songs are targeting the same listeners. When the original song is of a completely different genre than the new song, it has been found the new song is unlikely to be in competition with the original. It is likely to be found the competition to the original is limited because the group of listeners is different. When both songs are in the same genre the new piece may drown out the original and take its place, which indicates the creation of an economic hardship.

A. Every sentence in this paragraph contains either an unnecessary nominalization or passive voice.

B. The author should change the words "may drown out" in the last sentence because the author used passive voice.

C. The last sentence is a weak argument and the author should cut it.

D. Sometimes editing for a more concise style can show the author the strength of an argument because a dense writing style can cover up errors in reasoning.

Example 28-4

Review the following passage and decide which alternatives below are good edits. More than one answer may be correct. Note that citations are omitted.

The commercial nature of the work is a consideration when there is an examination of the purpose of the work. The fact that the work is commercial in nature does not mean that it negates consideration for fair use. If it is decided the work was created as more of a commentary than for profit, then an argument can be made for fair use. In order to prove that the song is more of a commentary or criticism, the defendant can try to show the new song does not unfairly interfere with the financial nature of the original. [98 words]

A. As a court examines a work, it considers whether the work's purpose is commercial. A work may be fair use and commercial if the defendant created it more for commentary than for profit. To show the work's nature is primarily to provide commentary, the defendant must demonstrate the new song does not unfairly interfere with the original's market. [58 words]

B. To prove fair use when there is a work commercial in nature, the courts examine whether the work interferes with the original's market. [23 words]

C. Courts consider the commercial nature of the work when there is an examination of the work's purpose. If the court decides the work was created for commentary and not for profit, then fair use is possible. The defendant can try to show the market of the original is not interfered with by the copy. [54 words]

D. Courts consider the commercial nature of a copy, although a commercial work can still be fair use. The defendant can demonstrate fair use by showing the new work is commentary that does not unfairly interfere with the original's market. [39 words]

EXPLANATIONS

Explanation 28-1

A is correct. This is a weak argument. Including it will weaken your other arguments. Cut it. **B** is also correct. The two instances are both in the first sentence: "could be mistaken" and "was found." **C** is incorrect. The grammar in sentence three is fine, although the style isn't concise or active. A good editor would delete the introductory phrase "In the case of *Seuss*" and make the verb active. Something similar to "the author copied seven recognizable features" would be a good solution. **D** is incorrect. Students often confuse present tense or a verb gerund (-ing) for passive voice. Both of those types of verbs are fine. Remember to ask yourself whether you can identify who is doing the action in the sentence. If you can't tell who did it, or if it uses the word "by" to identify the actor, it's passive voice.

Here is one way to edit the paragraph. The paragraph starts with counterargument and then answers the counterargument with why Olds should ultimately win this factor:

> Conversely, just as the *Seuss* court found that book buyers could confuse the copy with the original book because the two were so similar and in the same genre, listeners could mistake Olds' copy for the original because they are similar and in the same genre. But here, Olds takes far less of the original than the defendant in *Seuss*. Thus, consumers are far less likely to mistake the copy for the original and the court will probably not find Olds' copy interferes with Young's market.

Note that although this version adds words to strengthen the analogy, it still uses nearly 50 fewer words than the original.

Explanation 28-2

A is incorrect because an introductory paragraph is necessary for a well-organized, coherent document. It is true, however, that this particular introductory paragraph doesn't add much for the amount of words it uses. **B** is correct. A simpler thesis would be stronger: "Young is likely to lose his copyright infringement claim." **C** is incorrect. The phrase "there is no doubt that" adds little to the meaning of the sentence. Further, the sentence itself states the obvious because it essentially says "he will win if he can prove the case"—an obvious point that the author doesn't need to make. **D** is correct. The second sentence can be deleted entirely without a loss.

Here is one way to edit the paragraph:

> Young is unlikely to win a claim for copyright infringement because Olds can likely use the fair use defense. Courts examine the four factors for fair use below.

Explanation 28-3

A is correct. Here are the examples of the nominalizations or passive voice: "may be an infringement" (nominalization, "to infringe"); "make a determination" (nominalization, "to determine"); "it has been found" (passive voice, "courts have found"); "it is likely to be found" (passive voice, "a court will likely find" or just delete entirely); and "the creation of" (nominalization that the author can simply delete). *B* is incorrect. The phrase is not passive voice because we know who is doing the action: "*the new piece* may drown out." *C* is incorrect. The last sentence nicely sums up the argument that is the topic of the paragraph. *D* is correct and part of the magic of a good writing style. It's another reason for learning to write concisely.

Here is one way to edit the paragraph:

> A parody may infringe the copyright if it causes severe economic hardship by targeting the same listeners as the original. If the two songs are in different genres, they appeal to different listeners and are unlikely to compete for the same market.

This is a good edit of the passage, though it should include cites to authority.

Explanation 28-4

A is a good improvement. The edit saves lots of words by making nominalizations into active verbs. For example "is a consideration" becomes "it considers" and "there is an examination" becomes "as a court examines." Further, it eliminates passive voice: "it is decided"; "was created"; and "an argument can be made." It saves 50 words and is easy to follow. *B* is an extreme edit that probably doesn't preserve the meaning of the original passage. (Sometimes it's hard to tell the meaning of the original passage when the writing is particularly dense.) This edit eliminates the idea that courts consider whether the defendant created the copy as a commentary. It saves a lot of words, but unless you have decided the information about "more for commentary than for profit" is unimportant, the edit cuts too much. *C* saves words, but fails to minimize nominalizations and passive voice. You could shorten it by changing "when there is an examination of the work's purpose" to "when the court examines the work's purpose." The passage contains an example of passive voice in the third line: "was created." **D** is an excellent edit as long as the "created for commentary and not for profit" idea is clear enough. The verbs are active: "by showing" is not passive voice because we know who is doing it—the defendant. Depending on your goals for the passage, you might think carefully about whether you have cut needed emphasis. But you have saved 69 words that you can use to strengthen your argument in other ways.

Bringing It Together: Transitions and Coherence

Imagine that after reading your memo or brief, the reader puts it down and thinks to himself or herself, "Now, that was good. I get it." As a writer, this is your goal. One of the key aspects of achieving readability is coherence, which you can improve by following the tips in this chapter.

WHAT YOU NEED TO KNOW ABOUT TRANSITIONS AND COHERENCE

Coherence is hard to pinpoint because it comes from both content and writing style. Words and the ideas they convey must be consistent, logical, and related to each other throughout the document so that the reader can easily follow the writer's flow of thought between sentences, paragraphs, and sections.

No short list of steps can help you achieve coherence in your writing. In that regard, coherence is more of a guiding principle or characteristic of good writing rather than a concrete section or component. It starts with your clarity of thought about the relevant law and facts and it doesn't end until you've completed the final polishing revisions. But you can do several things to significantly increase your document's coherence at both the large-scale (structural) level and the small-scale (paragraph and sentence) level.

TIPS ON TRANSITIONS AND COHERENCE

Use introductory paragraphs—also known as roadmap or umbrella sections—to give the reader a big-picture view of what you say next. If you have several steps of analysis, an introductory paragraph can make it much easier for your reader to use and understand your document. For help with introductory sections, see Chapter 12.

For a memo's Discussion or a brief's Argument, use the organizational pattern readers are familiar with. This is the pattern explained in Chapter 6 and known variously as IRAC, CRAC, CREAC, CRuPAC, or the "organizational paradigm." Be especially careful to keep the rule statement and explanation separate from the application.

Use signpost words or phrases to keep the reader aware of your analysis's sequence and main points. For instance, sometimes you can enumerate your points as a list upfront ("Three exceptions exist for this requirement."). Then you can label each corresponding item in your analysis or argument as "First," "Second," and "Third." This works for various kinds of points—issues, elements, exceptions, questions, reasons, etc. (Put the number before the noun: i.e., "The first issue," "The second element," "The third exception," "The fourth question," "The fifth reason.") Note that it is "first," "second," and "third," and not "firstly," "secondly," and "thirdly."

In a persuasive document, point headings and subheadings help the reader find a particular section of a document and understand the logical flow of your argument. For help with point headings and subheadings, see Chapter 19.

To begin a paragraph coherently, use a well-crafted paragraph-thesis sentence. See Chapter 27 for more help with this.

Keep each paragraph focused on supporting the paragraph-thesis. Delete or move out any extraneous statements. The paragraph should have just one purpose. Consider this paragraph:

> A parody may permissibly copy original works to some extent because the nature of parody necessitates using some distinctive or memorable features of the original work to communicate that it is the subject of parody. *Campbell*, 510 U.S. at 588. For example, in *Campbell* the Supreme Court determined that 2 Live Crew's verbatim use of the first line of Roy Orbison's song "Oh, Pretty Woman" was permissible because it was necessary for the listener to "conjure up" the original. *Id.* Further, courts do not require parodies to take the minimum amount of copyrighted works needed for identification. *See Mattel*, 353 F.3d at 804. In *Mattel*, although the artist arguably could have used a smaller portion of the Barbie doll in his photography, the Ninth Circuit concluded that the artist's purpose and artistic medium justified the extent of copying. *Id.* Moreover, the court considered that the artist's photography was transformative because the

context in which the artist put the doll illuminated his view of Barbie's influence on societal gender roles. *Id.* at 802.

This paragraph is nicely unified on the point of the permissible amount of copying for a parody until the last line that begins "Moreover, . . ." At that point, the writer has put in an idea that goes to the first statutory fair use factor, the "purpose and character" of the work. This is a related point, but it is extraneous to this paragraph, which is focused on the third statutory fair use factor. It would be better to delete the last sentence or move it elsewhere.

Sequence your sentences in a logical order. A common sequence in legal writing is like a triangle that goes from a broad statement and narrows to specific support. A variation on this is to include a broader, general conclusion again at the end of the paragraph.

BROAD

Gross negligence "is the exercise of so slight a degree of care as to raise a presumption of conscious indifference to the consequences." *People v. Harris,* 104 Cal. Rptr. 3d 131, 134 (Ct. App. 2010). The objective test for gross negligence in cases involving vehicular manslaughter is whether a reasonable person in the defendant's position would have been aware of the dangers involved in talking on a cellular phone while driving. *Id.* For example, in *Tompkins,* the court held the defendant acted with gross negligence by driving and using a cell phone without a hands-free device because he "knew or should have known" that he was endangering others' lives. 89 Cal. Rptr. 3d 904, 909 (Ct. App. 2009). Likewise, in *Harris,* the court held that the defendant's subjective belief that it was safe for him to drive while talking on a cell phone was inconsequential because the test is objective. 104 Cal. Rptr. 3d at 135.

NARROW

Avoid long sentences, particularly lots of them in a row. Chapter 28 can help. As a general rule of thumb, a long sentence is 25 or more words or three to four lines of type. For instance, this sentence of 41 words is long and a bit hard to follow:

> The amount of the work used in copying, whether that is large or small, is deemed permissible by the extent of its purpose and character, such as to parody the original work without becoming a market substitute for the original work. *Campbell*, 510 U.S. at 587.

You could edit this to a sentence of 24 words that's much easier to read:

> The extent of permissible copying depends on its purpose and character, such as to parody without becoming a market substitute for the original work. *Campbell*, 510 U.S. at 587.

Here's another illustration of revising long sentences, reducing this long one:

> For the parodist to be successful at creating a parody, the reader must be able to identify the original work and this means that, due to the nature of parody, the parodist will often need to use some distinctive or memorable features that the audience will recognize. *Campbell*, 510 U.S. at 588.

to this shorter, easier-to-read version:

> Parody necessitates using some distinctive or memorable features of the original work so that the audience can recognize it as a parody of the original work. *Campbell*, 510 U.S. at 588.

Another strategy for avoiding long sentences is to break long sentences in two.

Use consistent terminology. Consider this passage:

> Item 303(a) of Regulation S-K requires the registrant to disclose any material changes in the mix and relative cost of its capital resources. 17 C.F.R. § 229.303 (2010). Substantial changes could include any resource-related trends, changes between equity and debt, or off-balance sheet arrangements. *Id.*

Once you've started with the concept of a "material change," do not vary this phrasing later if you're referring to the same thing. The reader will not know whether you mean the same thing if you vary the wording to "substantial change." Moreover, the phrase "material change" could be a legal term of art with a precise meaning (and if so, you should use quotation marks at least the first time you discuss it).

You can fix many sentence-level problems by keeping the subject and verb close together and using active voice. For help with sentence structure, refer to Chapter 26.

Keep paragraphs to a moderate length. As a rough benchmark, a paragraph that is three-quarters of a double-spaced page or less is typically a moderate length.

Use transitional words or phrases to connect your ideas between sentences and from paragraph to paragraph. Transitions signal to the reader how your ideas are connected and where your analysis is headed. Transitions might be as simple as a word like "Nevertheless," or "Furthermore," but you must carefully choose them and where you put them to properly convey your meaning. Here are some useful transitional words.

new or additional info:	additionally, furthermore, further, in addition, and
a list of coordinated ideas:	first, second, third
when giving examples:	for instance, for example, such as, to illustrate, specifically
time relationships:	before, after, previously, at the same time, later, then, subsequently
to show similarities:	likewise, analogously, similarly
for causation:	therefore, thus, consequently, accordingly, because
for contrasts:	although, but, even though, despite, even if, nevertheless, in contrast, even though
for emphasis:	moreover, above all, indeed
to concede a point:	although, granted, to be sure
more or less abstraction:	more generally, as a general matter, in general, specifically, more specifically, namely, in fact

You can also use a substantive transition or "dovetailing." To do this, begin a sentence with information you've already introduced to the reader and then add new information. This overlapping or dovetailing of key words or ideas adds coherence and makes it easier for the reader to digest your writing. In this example, we bolded certain words and phrases to illustrate dovetailing. (The bold should not appear in your work.)

Item 303(a) of Regulation S-K requires the registrant to disclose **any material changes** in the mix and relative cost of its capital resources. 17 C.F.R. § 229.303 (2010). **Material changes** could include any resource-related trends, changes between equity and debt, off-balance sheet arrangements, or **financial condition**. Id. Whereas section 303 concerns **material changes** to **financial** condition and the like, the comparable European Transparency Directive refers to principal risks more generally.

Remember, though, that you must have coherence in substance as well as style. No amount of transitions or dovetails will help you achieve coherence if your analysis doesn't make sense. Consider the following passage:

> The suspect killed the victim with a **gun**. **Guns** are often banned in states or are subject to waiting periods and permit requirements to reduce **crime**. Indeed, **crime**s like murder and robbery often involve **weapons**. **Weapons** are **dangerous**. Of course, **danger** comes from many sources; it could come from natural disasters or **extreme weather**. Such **weather** may be responsible for **death**. **This kind of death** is a tragedy.

EXAMPLES

Read the following examples. Each is based either on the cell phone manslaughter problem in Appendix A or the copyright and fair use problem in Appendix B. For each example, choose the best answer. Explain to yourself why you've chosen that answer. Then read the explanations in the last section of this chapter to check your work.

Example 29-1

Choose the best answer about the effectiveness of the transition word bolded in this passage:

> For a situation to rise to the level of an "emergency" and constitute a valid exception, there must be a risk of "imminent danger" threatening the driver or other individuals. *People v. Tompkins*, 89 Cal. Rptr. 3d 904, 909 (Ct. App. 2009); *People v. Newton*, 104 Cal. Rptr. 3d 138, 141 (Ct. App. 2010). **However**, in *Tompkins*, the court held that the defendant was not in an "emergency" situation when he called his family after learning that an earthquake had struck in their vicinity, because any potential danger to the defendant's family had passed by the time the defendant made the call. 89 Cal. Rptr. 3d at 909.

The choice of "However" is . . .

A. effective.
B. not effective and "Similarly," would be a good replacement.
C. not effective and "For example," would be a good replacement.
D. not effective and "Likewise," would be a good replacement.

Example 29-2

The four sentences in this paragraph aren't in a logical order. Rearrange them so that they make better sense.

> Like the *Campbell* defendants, who copied some lyrics from Roy Orbison's "Oh, Pretty Woman" to conjure up the original for purposes of parody, Olds accomplished the same with his song's refrain "stop knockin' the free world," which mirrors Young's phrasing. Although Olds used some of Young's lyrics, he did so to invoke and parody the original. Furthermore, as with the *Campbell* defendants, who transformed Roy Orbison's saccharine lyrics into a commentary on the harsh reality of street life, Olds has entirely reversed the anti-war message in Young's original song. Here, Olds targeted the anti-war message of Young's original song and transformed it into a social commentary about the importance of fighting for ideals.

Example 29-3

Identify the inconsistent terminology in this example. Replace with consistent terminology.

> Use of copyrighted material in a parody may fall under the fair use exception to the Copyright Act. *See* 17 U.S.C. § 107 (2006). To qualify for allowable use, parodists' work must fulfill the four factors of the permissibility test. *Id.* These factors include: "the purpose and character of the use, including whether such use is of a commercial nature or is for nonprofit educational purposes; the nature of the copyrighted work; the amount and substantiality of the portion used in relation to the copyrighted work as a whole; and the effect of the use upon the potential market for or value of the copyrighted work." *Id.*

Example 29-4

This paragraph for a draft objective memo is too long and is not unified around the paragraph-thesis sentence. Try to break this paragraph into two paragraphs in a logical way and write a paragraph-thesis sentence for the second paragraph.

> For a situation to rise to the level of an "emergency" and constitute a valid exception to section 23123 of the California Vehicle

Code, there must be "imminent danger" threatening the driver or other individuals. *People v. Tompkins*, 89 Cal. Rptr. 3d 904, 909 (Ct. App. 2009). For example, in *People v. Newton*, the court held that a genuine emergency existed when the defendant's wife began going into labor during a complicated pregnancy. 104 Cal. Rptr. 3d 138, 141 (Ct. App. 2010). Accordingly, the defendant had no obligation to pull over while driving when calling his wife's obstetrician. *Id.* By contrast, in *People v. Harris*, the court held that an emergency did not exist where a driver used his phone without a hands-free device to call a wedding party to inform them that he, the best man, would be late. 104 Cal. Rptr. 3d 131, 134 (Ct. App. 2010). Likewise in *People v. Tompkins*, the court held that the defendant was not in an "emergency" situation when he called his family after learning that an earthquake had struck in their vicinity, because any potential danger to himself and his family had passed by the time the defendant made the call. 89 Cal. Rptr. 3d at 909. Unlike in *Harris*, here there was real danger: the hazardous conditions of the road posed a threat to travelers. Our client, Ms. King, was calling to warn her friends of future danger, not simply checking in, like the defendant in *Tompkins*, to see how his family fared against a past threat. As in *Newton*, where the expecting father called his wife's obstetrician when his wife went into labor, King's cell phone use concerned a present emergency her friends were facing. King's friends were going to drive into the same perilous conditions that she was encountering, and warning them of the imminent danger constituted a justified emergency purpose.

EXPLANATIONS

Explanation 29-1

A is incorrect. "However" doesn't work well here because the sentence isn't a countervailing point, but rather an explanation or illustration of the rule. **B** is incorrect. Although in a sense there's a similarity between the statement of the rule and an explanation of how a court applied the rule in a precedent case, "Similarly," is not a precise word choice. The rule explanation is more explanatory than similar. **C** is correct. "For example," would be a good replacement because it expresses the relationship between the sentence and the preceding sentence. The rule explanation provides an example of how a court applied the rule. **D** is incorrect for the same reason B is incorrect.

Explanation 29-2

The following sentence order is more logical:

> Here, Olds targeted the anti-war message of Young's original song and transformed it into a social commentary about the importance of fighting for ideals. Although Olds used some of Young's lyrics, he did so to invoke and parody the original. Like the *Campbell* defendants, who copied some lyrics from Roy Orbison's "Oh, Pretty Woman" to conjure up the original for purposes of parody, Olds accomplished the same with his song's refrain "stop knockin' the free world," which mirrors Young's phrasing. Furthermore, as with the *Campbell* defendants, who transformed Roy Orbison's saccharine lyrics into a commentary on the harsh reality of street life, Olds has entirely reversed the anti-war message in Young's original song.

This revised sequencing puts the broad thesis sentence at the start of the paragraph. That is the point that the other sentences in the paragraph go toward proving or supporting. Following the thesis sentence are points of support, including analogical reasoning to precedent cases. The paragraph includes logical transitions such as the "Furthermore," that leads in to a sentence making an additional point on the same topic.

Explanation 29-3

The words in bold are unnecessary variations on the phrase "fair use." It would be better to keep "fair use" in those spots to avoid confusion about whether the writer is referring to the same thing or something different.

> Use of copyrighted material in a parody may fall under the fair use exception to the Copyright Act. *See* 17 U.S.C. § 107 (2006). To qualify for **allowable use**, parodists' work must fulfill the four factors of the **permissibility** test. *Id.* These factors include: "the purpose and character of the use, including whether such use is of a commercial nature or is for nonprofit educational purposes; the nature of the copyrighted work; the amount and substantiality of the portion used in relation to the copyrighted work as a whole; and the effect of the use upon the potential market for or value of the copyrighted work." *Id.*

Explanation 29-4

The example paragraph contains both rule statement and explanation about the applicable legal rules as well as rule application about how those rules will likely apply in a particular case at hand. A logical place to break this excessively long paragraph is where the switch to rule application occurs. In this example, that is at the sentence beginning "Unlike in *Harris*, here there was real danger present . . . ." The word "here" is a tip that the writer is talking about the instant case, namely Allison King's case in this example.

Once you break the paragraph in two, remember to review the new paragraphs to check that they each have well-crafted paragraph-thesis sentences and that the sentences in each paragraph are unified on the topic contained in the paragraph-thesis sentence and ordered in a logical sequence.

With this example, the paragraph-thesis sentence in the second paragraph can be revised in several ways. A simple solution would be to delete the lead-in "Unlike in *Harris*" because the paragraph does not go toward proving that narrow point of distinguishing King's case from *Harris*. Another improvement would be to more precisely echo the rule language in the sentence so that the application paragraph is clearly applying the rule established. We could change "real danger" to "imminent danger" and include the idea of this "constituting an emergency." Here's what it might look like once we break the paragraph in two where the application begins and we revise the paragraph-thesis sentence for that paragraph:

> For a situation to rise to the level of an "emergency" and constitute a valid exception to section 23123 of the California Vehicle Code, there must be "imminent danger" threatening the driver or other individuals. *People v. Tompkins*, 89 Cal. Rptr. 3d 904, 909 (Ct. App. 2009). For example, in *People v. Newton*, the court held that a genuine emergency existed when the defendant's wife began going into labor during a complicated pregnancy. 104 Cal. Rptr. 3d 138, 141 (Ct. App. 2010). Accordingly, the defendant had no obligation to pull over while driving when calling the hospital. *Id.* By contrast, in *People v. Harris*, the court held that an emergency did not exist where a driver used his phone without a hands-free device to call a wedding party to inform them that he, the best man, would be late. 104 Cal. Rptr. 3d 131, 134 (Ct. App. 2010). Likewise in *People v. Tompkins*, the court held that the defendant was not in an "emergency" situation when he called his family after learning that an earthquake had struck in their vicinity, because any potential danger to himself and his family had passed by the time the defendant made the call. 89 Cal. Rptr. 3d at 909.

Here, there was imminent danger constituting an emergency: The hazardous conditions of the road posed a threat to travelers. Our client, Ms. King, was calling to warn her friends of future danger, not simply checking in, like the defendant in *Tompkins*, to see how his family fared against a past threat. As in *Newton*, where the expecting father called his wife's obstetrician when his wife went into labor, King's cell phone use concerned a present emergency her friends were facing. King's friends were going to drive into the same perilous conditions that she was encountering, and warning them of the imminent danger constituted a justified emergency purpose.

The "Cell Phone Manslaughter" Problem

A

Our client, Allison King, has been charged with vehicular manslaughter in California. The facts that form the basis of the allegation are below.

On October 22, 2010, King was driving from Jenner to Gualala on State Highway 1. This road is well known for being a winding two-lane highway on the edge of a cliff with the sea below. The highway offers very few places to pull over. King planned to meet several friends from San Francisco for a weekend vacation on the coast near Gualala.

The night King was driving, the fog was rolling in from the ocean and driving conditions were even more hazardous than usual. King was terrified and kept her bearings in near-whiteout conditions by hugging the road on the side of the cliff. She also became concerned that the fog presented such dangerous driving conditions that she should warn her friends and suggest that they refrain from driving until road conditions improved.

King pulled out her cell phone and, while driving slowly along the cliff, she dialed one of her friends, June Coughlin, to give the warning. Her phone was not designed and configured to allow hands-free listening and talking. Suddenly a bicyclist appeared from out of the fog. King's car struck the cyclist, and he slipped across the road and over the cliff. The fall killed him. King has been charged with vehicular manslaughter.

The following California authorities may apply to this problem. (Note: the cases are fictional.)

Cal. Penal Code § 192. Manslaughter; voluntary, involuntary, and vehicular

Manslaughter is the unlawful killing of a human being without malice. It is of three kinds:

(a) Voluntary—upon a sudden quarrel or heat of passion.

(b) Involuntary—in the commission of an unlawful act, not amounting to felony; or in the commission of a lawful act which might produce death, in an unlawful manner, or without due caution and circumspection. This subdivision shall not apply to acts committed in the driving of a vehicle.

(c) Vehicular—

(1) Except as provided in subdivision (a) of Section 191.5, driving a vehicle in the commission of an unlawful act, not amounting to felony, and with gross negligence; or driving a vehicle in the commission of a lawful act which might produce death, in an unlawful manner, and with gross negligence. . . .

Cal. Penal Code § 191.5. Gross vehicular manslaughter while intoxicated

(a) Gross vehicular manslaughter while intoxicated is the unlawful killing of a human being without malice aforethought, in the driving of a vehicle, where the driving was in violation of Section 23140, 23152, or 23153 of the Vehicle Code, and the killing was either the proximate result of the commission of an unlawful act, not amounting to a felony, and with gross negligence, or the proximate result of the commission of a lawful act that might produce death, in an unlawful manner, and with gross negligence. . . .

Cal. Vehicle Code § 23123. Driving motor vehicle while using wireless telephone; penalty; exceptions

(a) A person shall not drive a motor vehicle while using a wireless telephone unless that telephone is specifically designed and configured to allow hands-free listening and talking, and is used in that manner while driving.

(b) A violation of this section is an infraction punishable by a base fine of twenty dollars ($20) for a first offense and fifty dollars ($50) for each subsequent offense.

(c) This section does not apply to a person using a wireless telephone for emergency purposes, including, but not limited to, an emergency call to a law enforcement agency, health care provider, fire department, or other emergency services agency or entity.

People v. Harris, 104 Cal. Rptr. 3d 131 (Ct. App. 2010)

On May 14, 2009, Harris was driving his car at approximately the speed limit, 45 mph. The vehicle in front of Harris was driven by Colter; Colter was preparing to turn right, and his turn signal was on. A pedestrian was crossing in the crosswalk, however, and Colter therefore had to stop before he could turn. Harris struck the back of Colter's car and Colter was killed. Skid marks at the scene reveal that Harris did not apply his brakes until his car was only three feet from Colter's vehicle. Harris was convicted of vehicular manslaughter under Cal. Penal Code § 192(c)(1) (West 2008), and he now appeals that conviction.

At the time of the accident, Harris was talking on a cellular phone without the benefit of a "hands-free" device. Harris admitted that he was aware it was a violation of California law to use a cellular phone while driving, but makes two contentions: (1) that he fits into the cell phone statute's exception for "emergencies"; and (2) that his actions did not constitute "gross negligence" under the manslaughter statute.

First, we hold that calling to inform a wedding party that the best man, Harris, would be late is not an "emergency" within the meaning of Cal. Vehicle Code § 23123(c) (West Supp. 2011). Harris' contention that pulling over to call would make him even later does not elevate the nature of the call to emergency status.

Second, as for whether the act was "gross negligence" under Cal. Penal Code § 192(c)(1) (West 2008), a reasonable person in Harris' position would have realized the risk involved in making the phone call while driving. "Gross negligence" is the exercise of so slight a degree of care as to raise a presumption of conscious indifference to the consequences. The test is objective: whether a reasonable person in the defendant's position would have been aware of the risk involved. If a *reasonable person* in defendant's position would have been aware of the risk involved, then defendant is presumed to have had such an awareness. The defendant's *lack* of such awareness does not preclude a finding of gross negligence if a reasonable person would have been so aware.

The fact that Harris was from Nevada and that the state of Nevada allows drivers to use cell phones while driving does not mitigate the risk. Harris' subjective belief in the safety of his act does not mitigate the fact that he should have known the danger involved. Therefore, we affirm Harris' vehicular manslaughter conviction.

People v. Tompkins, 89 Cal. Rptr. 3d 904 (Ct. App. 2009)

In the case before us today, Mr. Tompkins was convicted of vehicular manslaughter for causing the death of Jordan Smith while driving and simultaneously talking on his cell phone. To be guilty of vehicular manslaughter the state must show the defendant was "driving a vehicle in the commission of an unlawful act, not amounting to felony, and with gross negligence." Cal.

Penal Code § 192(c)(1) (West 2008). In this case, the unlawful act was the violation of Cal. Vehicle Code § 23123(a) (West Supp. 2011), driving a motor vehicle while using a wireless telephone that is not configured to allow hands-free listening and talking.

It is undisputed that Mr. Tompkins was driving and simultaneously speaking on his cell phone without a hands-free device when he struck and killed Mr. Smith. Tompkins contends, however, that the exception permitting use of a cell phone in case of an emergency, Cal. Vehicle Code § 23123(c) (West Supp. 2011), applies. Mr. Tompkins was driving from San Francisco to Los Angeles when he learned from a radio newscast that an earthquake measuring 6.9 on the Richter scale had struck the Bay Area. He called home to reassure himself that his wife and children were safe.

We hold that these facts do not constitute an emergency. An emergency implies imminent danger. Any danger to either Mr. Tompkins or his family had passed before the time of Tompkins' phone call. Further, as to the issue of gross negligence, Tompkins knew or should have known that driving while talking on his cell phone was endangering the lives of others. Therefore, we affirm the trial court's decision finding the defendant guilty of vehicular manslaughter.

People v. Newton, 104 Cal. Rptr. 3d 138 (Ct. App. 2010)

On December 20, 2009, Roger Newton was driving on Interstate 15 near San Bernardino, California. He was accompanied by his wife, Annette, who was seven months pregnant. Annette Newton had experienced several problems in the pregnancy, but had been free of problems for the previous three weeks. Suddenly, Mrs. Newton moaned in pain and announced she could "feel the baby coming." Mr. Newton immediately altered his course to head to St. Thomas Hospital in San Bernardino. He also used his cellular phone to call Mrs. Newton's obstetrician, hoping the doctor would meet the couple at the hospital. While on the phone, Newton did not see Julie Wolfe, who was jogging on the side of the road. The Newtons' car struck Ms. Wolfe and she died from injuries suffered in the accident. The Newtons' baby was born at the site of the accident.

Roger Newton was convicted of vehicular manslaughter. The trial court rejected his claim that calling his wife's doctor was an "emergency," stating that he could have pulled over to make the call. Further, the trial court explained that although the statute contemplates calls for emergency medical help, Newton was not calling doctors to the scene of an emergency; furthermore, there would be doctors at the hospital when the couple arrived.

We reverse Newton's vehicular manslaughter conviction because a genuine emergency existed and a reasonable person in Newton's shoes would have wanted the physician most familiar with his wife's pregnancy to meet the couple at the hospital. Gross negligence depends on the nature of the circumstances and was not present here.

The "Copyright and Fair Use" Problem

We represent Neil Young, a long-time rock musician who has stirred up some controversy with his latest concert tour and album, *Living with War*. The album includes songs entitled "Let's Impeach the President," "Lookin' for a Leader," and "Shock and Awe."

Young just found out that a relatively unknown young singer who uses the name Phil Olds has produced and is successfully marketing a rock song entitled "Stop Knockin' the Free World." Young holds the copyright on the lyrics to "Rockin' in the Free World," a song that was first included on an album released in 1989 and that has become an anti-war anthem.

"Rockin' in the Free World" was inspired by photos in a newspaper of the Ayatollah Khomeini's body being carried to his grave. These images showed mourners burning American flags in the street, which incited fear in Young's band due to their upcoming European tour. One band member commented that "whatever we do, we shouldn't go near the mideast. It's probably better we just keep on rockin' in the free world." Young then wrote the song.

Released several months prior to the collapse of the Berlin Wall, because of its chorus, which just repeats the phrase "Keep on rockin' in the free world," it became a de facto anthem for the fall of the Iron Curtain. The chorus reminds Americans of why we should improve on our faults and be proud of our strengths.

The lyrics of the song also criticize the administration of George H. W. Bush. The line "We got a thousand points of light/For the homeless man" refers to Bush's famous use of the phrase "a thousand points of light" in a call for volunteerism. The following line, "We got a kinder, gentler, machine gun hand," is a cynical take on another of his phrases: During the 1988 U.S. presidential campaign, he called for "a kinder and gentler nation."

The song received extensive radio play again shortly after the September 11, 2001, attacks, probably owing both to its celebration of "life in the free world" and for the lines "There's a lot of people sayin' we'd be better off dead/Don't feel like Satan, but I am to them," which was clearly taken as a reference to terrorism; the particular use of the word "Satan" was seen as reflecting the Islamist use of the phrase "the Great Satan" to refer to the United States.

But the song is as much about problems within the United States as overseas. The first line of the song, "Colors on the street/red, white, and blue," while certainly intended to evoke the colors of the U.S. flag, can also refer to gang colors. The second verse is a tribute to a drug addict who abandons her newborn baby in a trash can before returning to her drugs; in varying renditions of the song, this character is referred to as either a "woman" or a "girl."

A spliced version of the song also appeared during the end credits of Michael Moore's *Fahrenheit 9/11*, splicing the talk of war with the phrase "That's one more kid that'll never go to school/Never get to fall in love, never get to be cool," originally a tribute to the drug addict's abandoned child, now referencing a dead U.S. soldier in Iraq. In addition, many other famous bands regularly covered this song in concert.

About a year ago, Young says that a friend called and told him that he had just heard a parody of "Rockin' in the Free World"—Olds' song "Stop Knockin' the Free World"—on a talk radio program. The music appears to be identical to the original, but the words are different. Following is a comparison of the lyrics of the two songs. Olds' song champions pride in America without the critical element Young's song emphasizes; it purposely uses the lyrics and structure of Young's song, but is critical of Young's message of pacifism. Young wants to know how to stop Olds from using his lyrics. (The copyright on the musical composition, as opposed to the lyrics, is held jointly with members of Young's former band; we will concentrate only on the lyrics, not on the music.)

Young believes Olds' song infringes on his copyright. Olds is likely to claim his use of Young's song is protected as "fair use." Assume that a legal challenge would be filed in the Northern District of California.

Appendix B. The "Copyright and Fair Use" Problem

"Rockin' in the Free World"
Neil Young

There's colors on the street
Red, white and blue
People shufflin' their feet
People sleepin' in their shoes
But there's a warnin' sign on the road
    ahead
There's a lot of people sayin' we'd be
    better off dead
Don't feel like Satan, but I am to them
So I try to forget it, any way I can.

Keep on rockin' in the free world
Keep on rockin' in the free world
Keep on rockin' in the free world
Keep on rockin' in the free world

I see a woman in the night
With a baby in her hand
Under an old street light
Near a garbage can
Now she puts the kid away, and she's gone
    to get a hit
She hates her life, and what she's done to it
There's one more kid that will never go to
    school
Never get to fall in love, never get to be
    cool.

Keep on rockin' in the free world
Keep on rockin' in the free world
Keep on rockin' in the free world
Keep on rockin' in the free world

We got a thousand points of light
For the homeless man
We got a kinder, gentler
Machine gun hand
We got department stores and toilet paper
Got styrofoam boxes for the ozone layer
Got a man of the people, says keep hope
    alive
Got fuel to burn, got roads to drive.

Keep on rockin' in the free world
Keep on rockin' in the free world
Keep on rockin' in the free world
Keep on rockin' in the free world

"Stop Knockin' the Free World"
Phil Olds

There's flags on the street
Red, white and blue
People marchin' on their feet
People shakin' in their shoes
But there's a bright light on the road ahead
No more people sayin' we're better off red
Feel an obligation, to my fellow man
So I try to stop it, any way I can.

Stop knockin' the free world
Stop knockin' the free world
Stop knockin' the free world
Stop knockin' the free world

I see a family safe at home
Holding hands with their son
No need to roam
No place to run
Put the kids to bed, and then they start to
    pray
They love life, and what they've done today
There's one more child who will stay in
    school
Get to fall in love, glad he'll never be cool.

Stop knockin' the free world
Stop knockin' the free world
Stop knockin' the free world
Stop knockin' the free world

We got to shine our light
Build democracy
We got to show our strength
Fight theocracy
We got goods to buy and food to eat
Clothes for our body and shoes for our feet
Got a man of the people, says stay the
    course
Want fuel to burn, got to develop the
    source

Stop knockin' the free world
Stop knockin' the free world
Stop knockin' the free world
Stop knockin' the free world

The following statutes and cases (in summary form) may apply to this problem.

17 U.S.C. § 106. Exclusive rights in copyrighted works

Subject to sections 107 through 122, the owner of copyright under this title has the exclusive rights to do and to authorize any of the following:

(1) to reproduce the copyrighted work in copies or phonorecords;

(2) . . .

(3) to distribute copies or phonorecords of the copyrighted work to the public by sale or other transfer of ownership, or by rental, lease, or lending;

(4) in the case of literary, musical, dramatic, and choreographic works, pantomimes, and motion pictures and other audiovisual works, to perform the copyrighted work publicly; . . .

17 U.S.C. § 107. Limitations on exclusive rights: Fair use

Notwithstanding the provisions of section 106 . . . , the fair use of a copyrighted work, including such use by reproduction in copies or phonorecords or by any other means specified by that section, for purposes such as criticism, comment, news reporting, teaching (including multiple copies for classroom use), scholarship, or research, is not an infringement of copyright. In determining whether the use made of a work in any particular case is a fair use the factors to be considered shall include:

(1) the purpose and character of the use, including whether such use is of a commercial nature or is for nonprofit educational purposes;

(2) the nature of the copyrighted work;

(3) the amount and substantiality of the portion used in relation to the copyrighted work as a whole; and

(4) the effect of the use upon the potential market for or value of the copyrighted work. . . .

Campbell v. Acuff-Rose Music, Inc., 510 U.S. 569 (1994)

In 1964, Roy Orbison and William Dees wrote a rock ballad called "Oh, Pretty Woman" and assigned their rights to Acuff-Rose Music. Campbell and his popular rap music group, 2 Live Crew, wrote a rap song in 1989 entitled "Pretty Woman." After nearly a quarter of a million copies of the rap recording had been sold, Acuff-Rose Music sued to enforce their copyright. 2 Live Crew claims their commercial parody is a "fair use" within the meaning of the Copyright Act, 17 U.S.C. § 107. 2 Live Crew does not dispute that the song would infringe on the copyright absent a finding of fair use.

The fair use doctrine "permits [and requires] courts to avoid rigid application of the copyright statute when, on occasion, it would stifle the very creativity which that law is designed to foster." *Stewart v. Abend*, 495 U.S. 207, 236 (1990) (internal quotation marks and citation omitted). There are no bright-line rules, and the statute calls for case-by-case analysis. Similarly, nor may the four statutory factors be treated in isolation, one from another. The results must be weighed together, in light of the purposes of copyright.

I

The first factor, "the purpose and character of the use, including whether such use is of a commercial nature or is for nonprofit educational purposes," considers whether the use is for criticism, comment, or the like. The question is whether the new work "merely supersede[s] the objects" of the original creation, or instead "adds something new, with a further purpose or different character, altering the first with new expression, meaning, or message; it asks, in other words, whether and to what extent the new work is 'transformative.'" (Citations omitted.) Such transformative use is not absolutely necessary for a finding of fair use, but the goal of copyright, to promote science and the arts, is generally furthered by the creation of transformative works.

Parody has an obvious claim to transformative value. It can provide social benefit, by shedding light on an earlier work, and, in the process, creating a new one. Parody may or may not be fair use under § 107; parody, like any other use, has to work its way through the relevant factor, and be judged case by case.

Parody is transformative when it has "critical bearing on the substance or style of the original composition." The threshold question is whether a parodic character may reasonably be perceived.

2 Live Crew's song is transformative. The song could reasonably be perceived as commenting on the original or criticizing it. 2 Live Crew juxtaposes the romantic musings of a man whose fantasy comes true (with a prostitute), on the one hand, with degrading taunts, a bawdy demand for sex, and a sigh of relief from paternal responsibility on the other. The later words can be taken as a comment on the naivete of the original of an earlier day, as a rejection of its sentiment that ignores the ugliness of street life and the debasement that it signifies.

Furthermore, contrary to the court of appeals' ruling, which held that the commercial or nonprofit educational purpose of a work precluded a fair use finding, this is only one element of the first factor. Section 107(1) speaks of a broader investigation into "purpose and character."

2

The second statutory factor, "the nature of the copyrighted work," is generally disregarded in parody cases. It is not much help in this case, or in any parody case, since parodies almost invariably copy publicly known, expressive works.

3

The third factor asks whether "the amount and substantiality of the portion used in relation to the copyrighted work as a whole" is reasonable in relation to the purpose of the copying. The persuasiveness of a parodist's justification for the particular copying is significant, for we recognize that the extent of permissible copying varies with the purpose and character of the use.

When parody takes aim at a particular original work, the parody must be able to "conjure up" at least enough of that original to make the object of its critical wit recognizable. Hence, using some of the original's most distinctive or memorable features is common, as the audience will recognize them. Once enough has been taken to assure identification, how much more is reasonable will depend on the extent to which the song's overriding purpose and character is to parody the original or, in contrast, the likelihood that the parody may serve as a market substitute for the original. But using some characteristic features cannot be avoided.

Here, 2 Live Crew copied the characteristic opening bass riff (or musical phrase) of the original and the words of the first line copy the Orbison lyrics, arguably the "heart" of the original. But the question of fairness asks what else the parodist did besides go to the heart of the original. 2 Live Crew copied the bass riff and repeated it, but also produced otherwise distinctive sounds, interposing "scraper" noise, overlaying the music with solos in different keys, and altering the drum beat, changing the structure of the original song. The parody is not so insubstantial, as compared to the copying, that the third factor must be resolved as a matter of law against the parodists.

4

The fourth factor, "the effect of the use upon the potential market for or value of the copyrighted work," requires courts to consider not only the extent of market harm caused by the particular actions of the alleged infringer, but also "whether unrestricted and widespread conduct of the sort engaged in by the defendant . . . would result in a substantially adverse impact on the potential market" for the original. (Citations omitted.)

As to parody, it is more likely that the new work will not affect the market for the original because the parody and the original usually serve different market functions. We do not, of course, suggest that a parody may not harm the market at all, but when a lethal parody, like a scathing theater review, kills demand for the original, it does not produce a harm cognizable under the Copyright Act.

Since fair use is an affirmative defense, however, 2 Live Crew should have addressed the effect on the market for rap derivatives, not just demonstrated that there was no likely effect on the market for the original. Affidavits addressing the likely effect of 2 Live Crew's parodic rap song on the market for a non-parody, rap version of "Oh, Pretty Woman" should also have been submitted. This evidentiary hole can be plugged on remand.

In conclusion, it was error for the Court of Appeals to conclude that the commercial nature of 2 Live Crew's parody of "Oh, Pretty Woman" rendered it presumptively unfair. The court also erred in holding that 2 Live Crew had necessarily copied excessively from the Orbison original, considering the parodic purpose of the use. We therefore reverse the judgment of the Court of Appeals and remand the case for further proceedings consistent with this opinion.

Appendix A to *Opinion of the Court*	*Appendix B to* *Opinion to the Court*
"Oh, Pretty Woman" by Roy Orbison and William Dees	"Pretty Woman" as recorded by 2 Live Crew
Pretty Woman, walking down the street	Pretty woman walkin' down the street
Pretty Woman, the kind I like to meet	Pretty woman girl you look so sweet
Pretty Woman, I don't believe you, you're not the truth	Pretty woman you bring me down to that knee
No one could look as good as you	Pretty woman you make me wanna beg please
Mercy	Oh, pretty woman
Pretty Woman, won't you pardon me	Big hairy woman you need to shave that stuff
Pretty Woman, I couldn't help but see	Big hairy woman you know I bet it's tough
Pretty Woman, that you look lovely as can be	Big hairy woman all that hair it ain't legit
Are you lonely just like me?	'Cause you look like 'Cousin It'
Pretty Woman, stop a while	Big hairy woman
Pretty Woman, talk a while	Bald headed woman girl your hair won't grow
Pretty Woman give your smile to me	Bald headed woman you got a teeny weeny afro
Pretty Woman, yeah, yeah, yeah	Bald headed woman you know your hair could look nice
Pretty Woman, look my way	Bald headed woman first you got to roll it with rice

Pretty Woman, say you'll stay with
    me
	Bald headed woman here, let me get this hunk of
	    biz for ya

'Cause I need you, I'll treat you right	Ya know what I'm saying you look better than rice a roni
Come to me baby, Be mine tonight	Oh bald headed woman
Pretty Woman, don't walk on by	Big hairy woman come on in
Pretty Woman, don't make me cry	And don't forget your bald headed friend
Pretty Woman, don't walk away	Hey pretty woman let the boys
Hey, O.K.	Jump in
If that's the way it must be, O.K.	Two timin' woman girl you know you ain't right
I guess I'll go on home, it's late	Two timin' woman you's out with my boy last night
There'll be tomorrow night, but wait!	Two timin' woman that takes a load off my mind
What do I see?	Two timin' woman now I know the baby ain't mine
Is she walking back to me?	Oh, two timin' woman
Yeah, she's walking back to me!	Oh pretty woman
Oh, Pretty Woman	

Dr. Seuss Enters., L.P. v. Penguin Books USA, Inc., 109 F.3d 1394 (9th Cir. 1997)

We must decide whether a poetic account of the O.J. Simpson double murder trial entitled *The Cat NOT in the Hat! A Parody by Dr. Juice*, presents a sufficient showing of copyright and trademark infringement of the well-known *The Cat in the Hat* by Dr. Seuss.

Under the pseudonym "Dr. Seuss," at least 47 books were published over sixty years, with approximately 35 million copies currently in print worldwide. The books use simple, rhyming, repetitive language, accompanied by characters that are recognizable by and appealing to children.

The Cat in the Hat involves a mischievous but well-meaning character, the Cat, who continues to be among the most famous and well recognized of the Dr. Seuss creations. The Cat is almost always depicted with his distinctive scrunched and somewhat shabby red and white stovepipe hat. Almost 40 years later, Penguin Books published *The Cat NOT in the Hat!* satirizing the O.J. Simpson double murder trial. Seuss sued for copyright infringement, and Penguin Books claimed fair use for a parody. The court therefore applied the four factors stated in § 107 of the Copyright Act.

I

Under the first factor, "the purpose and character of the use, including whether such use is of a commercial nature or is for nonprofit educational purposes," the inquiry is whether *The Cat NOT in the Hat!* merely supersedes the Dr. Seuss creations, or whether and to what extent the new work is "transformative," i.e., altering *The Cat in the Hat* with new expression, meaning or message. Looking at *The Cat NOT in the Hat!* itself, the first two pages present a view of Los Angeles, with particular emphasis on the connection with Brentwood, given the depiction of the news camera lights. The story begins as follows:

> A happy town
> Inside L.A.
> Where rich folks play
> The day away.
> But under the moon
> The 12th of June.
> Two victims flail
> Assault! Assail!
> Somebody will go to jail!
> Who will it be?
> Oh my! Oh me!

The third page reads: "One Knife?/Two Knife?/Red Knife/Dead Wife." This stanza no doubt mimics the first poem in Dr. Seuss' *One Fish Two Fish Red Fish Blue Fish*: "One fish/two fish/red fish/blue fish. Black fish/blue fish/old fish/new fish." Throughout the book, these stanzas and the illustrations simply retell the Simpson tale. Although *The Cat NOT in the Hat!* does broadly mimic Dr. Seuss' characteristic style, it does not hold his style up to ridicule. The book merely uses the Cat's stovepipe hat, the narrator ("Dr. Juice"), and the title (*The Cat NOT in the Hat!*) "to get attention" or maybe even "to avoid the drudgery in working up something fresh." *Campbell*, 510 U.S. at 580. Because there is no effort to create a transformative work with "new expression, meaning, or message," the infringing work's commercial use further cuts against the fair use defense. *Id.* at 579.

2

While the second statutory factor, "the nature of the copyrighted work," has not been terribly significant in the overall fair use balancing, the creativity, imagination and originality embodied in *The Cat in the Hat* and its central character tilts the scale against fair use.

3

The third factor, "the amount and substantiality of the portion used in relation to the copyrighted work as a whole," raises the question of substantial similarity. "The Cat in the Hat" is the central character. We have no doubt that the Cat's image is the highly expressive core of Dr. Seuss' work. Penguin Books insists that The Cat in the Hat is the vehicle for their parody because of the similarities between the two stories: Nicole Brown and Ronald Goldman were surprised by a "Cat" (O.J. Simpson) who committed acts contrary to moral and legal authority. The prosecution of Simpson created a horrible mess, in which the defense team seemed to impose "tricks" on an unwilling public, resulting in a verdict that a substantial segment of the public regarded as astonishing. Just as *The Cat in the Hat* ends with the moral dilemma of whether the children should tell their mother about their visitor that afternoon, *The Cat NOT in the Hat!* ends with a similar moral dilemma:

> JUICE
> +ST
> JUSTICE
> Hmm . . . take the word JUICE.
> Then add ST.
> Between the U and I, you see.
> And then you have JUSTICE.
> Or maybe you don't.

> Maybe we will.
> And maybe we won't.
> 'Cause if the Cat didn't do it?
> Then who? Then who?
> Was it him?
> Was it her?
> Was it me?
> Was it you?
> Oh me! Oh my!
> Oh my! Oh me!
> The murderer is running free.

We agree with the district court that Penguin's fair use defense is "completely unconvincing."

4

The fourth factor is "the effect of the use upon the potential market for or value of the copyrighted work." The good will and reputation associated with Dr. Seuss' work is substantial. Because, on the facts presented, Penguin's use of *The Cat in the Hat* original was non-transformative, and admittedly commercial, we conclude that market substitution is at least more certain, and market harm may be more readily inferred. Especially because the market was children, who could easily mistake the copy for the original, a negative effect is likely.

Since fair use is an affirmative defense, Penguin must present favorable evidence about relevant markets. Given their failure to submit evidence on this point, Penguin is not entitled to relief.

Affirmed.

Mattel Inc. v. Walking Mountain Prods., 353 F.3d 792 (9th Cir. 2003)

Mattel asks us to prohibit artist Thomas Forsythe from producing and selling photographs containing Mattel's "Barbie" doll. Forsythe, aka "Walking Mountain Productions," is a photographer who produces photographs with social and political overtones. In 1997, Forsythe developed a series of 78 photographs entitled "Food Chain Barbie," in which he depicted Barbie in various absurd and often sexualized positions. Forsythe generally depicts one or more nude Barbie dolls juxtaposed with vintage kitchen appliances.

Forsythe chose to parody Barbie in his photographs because he believes that "Barbie is the most enduring of those products that feed on the insecurities of our beauty and perfection-obsessed consumer culture." His photos critique the objectification of women associated with Barbie and "the societal acceptance of women as objects." Forsythe's market success was limited, earning him a total of $3,659.

The Copyright Act seeks to promote the progress of science and art by protecting artistic and scientific works while encouraging the development and evolution of new works. *See Campbell v. Acuff-Rose Music, Inc.*, 510 U.S. 569, 575-76 (1994). The fair use exception excludes from copyright restrictions certain works, such as those that criticize and comment on another work. 17 U.S.C. § 107. The primary intent of fair use is to weigh the rights of the original owner against the benefit that the secondary use provides to society.

To determine whether a work constitutes fair use, we engage in a case-by-case analysis and a flexible balancing of relevant factors. *Campbell*, 510 U.S. at 577-78. The factors are "to be explored, and the results weighed together, in light of the purposes of copyright." *Id.* at 578.

The district court granted Forsythe's motion for summary judgment on Mattel's claim of copyright infringement. We review de novo a grant of summary judgment. *See Oliver v. Keller*, 289 F.3d 623, 626 (9th Cir. 2002). We also review the district court's finding of fair use under the Copyright Act, a mixed question of law and fact, by the same de novo standard. *Kelly v. Arriba Soft Corp.*, 336 F.3d 811, 817 (9th Cir. 2003).

A. Purpose and character of use

The first factor asks "to what extent the new work is transformative." *Campbell*, 510 U.S. at 579. A work must add "something new, with a further purpose or different character, altering the first with new expression, meaning, or message." *Id.* Parodic works, like other works that comment and criticize, are by their nature often sufficiently transformative to fit clearly under the fair use exception. *Id.*

In assessing whether Forsythe's photographs parody Barbie, Mattel urges us to ignore context—both the social context of Forsythe's work and the actual context in which Mattel's copyrighted works are placed in Forsythe's photographs. However, "in parody, as in news reporting, context is everything." *Id.* at 588 (citations omitted). We conclude that Forsythe's work may reasonably be perceived as a parody of Barbie.

Mattel has established Barbie as "the ideal American woman." Mattel's advertisements show these plastic dolls dressed in various outfits, leading glamorous lifestyles and engaged in exciting activities, representing women's traditional role positively. To sell its product, Mattel uses associations of beauty, wealth, and glamour.

Forsythe turns this image on its head with his photographs of Barbies in often ridiculous and apparently dangerous situations. In some of Forsythe's photos, Barbie is about to be destroyed or harmed by domestic life in the form of kitchen appliances. In other photographs, Forsythe conveys a sexualized perspective of Barbie by showing the nude doll in sexually suggestive contexts. It is not difficult to see the commentary that Forsythe intended or the harm that he perceived in Barbie's influence on gender roles and the position of women in society.

Another element of the first factor analysis is whether the work's "purpose" was commercial or had a non-profit aim. *Campbell*, 510 U.S. at 584. Clearly, Forsythe had a commercial expectation and presumably hoped to find a market for his art. However, given the extremely transformative nature and parodic quality of Forsythe's work, its commercial qualities become less important. However one may feel about his message, his photographs parody Barbie and everything Mattel's doll has come to signify. We find that this factor weighs heavily in favor of Forsythe.

B. Nature of the copyrighted work

The second factor typically has not been terribly useful in the overall fair use balancing. In any event, it may weigh slightly against Forsythe.

C. Amount and substantiality of the portion used

Under the third factor, the "extent of permissible copying varies with the purpose and character of the use." *Campbell*, 510 U.S. at 586-87. Mattel argues that Forsythe used the entirety of its copyrighted work and that this factor weighs against him. Mattel contends that Forsythe could have used less of the Barbie figure by, for example, limiting his photos to the Barbie heads.

First, Forsythe did not simply copy the work "verbatim" with "little added or changed." *Id.* at 587-88. Forsythe did not display the entire Barbie head and body in his photographs. Second, Mattel attempts to benefit from the somewhat unique nature of the copyrighted work in this case. Copyright infringement actions generally involve songs, video, or written works, which are naturally severable. Here, short of severing the doll, Forsythe must add to it by creating a context around it and capturing that context in a photograph. Forsythe's use of the entire doll and his use of dismembered parts of the doll are incorporated into the new work but emerge imbued with a different character.

Moreover, Forsythe was justified in the amount of Mattel's copyrighted work that he used in his photographs. We do not require parodic works to take the absolute minimum amount of the copyrighted work possible. As the Supreme Court stated in *Campbell*, "once enough has been taken to assure identification, how much more is reasonable will depend, say, on the extent to which the [work's] overriding purpose and character is to parody the original or, in contrast, the likelihood that the parody may serve as a market substitute for the original." *Id.* at 587. We conclude that the extent of Forsythe's copying of the Barbie figure and head was justifiable in light of his parodic purpose of criticizing stereotypical feminine roles in society and the medium used. This factor weighs in his favor.

D. Effect of the use upon potential market

The fourth factor considers whether actual market harm resulted from the defendant's use of plaintiff's protected material. Because of the parodic nature of Forsythe's work, it is highly unlikely that it will substitute for products in Mattel's markets or licenses. In *Campbell*, the Court clearly stated, "as to parody pure and simple, it is more likely that the new work will not affect the market for the original in a way cognizable under this factor." 510 U.S. at 591. Forsythe's work could only reasonably substitute for a work in the market for adult-oriented artistic photographs of Barbie. We think it safe to assume that Mattel will not enter such a market. Nor is it likely that Mattel would license an artist to create a work that is so critical of Barbie. Hence, Forsythe's works do not negatively affect any derivative work by Mattel.

Furthermore, this factor does not recognize a decrease in value of a copyrighted work that may result from a particularly powerful critical work. *Id.* at 593 ("The fact that a parody may impair the market for derivative uses by the very effectiveness of its critical commentary is no more relevant under copyright than the like threat to the original market . . .").

Having balanced the four § 107 fair use factors, we hold that Forsythe's work constitutes fair use.

Fisher v. Dees, 794 F.2d 432 (9th Cir. 1986)

FACTUAL AND PROCEDURAL BACKGROUND

The plaintiffs-appellants, Marvin Fisher and Jack Segal (the composers), composed and own the copyright to the '50s standard "When Sunny Gets Blue" (the song). In late 1984, a law firm representing the defendants-appellees contacted Fisher and requested permission to use part or all of the music to "When Sunny Gets Blue" in order to create a comedic and inoffensive version of the song. Fisher refused the request.

A few months later, Dees released a comedy record album called *Put It Where the Moon Don't Shine*. One cut on the album, entitled "When Sonny Sniffs Glue" (the parody), is an obvious take-off on the composers' song. The parody copies the first six of the song's thirty-eight bars of music—its recognizable main theme. In addition, it changes the original's opening lyrics—"When Sunny gets blue, her eyes get gray and cloudy, then the rain begins to fall" to "When Sonny sniffs glue, her eyes get red and bulgy, then her hair begins to fall." The parody runs for 29 seconds of the approximately forty minutes of material on Dees's album.

DISCUSSION

Dees claims copying of the song for purposes of parody constituted a fair use. We agree.

Overview of the fair-use doctrine

The fair-use doctrine was initially developed by courts as an equitable defense to copyright infringement. In effect, the doctrine creates a limited privilege in those other than the owner of a copyright to use the copyrighted material in a reasonable manner without the owner's consent. (Citations omitted.) In restating the fair-use doctrine Congress enumerated four non-exclusive factors for courts to consider:

(1) the purpose and character of the use, including whether such use is of a commercial nature or is for nonprofit educational purposes;
(2) the nature of the copyrighted work;
(3) the amount and substantiality of the portion used in relation to the copyrighted work as a whole; and
(4) the effect of the use upon the potential market for or value of the copyrighted work.

17 U.S.C. § 107 (1982). In addition, in the legislative notes accompanying the provision, Congress listed examples "of the sort of activities the courts might regard as fair use under the circumstances." Id. § 107 historical and revision notes (1982). Congress named parody as one of these activities. Nonetheless, parody was not classified as a *presumptively* fair use. Each assertion of the "parody defense" must be considered individually, in light of the statutory factors, reason, experience, and, of course, the general principles developed in past cases. (Citations omitted.)

Applying the fair-use test

The subject of the parody

The composers assert that the parody, although it borrows from the original work, was not "directed" at the original. That is, a humorous or satiric work deserves protection under the fair-use doctrine only if the copied work is at least partly the target of the work in question. Otherwise, there is no need to "conjure up" the original in the audience's mind and no justification for borrowing from it. (Citations omitted.)

We requested counsel to provide us with tapes of both Dees's parody and the original (as sung by Johnny Mathis). Although we have no illusions of musical expertise, it was clear to us that Dees's version was intended to poke fun at the composers' song, and at Mr. Mathis's rather singular vocal range. We reject the notion that the song was used merely as a vehicle to achieve a comedic objective unrelated to the song, its place and time.

The economic effect of the use

Thus, we must turn our attention to the fourth factor in the fair-use analysis—"the effect of the use upon the potential market for or value of the copyrighted work," 17 U.S.C. § 107(4). This factor, not surprisingly, "is undoubtedly the single most important element of fair use." In assessing the economic effect of the parody, the parody's critical impact must be excluded. Through its critical function, a parody may quite legitimately aim at garroting the original, destroying it commercially as well as artistically. (Citation and quotation marks omitted.)

Copyright law is not designed to stifle critics. "'Destructive' parodies play an important role in social and literary criticism and thus merit protection even though they may discourage or discredit an original author." Accordingly, the economic effect of a parody with which we are concerned is not its potential to destroy or diminish the market for the original—any bad review can have that effect—but rather whether it *fulfills the demand* for the original. Biting criticism suppresses demand; copyright infringement usurps it. Thus, infringement occurs when a parody supplants the original in markets the original is aimed at, or in which the original is, or has reasonable potential to become, commercially valuable. (Citations omitted.)

This is not a case in which commercial substitution is likely. "When Sunny Gets Blue" is "a lyrical song concerning or relating to a woman's feelings about lost love and her chance for . . . happiness again." Appellants' Opening Brief at 3. By contrast, the parody is a 29-second recording concerning a woman who sniffs glue, which "ends with noise and laughter mixed into the song." We do not believe that consumers desirous of hearing a romantic and nostalgic ballad such as the composers' song would be satisfied to purchase the parody instead. Nor are those fond of parody likely to consider "When Sunny Gets Blue" a source of satisfaction. The two works do not fulfill the same demand. Consequently, the parody has no cognizable economic effect on the original.

The amount and substantiality of the taking

This court has also consistently focused on the third fair-use factor—the amount and substantiality of the taking, 17 U.S.C. § 107(3). Thus far, however, we have provided few concrete guidelines; we have merely sketched the outer boundaries of the inquiry. On the one hand, "substantial copying by a defendant, combined with the fact that the portion copied constituted a substantial part of the defendant's work," does not automatically preclude the fair use defense. On the other hand, "copying that is virtually complete or almost verbatim" will not be protected. (Citations omitted.)

Like a speech, a song is difficult to parody effectively without exact or near-exact copying. If the would-be parodist varies the music or meter of the original substantially, it simply will not be recognizable to the general audience. This "special need for accuracy" provides some license for "closer" parody. To be sure, that license is not limitless: the parodist's desire to make the best parody must be balanced against the rights of the copyright owner in his original expressions. (Citation and quotation marks omitted.) We think the balance tips in the parodists' favor here. In view of the parody's medium, its purposes, and its brevity, it takes no more from the original than is necessary to accomplish reasonably its parodic purpose.

Summation

We conclude that "When Sonny Sniffs Glue" is a parody deserving of fair-use protection as a matter of law. Thus, we affirm the district court's grant of summary judgment on the copyright claim.

Index

Index